THE CASE THAT SHOCKED
THE CONSCIENCE OF A NATION

Jim Keegstra taught his Eckville high school students that a Jewish conspiracy was manipulating people and governments in an ongoing attempt to control the world. Such theories are not new, of course. They are the basis of blood libel accusations that date back to the Dark Ages. But this is the 1980s, and Canada is a modern, democratic society. The shock surrounding this revelation was compounded when reporters discovered that Keegstra had been teaching his lessons in hate for over a decade—and that the teacher had convinced many of the young people in Eckville that the Nazi murder of six million Jews never took place.

"[He was] a forceful teacher [who kept] excellent control of his class."

—Earl A. Clark, Deputy Superintendent
of the School Board

"He's the most interesting teacher we've had."

—Student, Eckville High School

"We must get rid of every living Jew so that we can live in peace and freedom."

—From an essay written for Keegstra's
social studies class

"I have never seen such anti-Semitism."

—Ben Kayfetz, Canadian Jewish Congress

A TRUST BETRAYED

THE KEEGSTRA AFFAIR

David Bercuson &
Douglas Wertheimer

SEAL BOOKS

McClelland-Bantam, Inc.

Toronto

A TRUST BETRAYED

A Seal Book / published by arrangement with
Doubleday Canada Ltd.

PRINTING HISTORY
Doubleday Canada edition published November 1985
Seal edition / February 1987

ISBN 0-7704-2155-5

Seal Books are published by McClelland and Stewart-Bantam
Limited. Its trademark, consisting of the words "Seal Books" and the
portrayal of a seal, is the property of McClelland and Stewart-
Bantam Limited, 60 St. Clair Avenue East, Suite 601, Toronto,
Ontario M4T 1N5 Canada. This trademark has been duly registered
in the Trademarks Office of Canada. The trademark, consisting of
the words "Bantam" and the portrayal of a rooster, is the property of
and is used with the consent of Bantam Books, Inc., 666 Fifth
Avenue, New York, New York 10103. This trademark has been duly
registered in the Trademarks Office of Canada and elsewhere.

PRINTED IN CANADA

COVER PRINTED IN U.S.A.

U   0 9 8 7 6 5 4 3 2 1

for
Gila, Saul & Aaron
Michael & Sharon

Contents

Preface

IN THE EIGHTH DECADE of the 20th century, in a classroom in western Canada, a school teacher was found to be providing instruction based on fantasies about the Jewish people and their religion which had originated in medieval Christian Europe. This book is about the man behind those myths, about the system and environment which tolerated his teaching for so many years, and about the ways in which elements in society reacted to the affair and its implications.

For nearly three years, Jim Keegstra the teacher, and his classroom in Eckville, Alberta, captured headlines across Canada. In hundreds of newspapers, in thousands of articles, and in millions of words, this affair has been described, debated, and analyzed. Since the famous Scopes Monkey Trial sixty years ago, perhaps no similar case in North America has received so much sustained attention. That this has been so is an indication that what occurred was perceived as touching on issues—such as moral responsibility and the purpose of education—which transcend time and place.

A number of significant aspects of the Keegstra affair are treated in this book for the first time. We have included accounts of the earliest attempts to make known what Keegstra was teaching; of the crucial leadership role played by the press; of the historic meeting of Jewish leaders of Alberta with the premier of the province; and an assessment of the responses made by the Jewish community, and by Christian communities, to a perceived resurgence in anti-Semitic sentiment. Drawing on more than two dozen interviews (some of which were conducted during the heat of the events described), an extensive collection of newspaper articles, access to confidential and private archives, and personal knowledge, we have attempted to provide a fresh understanding of some of the controversies which raged around Jim Keegstra.

In this regard, readers may find it useful to have a summary of our principal conclusions.

The world-view of Jim Keegstra, far from being an erratic, *ad hoc* creation, is an internally consistent outlook based on paranoid fantasies about a Jewish world-conspiracy bent on controlling, and then destroying, Christianity. The blueprint for a secret plot to control all governments is purportedly set down in the Talmud. It is our conclusion that Keegstra discovered these medieval myths in modern anti-Semitic books, which repeat them, in the monetary philosophy of the Douglasite wing of the Social Credit movement, which revolves around them, and in the New Testament, which he believes supports them.

In referring to well-known non-Jews such as the German philosopher Hegel, the Russian revolutionary Lenin, or the American philanthropist Rockefeller as "Jews," Keegstra was not engaging in a random name-calling exercise. He was sorting people into his dualistic world, motivated by the belief that the Jew is an evil principle. He thus gave new meaning to the famous phrase of the late 19th-century anti-Semite Karl Lueger, who said: "I decide who is a Jew."[1]

For more than a decade, Keegstra fed students in Eckville High School a steady diet of biased statements principally about Jews, but also about Catholics, Blacks, and others. We found that these teachings were known to some extent to Keegstra's colleagues, to parents, and to the school's principals. Apathy, complacency, and conformist pressures prevented most from speaking out against what was occurring. Others sympathized with Keegstra's worldview, or found him to be a "likeable villain."

Yet there were a number of parents prior to 1982 who refused to accept the Keegstra situation as normal, and attempted to protest what was going on. They failed in their efforts because the system failed. We trace this failure to an educational "Age of Aquarius" which, during the late 1960s and early 1970s, had resulted in the loosening of standards of teaching and supervision in the classrooms of Alberta schools.

Over a year passed between September 1981—when Robert David, the Superintendent of the Lacombe County School Board, first heard of Jim Keegstra—and December 1982, when the School Board fired him. Many have viewed this as proof of a dilatory approach to a serious problem. We found, however, that from the outset David was aware of the difficulty of firing a teacher in Alberta. During the 1970s, ten dismissal cases in the province were appealed to boards of reference; only two firings were upheld. David's approach to the Keegstra case, in light of obstacles confronting such an action, was judicious and effective.

Although there was a widespread sense of public outrage against those perceived to be implicated by Keegstra's classroom activities, the officials responsible for the education of Alberta's children were also mindful of other issues. One could hardly fail to notice the denunciation of Keegstra by Dave King, the Alberta Minister of Education. At the same time, King grasped the opportunity which he felt the affair offered to pursue initiatives previously stalled in the educational field.

The Alberta Teachers' Association was aware of King's tactics, and of the way in which his proposed changes would affect it. In part, we believe that may explain why the ATA's main attitude to Keegstra was to treat him as if he were an auto worker who had been drilling holes in the wrong place, rather than as an educator who betrayed the trust that had been placed in him. To the ATA, differences between themselves and the Department of Education loomed larger than the misdirected actions of a single individual.

When Keegstra's classroom teachings were first publicized, many observers believed that the Alberta Social Studies Curriculum was at least partially to blame for an out-of-control situation. It was argued that the Eckville teacher could never have taught his delusionary myths about a Jewish world-conspiracy had the curriculum emphasized the discipline of history, instead of promoting a "values education" and "social issues" orientation. This assessment, however, is incorrect, since Keegstra in fact never taught the prescribed curriculum.

Our research has shown that the tremendous early media attention focused on the Keegstra affair was the result of a conscious decision to publicize a sense of outrage at what had occurred. It is unlikely that Keegstra would have become a *cause célèbre* had the media not become convinced of the integrity of this passionate response. The media campaign was initiated and conducted mainly by Herb Katz, who held the volunteer position of head of the Community Relations Council of the Jewish Federation of Edmonton.

Although there were exceptions, we found that Christian communities in Alberta hesitated at first to denounce the anti-Semitic teachings of a self-proclaimed devout Christian, and shied away from providing outspoken moral leadership. In this they were not different from the Alberta government of Peter Lougheed, which for a time found it difficult to empathize with the agony and the moral outrage of many of the province's Jews. In both instances there were reasons for this reluctance and this aloofness, and there is no indication that it was rooted in an unspoken sympathy for Keegstra's teachings.

In the absence of moral leadership from elected officials or church leaders in Alberta, it fell primarily to the newspaper press of Alberta to cover, expose, and respond to an emotionally-charged situation. In this way, the secular daily and weekly press became the voice of conscience and ethical behavior. No publication reacted with greater understanding of the issues, or provided more impressive editorial comment, than the *Edmonton Journal*.

Nonetheless, there were shortcomings in the newspaper coverage of the Keegstra affair. We found that it tended to be narrowly regional. It focused excessive attention on the "Holocaust denial" pronouncements of Keegstra, Stephen Stiles, and others, losing sight of the essence of Keegstra's thought, which lay in the Jewish world-conspiracy myth. In its approach to the issue, the Alberta press was deeply influenced by the attitudes of the Jewish communities in Alberta.

Although major national Jewish organizations applauded the decision of the Alberta Attorney General to prosecute Keegstra for violating the hate promotion section of the Criminal Code of Canada, there were those—both Jews and non-Jews—who were convinced that it was virtually impossible to enforce and that it ought to be changed. Many factors entered into the thinking of the Attorney General as he contemplated Keegstra's actions in the light of the existing law. The final decision was reached without any involvement from the Jewish community. The decision to lay charges was the responsibility of the Alberta Attorney General and the Premier.

In writing this book, we have sought to interview a broad range of people. Unfortunately, a number of individuals refused to be interviewed by us, and we are conscious of the obstacle which this has presented. Those who refused to be interviewed during the preparation of this book were Art Cowley, President of the Alberta Teachers' Association; Frank Flanagan, former Superintendent of the Lacombe County School Board; Jim Keegstra; David King, Alberta Minister of Education; Peter Lougheed, Premier of Alberta; and Ed Olsen, Principal of Eckville Junior-Senior High School. It was a condition of some of those whom we have quoted or cited in this book that their names not be revealed.

Many people have helped us in the preparation of this work. We are especially grateful for permission to consult

the collection of documents at the Jewish Federation of
Edmonton. For the loan of private materials, and for
assistance in locating secondary material, we wish to thank
Marg Andrew, C. C. Aronsfeld, Carl Bond, Art Carritt, the
Canadian Jewish Congress (Toronto and Vancouver Re-
gions), Sheldon Chumir, Professor Norman Chon, R. K.
David, Dr. N. Merrill Distad, Jack Downey, Herb Katz,
Manuel Prutschi, Alan Shefman, and M. J. Silverman. The
research assistance of Darlene Zdunich and Lenor Kusner
has been most valuable to us. We want to especially thank
Denise Schon, Senior Editor of Doubleday Canada Limited, who showed faith in this project from the beginning,
and enhanced it by the professional attention which she
gave it.

Finally, this book would not have been undertaken or
completed without the understanding, support, and assistance of Gila Wertheimer. Of course, we alone are responsible for all errors of omission or commission.

DAVID J. BERCUSON
DOUGLAS WERTHEIMER
Calgary, August 1985

Introduction

IN THE SPRING of 1983 the attention of Canadians was focused on a small town in the western province of Alberta. There Jim Keegstra, a small town high school teacher, had taught his students that a Jewish conspiracy manipulated people and governments in an ongoing attempt to control the world.

Such theories are not new, of course. They are the basis of blood libel accusations that date back to the Dark Ages. But this is the 1980s, and Canada is a modern, democratic society. The shock surrounding this revelation was compounded when reporters discovered that Keegstra had been teaching his lessons in hate for over a decade. When the press descended on the small town—Eckville, Alberta—to interview some of Keegstra's students, they discovered that the teacher had convinced many of the young people that the Nazi murder of six million Jews never took place. He had persuaded many that Jews had manipulated world events since at least as far back as the French Revolution in their efforts to take over the world, that Jews were obliged by their religion to hate Christians and rob and steal from them and that Jews engaged in a variety of perverted sexual practises in their worship of the anti-Christ.

Jim Keegstra was born, raised and educated in Alberta. He holds a university degree in education from one of the best new universities in western Canada. He started his career as a teacher in the late 1960s and taught at a number of small town schools before landing a permanent job in Eckville in 1968. He is a fundamentalist Christian who absorbed a great deal of anti-Semitism while growing up in rural Alberta in the 1930s. Within a few short years of taking up his teaching position in Eckville, he began to introduce his anti-Jewish views into the classroom. Keegstra diligently studied the basic anti-Jewish texts of today, most of which he obtained through a right-wing group known as the Canadian League of Rights. These books, which have become the stock-in-trade of anti-Jewish hate groups around the world, are largely published and distributed in the United States by organizations such as Liberty Bell Press, Noontide Press and the Institute for Historical Review. As Keegstra read, he passed more and more of what he learned on to his students. Although some parents and teachers in Eckville knew what he was doing, no one tried to stop him until 1982, when a new school superintendent became aware of what was happening in Eckville. It took a year to go through all the steps necessary to fire Keegstra, as he was a tenured teacher.

Keegstra eventually lost his teaching license and was charged under Canadian criminal law with deliberately fomenting hate against an identifiable group. His trial stretched out for over three months, from early April 1985 to late July. When it was over, Keegstra was convicted. But the trial left many questions unanswered: How could this have happened in Canada? How could Keegstra have taught his anti-Jewish message for so long? Where did his ideas come from? How much of what happened was unique to Alberta and western Canada? What exactly did he teach his students and how? Why did it take so long to dismiss him? Why did the Teachers' Association help him defend himself against his dismissal? Could something similar have happened anywhere else in Canada or in the United States?

This book contains the answers to some of these questions. Others can be answered only by inference. It should be clear to anyone who reads this story that complacency can undermine the integrity of *any* educational system, *anywhere*. The Keegstra story took place in a province in western Canada, but it could have happened in Ontario or New York State or California. That is the most chilling message of Jim Keegstra's betrayal of trust.

1

The World of Jim Keegstra

THE FIRST CLUE that most Canadians had to the world of Jim Keegstra was flashed across the television screens of the nation on the night of Monday, May 2, 1983, when CBC television's "The Journal" went on the air. The entire program that evening was devoted to the Keegstra affair with the airing of a documentary entitled "Lessons in Hate," produced by Morris Karp, which had been shot in Eckville following Keegstra's dismissal. About one-third of the way into the program, CBC's Linden MacIntyre was shown interviewing Keegstra in his Eckville mobile home. Keegstra sat in a big easy chair, checked shirt rolled up at the sleeves, beside his television set and rubber plant. On the table in front of him was a pile of the books that had become the foundation of his thinking.

MacIntyre was barely able to hide his indignation: "I come back to the fact that you have conditioned a young person to go out into the world and hate a Jew," he told Keegstra. "The first Jew he meets is going to be regarded by him as an enemy—somebody who wants to enslave him."

"They do," Keegstra answered, "if you read Jewish literature, Jewish literature is clear . . . and it says bluntly that the *goy**—which means beast—are to be the slaves of the Jew. And that Jew here means the Judaic, talmudic, rabbinical Jew."[1]

Jewish literature, in fact, says no such thing. Jews are required to act fairly and ethically towards all persons regardless of race or religion. Jews believe that all people who worship God are eligible to take part in the world to come. But Jim Keegstra does not believe this, and for more than a decade he taught high school students in Eckville, Alberta that Jews are evil and scheme to enslave Christians and destroy Christianity. When Keegstra was fired by his employer, the Lacombe County Board of Education, in December 1982, Canadians began to learn the shocking truth about his teachings. They started to pay close attention to the small Alberta community in which he lived and taught.

— I —

In the spring of 1983, a small town in central Alberta suddenly dominated the news across Canada. Eckville, with a little more than 800 people, seemed to become the media capital of the country. Television film crews, reporters and photographers took thousands of pictures, shot countless meters of film and tried to interview almost everyone in town.

The main focus of the attention was a low, concrete and brick building in the center of town, Eckville Junior/Senior High School, and the students and teachers who taught and learned there. This was the place where Jim Keegstra had betrayed his trust as a teacher and taught Eckville children that Catholics are in league with Communism; that Blacks are inferior to whites; that bankers, capitalists and lawyers are evil perverters of the free enterprise system; and that a Jewish conspiracy has been manipulating people and events for centuries in a plot to destroy Christianity and

---

*In Hebrew, the word *goy* means a crowd, a people, or a nation. The plural form, *goyim*, is used in the sense of "*other* nations," i.e., non-Jews. The term used for Christians is *Notzrim* (Nazarenes).

enslave the world. Jim Keegstra had made Eckville famous, but for all the wrong reasons.

Eckville never sought the national attention devoted to it; few Eckvillians would have welcomed it. The town is not much different from hundreds of other small communities scattered across the Canadian west. It is located in the rolling parkland of central Alberta about halfway between Edmonton and Calgary. It is just north of Provincial Highway 11, which runs from Red Deer to Rocky Mountain House. Eckville is a rural community. Most of its residents are connected in one way or another to farming or to the oil and gas business.

Visiting Eckville is something of an anti-climax after all the national attention that has been devoted to it since Keegstra was dismissed from Eckville High School in December 1982. Heading west on Highway 11, it is easy to speed past the green sign announcing the turnoff for this infamous small town just a few kilometers north of the main road. A right turn just before a Husky gas station, and a short drive through rolling farm country bring visitors to another sign announcing, "Welcome to Eckville, a good community to live in." The sign, one suspects, has been photographed hundreds of times by now.

However, with all the publicity, Eckville is still a modest little place and, in many ways, a typical rural Canadian community. There are two grain elevators by the railway tracks, two churches (one Presbyterian and one United Church of Canada), the high school and, at the center of town near Eckville's only traffic light, two streets lined on both sides with small frame and stucco commercial buildings. Most of the stores are closed and empty but on one corner of the town's main intersection stands a building somewhat larger than the others. It houses Carritt's Turbo station, which on principle has always sold gasoline in gallons only. The same building also houses the office of the *Eckville Examiner*, the weekly town newspaper, which helped break the Keegstra story in a courageous episode in the history of Canadian journalism.

But first, what about the history of Eckville itself? The

community was established just after the turn of the century on land donated to local settlers by Arthur Eckford, who gave his name to the settlement.[2] The first school was built in 1906 and by 1910 the little community was a bustling village with a post office, hotel, feed barn and cheese factory. Proud residents named their four streets Main, Dominion, Willow and Prince. The coming of the railway in 1912 brought the promise of better things but the First World War interrupted Eckville's slow and steady growth. The community's first bank was not established until 1918. By then pioneer days had just about passed and Eckvillians got down to the necessary but not always easy job of learning to live with each other.

Although the majority of Eckville's residents were immigrants from Britain, a large number of Estonian and Finnish settlers had also put down roots in the district. They brought with them the religious and political divisions that had often marred the peace of the old country. Some were conservative Protestants; others were atheistic socialists. They were to leave their mark on local politics for years to come. Sylvan Lake, several kilometers east of Eckville on Highway 11, was for many years the site of a summer camp for the children of Alberta Communists.

Althought Eckville became an incorporated village in 1921, the community grew slowly until the Second World War. There were not enough residents to qualify it as an incorporated town until 1966. By then Eckvillians were enjoying running water and electricity—both having arrived only after the war. They also had a small hospital, a hotel and a beer parlor. As the community grew, so did the need for schooling. The village school was absorbed into the Lacombe School Division in the 1940s. Following this, the school building was expanded to accommodate grades one through twelve. When Eckville began to grow rapidly in the 1960s due to a small local oil and natural gas boom, a second building was constructed for the elementary classes. This left junior and senior high in the building they now occupy, not far from the center of town.

Eckville has recently acquired a reputation for bigotry

and religious narrow-mindedness. Since the Keegstra affair exploded onto the front pages of Canadian newspapers, Eckville has been branded as the town that tolerated hatred in its schools. It became all too easy to paint Eckville as the typical Alberta "buckle on the Bible Belt" in a national show of self-righteousness that mixed blind prejudice with a failure to understand what the Keegstra affair was all about.

Contrary to what many have supposed, there is no particularly strong church-going tradition in the town. The great majority of the residents are members of main-line Protestant churches. About twenty percent are Catholics, who were also the targets of Keegstra's bigotry.[3] Eckvillians are no more abstemious than other Canadians, and the town's high school students go to dances and parties, drink beer, drive fast and neck on country roads like a lot of other teenagers. The same summer that all of Canada was talking about Jim Keegstra was the summer that Eckville hosted its first male stripper, who performed at the local hotel. The staid ladies of this allegedly straight-laced town mobbed him and sent him scratched and screaming out the window of his hotel room looking for safety.[4]

How culpable were Eckvillians in the Keegstra affair? It is unlikely that the teachings of a prominent local teacher could have gone undiscovered for very long. Keegstra's career in town politics and his popularity among students made him stand out. Many Eckvillians came to his defence after he ran into trouble with the Lacombe County Board of Education, and several members of the town council even wrote letters of support for him. It must be remembered, however, that in a small town where everyone knows everyone else, it is difficult to go against the grain on any matter, let alone one as serious as the teachings of Jim Keegstra. It must also be remembered that three of the people most directly responsible for Keegstra's dismissal, Margaret Andrew, Susan Maddox and Kevin McEntee, were all Eckville residents.

If most Eckvillians can be collectively accused of anything over the fourteen-year span of Keegstra's teachings, it is apathy. As one Eckville mother put it, "We were so busy running the farm, taking our kids to 4-H, figure skating and everything else, we never took the time to read their school work."[5] But then, many other Canadian parents are probably guilty of the same thing. It might not have mattered so much if Jim Keegstra, a man with a mission, had not taken a position at Eckville High School.

— II —

Jim Keegstra was born to Dutch immigrant parents, the last of seven children, in Vulcan, Alberta on March 30, 1934. Anna and Klaas Keegstra had immigrated to Canada in 1928 from the island of Friesland in Holland. Like most agricultural immigrants from the Netherlands, they were strong Calvinists, belonging to the Dutch Reformed Church. The family lived in the tiny hamlet of Kircaldy, just south of Vulcan, which is itself situated eighty kilometers southeast of Calgary.

The area had been a destination for Dutch immigrants since shortly after the turn of the century, when the Dutch Reformed Church encouraged poor Hollanders to move to Canada to help spread the Calvinist faith. Religion played an important part in the settlers' lives. In the years prior to the arrival of the Keegstras congregations were established in the small southern Alberta communities of Granum, Nobleford and Burdet, not far from where the Keegstras were to live.[6]

The Keegstras were very poor when they arrived in Canada and Klaas was forced to work for some years on a dairy farm. The Depression, which first hit western Canada with full force in the spring of 1930, made matters worse. Prices for wheat and other grains plummetted; the market for sugar beets dried up. Farmers all over southern Alberta were driven into bankruptcy.

Nature added to the disaster as the rainfall on the southern prairies diminished. This caused a huge dustbowl to envelop much of the area known as Palliser's Triangle, which encompasses southeastern Alberta, southern Saskatchewan and southwestern Manitoba. It is no wonder that the Keegstras soon moved. First they went to Cross-field, about forty kilometers north of Calgary and away from the worst drought and Depression. Then they moved on to Alhambra, about halfway between Eckville and Rocky Mountain House. This is where Jim Keegstra completed high school in 1954.

The young Keegstra had little interest in farming. By the early 1950s he had decided, instead, to be an auto mechanic. For several years following his graduation from high school, he learned the mechanic's trade. He served an apprenticeship and received his auto mechanics papers in Carstairs, Alberta, in 1957. The previous year he had married Lorraine, and perhaps he began to think that his chosen vocation would not provide a good enough economic foundation to raise a family. In 1959 he entered the University of Alberta at Calgary (now the University of Calgary) to study for a Bachelor of Education degree with a specialization in industrial arts. Keegstra was a hard worker. He attended university classes while supporting himself and his growing family by working as a mechanic and also by teaching. After his graduation from university in 1967, he took summer courses in social studies to upgrade his degree.[7]

— III —

Jim Keegstra is a self-made man and a strong individualist. His religious and political development reflected both his poverty-stricken youth and the individualism that grew out of his prairie farming environment. His family were strong Fundamentalist Protestants, believing in the literal truth of the Bible. They were also loyal Social Crediters and Jim Keegstra developed a strong allegiance to both traditions in his youth.

When the Keegstras first arrived in Canada, they were members of the Dutch Reformed Church. Like many pioneers, however, they soon left their old faith in search of a church more suited to their adopted environment. Calvinism may be considered a rather austere doctrine by some. It is a faith which places a strong emphasis on intellect and which is more in tune with modern scientific theories about human beings and their environment than many other, more conservative dogmas. The faith of Calvinists does not rest on a literal interpretation of the Bible or on strong, emotional declarations or experiences of salvation. It is more a religion of the head than of the heart. As such, it has never had a strong appeal to North Americans living and working in farm and pioneer communities. Instead, they have traditionally been drawn to Evangelism—a religious tradition which strongly emphasizes emotion and faith—and Fundamentalism, which is based on the literal acceptance of the Bible.

Keegstra and his parents remained true to the basic tenets of Calvinism—a belief in the unchanging nature of Jesus Christ, a rejection of ostentation and the answering to God for all human activity and enterprise. However they were also drawn towards less pragmatic and more emotional "heart"-oriented creeds. Fundamentalist and Evangelical churches generally reject modern Biblical criticism, scientific theories that are perceived to conflict with the Bible (such as evolution) and liberalism in personal morality and politics. The Keegstras, like other farm and pioneer families, were undoubtedly drawn to such churches by the rugged individualism embodied in them, their own need for self-reliance and the guide to daily living and personal conduct provided through intensive Bible study.

In the southern Alberta of the early 1930s, Evangelism and Fundamentalism went hand-in-hand with the Social Credit doctrines preached by William Aberhart. "Bible Bill" was a mathematics teacher, principal of Crescent Heights High School in Calgary and head of the Calgary Prophetic Bible Institute. By the early 1930s he had built up a large following in southern Alberta through his Sunday broadcasts over CFCN radio. In the depths of the Depression, Aberhart discovered the theory of Social Credit, first developed in England by British engineer Major C.H. Douglas in the early 1920s.

Aberhart became an instant convert. Social Credit

appealed to him because it was a relatively simple idea which appeared to explain what had gone wrong with the economic system. Aberhart began to preach Social Credit doctrine in his religious broadcasts and by 1935 was able to lead a Social Credit government to power in Edmonton. Douglas, the originator of the theory, believed that there was nothing wrong with society's productive capacity, but that the ability of the people to purchase was restricted by the large sums that had to be directed towards the payment of interest on loans. These loans, made by a conspiracy of international bankers, Douglas wrote, were destroying the vitality of the capitalist system. In his view, the bankers could be stopped only by the introduction of Social Credit—a system of debt-free dividend payments in cash from the government to the consumers.[8] Social Credit, in effect, absolved the farmers, workers and small business people of any blame in the economic collapse. It placed the responsibility squarely on a clique of evil bankers. The theory appeared to provide a solution to the Depression. It bypassed the more radical proposals of socialists and Communists. Furthermore, it was easy to understand and to explain to the ordinary citizens of Alberta.

Social Credit appealed strongly to people like the Keegstra family, whose world was collapsing around them. It promised recovery for the Depression-wracked farm country of southern Alberta. It was sold by one of the most effective radio evangelists in Canadian history. Also, it fit in well with the notion that the honest, God-fearing folks who had farmed their land and attended their churches had been victimized by an evil group of social parasites. Not the least of the new theory's appeal was Aberhart's promise to start his Social Credit administration with a straight cash grant of $25 to all Albertans.

The Keegstras became strong Social Creditors and young Jim followed in their footsteps. He attended Aberhart's Calgary Prophetic Bible Institute and in 1957 joined the Social Credit party. By the time Jim Keegstra finished university in 1967 he had read most of the writings of Major Douglas.[9] His strong attachment to Social Credit was rooted in his Protestant fundamentalism. He believes that its philosophy is based on the Bible and on "Christian principles" such as individualism, freedom and free enterprise.[10]

Keegstra's view of the world is a view dominated by the Jews. He first encountered these people in his Bible and in the anti-Semitic pamphlets and booklets he read as he grew up. He himself has admitted to having met only a very small number of Jews in his youth—his father's tailor, and some cattle buyers who worked near Rocky Mountain House.[11]

As a strong believer in the literal truth of the Bible, Keegstra noted that the Jews neither believe in the divinity of Jesus, nor follow his teachings. He also knew that in passages in the New Testament they are condemned for their refusal to follow Jesus. In Chapter 8 of the Gospel of St. John, for example—one often cited by Keegstra—Jesus tells a group of Jews: "Ye are of your father the devil."[12] Few modern Christians take these words literally, but Keegstra doubts neither the truth of the event nor the accuracy of Jesus' accusation. To him, therefore, the Jews were not merely non-Christian. They were and are actively anti-Christian, serving the purposes of the devil and the anti-Christ, and posing a mortal threat to Christianity. The Jews, he told a reporter in 1983, "hate Christ," and were and are "out to destroy" Christianity. There could not, therefore, be any fraternization between Jews and Christians.[13]

Keegstra claims to have become interested in the Jews through his reading of the Bible and to have wandered into the study of the Talmud in search of the true nature of Judaism. While in fact there are two distinct Talmuds—the Babylonian and the Jerusalem—it is the Babylonian Talmud which is the more frequently studied of the two. Its 6,000 folio pages, in Hebrew and in Aramaic, contain a record of oral debates and discussions in the great academies of Babylon on legal issues affecting every aspect of Jewish life. But it is much more than that. It is a vast "sea," a storehouse of information connected with the life, habits, views and superstitions of both the Jews and non-Jews. It represents several hundred years of tradition, covering a period which ended around 500 C.E. The Talmud is so massive and all-encompassing that is can only be mastered after years of study.

Keegstra never made such an effort. His Talmudic "studies" consisted of reading and absorbing anti-Semitic works such as an eighty-eight-page booklet first published in Czarist Russia in 1892. This booklet, entitled *The Talmud Unmasked: The Secret Rabbinical Teachings Concerning Christians*, was written by Rev. Justinus Bonaventura Pranaitis, Professor of Hebrew Language at the Imperial Ecclesiastical Academy of the Roman Catholic Church in St. Petersburg. Pranaitis had a long career as a dedicated Jew-hater. He apparently also had a criminal record. In 1911, he appeared as a witness for the prosecution in the infamous trial of Mendel Beilis, in Kiev. Beilis had been charged with murdering a twelve-year-old boy in order to use the blood of a Christian child in Jewish ritual. Pranaitis claimed that the killing had all the characteristics of a ritual murder by Jews.

Pranaitis' masterwork, *The Talmud Unmasked*, contains a number of excerpts of Talmudic text concerning Jewish relations with, and attitudes towards, non-Jews. These have been mis-translated and taken out of context to show that Judaism is viciously anti-Christian. There can be little doubt that Keegstra's views on Judaism were strongly influenced by this and similar works. Many of the claims he repeats most often—that Jews consider it a sin to sell property to a non-Jew; that Jews are prohibited from giving gifts to non-Jews or from praising them in any way; that Jews consider Mary, mother of Jesus, to have been a prostitute and Jesus a bastard—are outlined clearly in *The Talmud Unmasked*. The booklet falsely claims, in fact, that *any* anti-Christian act, from murder of Christians to theft of Christian property is not only condoned but actually advocated by the Talmud.[14]

There are, indeed, less than flattering references to Jesus and Christianity in the thousands of pages of Talmudic text. It should not be surprising that a work so massive and diverse should contain such material. It was, one must remember, compiled after five centuries of growing Christian-Jewish conflict, which had seen Christianity—a bitter rival of Judaism—emerge triumphant in the Roman Empire, and which had produced mass persecutions of Jews. But references to Christianity in the Talmud are actually relatively few. It certainly presents none of the gross distortions contained in *The Talmud Unmasked*. The Talmud was, and is, a guide to everyday life for Jews, who are required to fulfill their convenant with God by following God's commandments. It is the Talmud which basically tells them what God has commanded, by interpreting Biblical law and showing how it is to be applied in everyday situations.

The Talmud Unmasked purports to prove, however, that the Talmud really exists for another reason—to guide Jews in their war against Christianity. A good example is the claim advanced on page 73 of the booklet, one often mentioned by Keegstra himself. Pranaitis states that "A Jew may lie and perjure himself to condemn a Christian." The assertion is based on a portion of Talmudic text (Baba Kama 113a) concerning the need for Jews to treat the property of *heathens* with the same respect they hold for Jewish property. In the folio pages of analysis and debate devoted to this subject, the Talmud clearly prohibits Jews from robbing heathens, keeping their lost property or swearing false oaths against them, And yet *The Talmud Unmasked* asserts not only that the passage refers to Christians, but that the Talmud permits this type of unethical behavior.

From publications such as this, freely available throughout Canada, the United States and elsewhere, Keegstra undoubtedly came to believe some of the most vicious libels ever spread about the Jews. *The Talmud Unmasked* is published in the United States by Liberty Bell Publications, owned by self-professed Nazi, George P. Dietz ("I and my associates live and breathe National Socialism every waking moment"). The same organization also distributes other anti-Jewish material ranging from Hitler's political testament, *Mein Kampf*, to bumper stickers that

began to study the Talmud, only to discover a truth about
13th-century Europe. It was at that time that Christians
expressions of an anti-Jewish spirit which has its roots in
of Pranaitis and Dilling, they are no more than modern-day
Notwithstanding these differences between the wor...

Press.
been called
the United States
Jewish organizations as th...

for Historical Review, which specializes in Holocaust denial
publications.[16] The Dilling book focuses on the same theme
as *The Talmud Unmasked:* Judaism is actively anti-
Christian. Dilling, like Pranaitis, used excerpts from the
Talmud to prove her case and many of her points were lifted
directly from *The Talmud Unmasked*. Dilling's main thesis
is that Judaism is not based on the Hebrew Bible (the Old
Testament), but upon the Babylonian Talmud, which she
describes as a pornographic, anti-Gentile, anti-Christian
document written by the Pharisees.

Dilling's work ranges much farther afield than did *The
Talmud Unmasked*, however. The older book aimed to show
only that Jews were anti-Christian and that Judaism
condoned all forms of anti-Christian activity. Dilling, on the
other hand, also aimed to demonstrate that Judaism is
depraved in its own right and has laid the foundation for,
and worked actively with, Communism. *The Jewish Religion* sets out to show that Jews are allowed to commit all
sorts of sexual perversions from the buggery of children to
intercourse with animals, and that prominent Jews played a
major role in the success of the Bolshevik revolution of
1917. All of these themes have been repeated by Jim
Keegstra in the classroom and in interviews with the
press.[17]

Judaism of which they had been unaware: that it is more than a Biblical religion. As they came to understand the way in which the Talmud had shaped and guided the lives of Jews, they concluded that the Jews had severed their historic relationship with Christianity. Jews, they believed, could no longer be considered the "People of the Book" because the Bible had become of less importance to them in their daily lives than the Talmud. Moreover, they thought that the Talmud was a work which contained defamatory statements about Christianity. From that time, the Talmud was banned, burned and censored in Europe.

In the 19th century, anti-Semites once again attacked Judaism through the Talmud. Johann Eisenmenger's vicious anti-Talmudic polemic, *Entdecktes Judenthum (Judaism Unmasked)*, first published in 1699, was reissued in 1893. Among similar works available then were August Rohling's *Der Talmudjude* (1871), Hippolyte Lutostanski's three-volume *Talmud and the Jews* (1879–80) and Pranaitis' *The Talmud Unmasked*.

The fantasy which conceived of the Talmud as an anti-Christian work, and the myth of the Jewish world-conspiracy, were two of the key elements in Keegstra's thinking about the Jews. He imbibed these ideas from modern works which repeat these century-old delusions. Today it is no longer alleged that Jews desecrate the wafer used by Catholics in the Eucharist ceremony, or that Jews murder Christians in order to use their blood for Passover rituals. The conspiracy myth and attacks on the Talmud, however, have proven more durable weapons in the anti-Semite's arsenal. Whatever the psychological appeal of these myths to Jim Keegstra, he not only absorbed them, but conveyed them to students in his classroom.[18]

Did Keegstra turn to such writings because he was already an anti-Semite, or did he become an anti-Semite because he read them? It is likely that he himself could not or would not answer this question. He, of course, denies hating Jews at all. But one thing is clear: Keegstra's religious views and his "self-education" about the Talmud soon led him much farther afield in his pursuit of a supposed Jewish plot against civilization.

Thus Keegstra questioned the doctrine that Christ's Second Coming and personal reign on earth would precede (rather than conclude) the millennium. This belief, known as premillennialism, was a cornerstone of the thinking of many Fundamentalist students of prophecy in 19th-century Britain and America. Moreover, it was usually bound to what some Christians thought was another part of the Divine schema, the restoration of the Jews to the Holy Land. The Baptists are one of the many denominations in North America who still believe in premillennialism. Keegstra noted that he had once been "nabbed, seduced really, by the Baptists," but he had later rejected their premillennialist views.

Keegstra's rejection of this doctrine and his consequent move from the Baptists and from the Church of the Nazarene to the Diamond Valley Full Gospel Church, near Eckville (where his son Larry is pastor) are more than matters of technical interest. Since it was bound to a conception of the future in which the Jews would be restored to God's favor, the rejection of premillennialism involved a reconsideration of the role of the Jews in history. A person such as Keegstra, already inclined to a negative attitude towards Jews, could readily conclude that they no longer play a role in the Divine plan. Indeed, he could maintain that the "Israel of God" in the New Testament is a reference not to Jews, but to the Christian churches.[19]

Jim Keegstra clearly sees himself as a solitary soldier in a war against the forces of the anti-Christ. In his imaginary world, the Jews are determined to destroy Christianity, which is the one real obstacle to their Satanic aims because it is the basis for whatever freedom is left in the world today. There is a direct link between Judaism, Communism and socialism in his mind, because "all are materialistic, all are internationalists and all advocate the abolition of private property."[20]

By the time Jim Keegstra was fired from his teaching post at Eckville High School, his anti-Jewish views had become complex and all-encompassing. They far surpassed the simple anti-Jewish prejudice of his youth. It is impossible to know the full story of the development of those views. But there can be little doubt that the process was well on its way before Jim Keegstra ever stood in front of an Alberta classroom.

— IV —

Keegstra's teaching career began in 1961 in Cremona, a small town (population 365) about sixty-five kilometers north of Calgary. He taught industrial arts, science and mathematics at the local high school. Keegstra was attending the University of Alberta at Calgary at the time, working towards his B. Ed. He took summer courses in order to broaden the range of subjects he might teach. Although he later specialized in teaching modern history in his social studies courses, he took only two history courses at the university, one in Canadian and the other in European history.

In 1963, Jim Keegstra left Cremona and moved with his family to Red Deer, where he was employed at the Lindsay Thurder Composite High School teaching automotive mechanics. In 1966 he moved again, this time to Medicine Hat. There, for the first time, he taught social studies and law, as well as his usual industrial arts subjects. According to his own recollection, he taught social studies "by the book" in the beginning, but found the texts too left wing for his tastes. "They were written primarily by socialists and a socialist has an awfully thick pair of red glasses." He later recounted, "Things come out awfully red." Keegstra, always the individualist, then began to do his own "research" into world history and began to teach his own version of it. He saw it as his responsibility as a teacher "not to use old junk."[21]

Keegstra was graduated from university in 1967 and, armed with his new degree, sought a permanent teaching position. He found one in Eckville in 1968. There he joined a small staff, all of whom taught a wide range of subjects. Although Keegstra initially taught only automotives and industrial arts, it was not long before he began to teach social studies, law, mathematics and science to both junior and senior high school classes. Keegstra was able to introduce his own brand of anti-Jewish history into the classroom because he was not restricted to the subject areas he had specialized in—industrial arts and automotives. Although he has scant training as a social studies expert, he ended up teaching many of the social studies classes at Eckville High School. How did this happen?

In Alberta, as in many other jurisdictions, teachers are trained to be teachers. They are not necessarily trained to be experts in a certain subject or subjects although they may, in fact, take heavy course concentrations in fields such as history or biology. A teacher who has specialized in industrial arts, therefore, is considered a teacher first and an industrial arts specialist second. Because he or she holds a B.Ed., a teacher is often thought to be capable of teaching *any* subject, not just in his or her area of specialization.

School officials would obviously, under most conditions, prefer to employ teachers to teach specific subjects who had been especially trained in those subjects. However, this is not always possible. In many small jurisdictions—rural school districts—it is in fact often impossible. At the time of Keegstra's dismissal, he was one of only seven fulltime teachers at the school, including the principal, Ed Olsen. Since Keegstra appeared to be an effective teacher, was well liked by the students and had taken social studies subjects at university, it was natural that he would quickly become one of the school's regular social studies teachers. This gave him the opportunity to introduce his anti-Jewish theories into an otherwise conventional educational curriculum.

Keegstra had little trouble fitting into the community

of Eckville. He attended the Diamond Valley Full Gospel
Church and became a deacon and Sunday School teacher
there. The church, a log structure located in the wooded
Diamond Valley not far from Eckville, is Fundamentalist
and Evangelical, but not millennialist. In 1974, Keegstra
ran for Eckville town council. He and six other incumbents
were elected by acclamation to the seven-member body.
He was re-elected by acclamation in 1977 and won the
mayoralty of Eckville, again by acclamation, in 1980.

In spite of his leadership activities in the community,
people in Eckville did not know quite what to make of Jim
Keegstra. On the one hand he was personable, religious
and obviously hard working. On the other hand, he kept to
himself much of the time, rarely socializing with the
townspeople and restricting himself to a small circle of
friends from his church. It is clear that he was respected,
for the most part, and developed a reputation as a real
Christian. Fellow social studies teacher Joe Lindberg
considers Keegstra to be a committed and charitable
Christian. The Keegstras sometimes opened their home to
destitute people, including ex-convicts from the provincial
jail at Bowden, because they believed it was their Christian
duty to help others as long as there was something to put on
the table.

Keegstra was and is a loner. Shortly before his trial in
the spring of 1985, he told reporter Ross Henderson of the
Red Deer Advocate that he always found meeting people "a
little hard" because he is not "an outgoing type of person."[22]
In the classroom, however, Keegstra came into his own. He
often came to school early to prepare for his students and to
offer them advice or help if they required it. He kept strict
disciplinary control of his students and was clearly in charge
at all times. This is an ability highly prized in high school
teachers.

Keegstra seems to have developed an especially close
relationship with some of the boys, helping them to fix their
cars after school and ready to lend an ear to their problems.
His relationship with the girls was much frostier—Keegstra

never hid his extreme distaste for anything smacking of feminism. A tall rangy man, well groomed, with a predilection for sunglasses and wide belts, and with his graying hair slicked back in the style of the 1950s, he clearly appealed to the macho in the Eckville boys, despite his disapproval of the drinking and partying which dominated the social life of this typical rural high school community. There is no doubt that Keegstra was able to develop strong bonds with some of his students, although others were repelled by his mannerisms and the message he taught in class.

Jim Keegstra is a true believer. There is no evidence that he was, or is, at all cynical about the message of hate that he taught in the classroom. He lives in an imaginary world run by Jewish conspirators who exist behind the scenes in a variety of guises controlling and manipulating the events which determine the course of human history. He has come to believe in them as others might believe in fairies or leprechauns. Having converted himself to this conspiratorial view, he is intent on converting others, warning them of the "truths" that only he and a handful of others can see. Keegstra decided long ago to take on the conventional world, to save it from those who lurk in the shadows to destroy it. He sees himself as a soldier for Jesus, fighting against the conspiracy of the anti-Christ. He seems determined to fight his righteous battle despite the cost, and regardless of the suffering it might bring to him.

His son Larry reflected this strong conviction in a letter to the *Eckville Examiner* published after his father's defeat in his bid for re-election to the mayoralty of Eckville following his dismissal from his teaching post. "As I scan the results of our town election, I am reminded of the words of Jesus as He looked out over the city: 'O Jerusalem, Jerusalem, thou that killest the prophets, and stonest them which are sent unto thee' . . ."23

In Jim Keegstra's battle against the lurking forces of evil, there is no more room for compromise than there was in Jesus' struggle to establish the Kingdom of Heaven, at least in Keegstra's mind. He is, he believes, following in his

Lord's footsteps. It is not he who is wrong; it is main-line Christianity which has now eschewed the anti-Semitism that was once a part of Christian dogma. Keegstra believes that he and only a few others have seen the light of truth; it is the rest of the world which fails to understand.

2

The Roots of Anti-Semitism

JIM KEEGSTRA DOES NOT aim simply to keep Jews out of the local club or to bar them from his neighborhood. His is not the prejudice of some of society's upper crust, with its slurs about pushy Jews or its jokes about Jewish businesspeople. Jim Keegstra, and those like him, are the current representatives of a way of thinking that goes back two thousand years.

Long before Hitler came to power and raised the racial theories of 19th-century crackpot philosophers and pseudoscientists into Nazism, the notion of a "Jewish conspiracy" existed and set the stage for genocide. Although Keegstra lives and taught in a small town in Alberta, he is a kindred spirit to others like him—stretching back into history and across the globe—who have taken their inspiration from their own biased interpretation of the New Testament and from malevolent medieval beliefs. Whether or not Keegstra succeeded in teaching his students to be biased or prejudiced against Jews, he taught them the very same world view which kindled and sustained the Holocaust.

— I —

The idea that Jews are demonic and conspiratorial, that they aim to enslave others through deceit and manipulation, has its origins in the New Testament. In New Testament times some early Christians, including several leaders of the new religion, mounted a campaign to show that the Jewish people of the day had been led against Jesus by the group known as the Pharisees. Anti-Pharisaic references abound in the New Testament and in early Christian writings despite the fact that Jesus' teachings were closer to those of the Pharisees than to those of most other groups in ancient Palestine. In truth, the Pharisees were the founders of modern, rabbinical Judaism. They were the bitter enemies of the Sadducees, who supported the continuation of temple worship and collaborated with the Roman rulers of the day. Keegstra's remonstrations against "rabbinical Judaism" are an echo of the ancient Christian campaign against Pharisaism.

That campaign was made even more bitter by the increasing popularization, in the early centuries of Christianity, of the notion that only those people who had become Christians were the inheritors of God's covenant with Israel. The new Christians believed that the life, death and resurrection of Christ was a new covenant between God and those who believed in His Son. It was to replace the old covenant between God and the Jews. The Gospel of St. John had quoted Jesus accusing the Jews of being the sons of the devil, and ancient Christian theologians such as St. John Chrysostom took up the message in order to discredit the rival faith. In an effort to terrorize the Jewish Christians of Antioch into a final breach with their parent religion, he called the synagogue "the temple of demons . . . the cavern of devils . . . a gulf and abyss of perdition." St. Augustine wrote that the Jews, who had once been the favorite sons of God, had been transformed, instead, into children of the devil. But this was not all. Jews were also said to be in league with the anti-Christ, whose tyrannical reign, according to the Book of Revelation, is to precede the second coming of Christ.[1]

Most hatred of Jews in the early Christian era was based on the charge of Deicide—the accusation that the Jews had murdered Christ and the assumption that all Jews, everywhere and throughout the ages, were guilty of this crime and destined to suffer for it. Since many early Christians believed this, it was also easy for them to accept almost any accusation leveled against the Jews, no matter how foul or fantastic. The centuries after the fall of the Roman Empire—the Dark Ages—were a time of fear and suspicion throughout Europe and many Christians were all too ready to believe that Jews were engaging in witchcraft in order to advance the cause of their master, the devil.

At the time of the First Crusade, such legends and myths became a rationale for the slaughter of Jews in Europe and Palestine. Many of the Crusaders, especially in the Rhine River valley in Germany, could not wait to get to the Holy Land to conduct their war on non-Christians, especially when the Jews whom they believed to be allies of the anti-Christ were so close at hand.

By the 12th century the Jews were being accused of murdering Christian children to use their blood in baking of the Passover *matzot* (unleavened bread), desecrating hosts in churches, poisoning wells, conducting black magic and weaving spells against Christianity. Popes and bishops frequently condemned these anti-Jewish myths, but they nevertheless became part of the popular culture of European peasant society and were often encouraged by local priests, friars and nuns.

The spread of the notion that Jews were purveyors of black magic and dark rituals was undoubtedly intensified by the exclusion of Jews from the larger society, which began with the enclosure of the first ghetto in Venice in 1516. Prior to this there had been no restrictions on where Jews could live although, as an oft-persecuted minority, they usually chose to live together. The ghetto walls closed the

Jews off from the rest of Europe, enhancing the aura of mystery surrounding them.

The alien nature of Jews and Judaism had its roots in pre-Christian times, when Jews had consistently refused to adopt the gods of a succession of conquerors—a practice that was almost standard in the ancient world with its more or less interchangeable deities. The ghetto, and the special anti-Jewish laws and practices—from the Jew Tax to the Jew Hat—strengthened the separateness. They deepened the conviction of many Christians that the Jews were devil worshippers and doers of evil.

The French Revolution was the beginning of the end for the ghetto. When the National Assembly granted full citizenship to French Jews in 1791, one era in the relationship of Jews to Christians in Europe began to come to a close. Another began to open up. In the ghetto era Jews were a people apart, easily defined and saddled with a permanently inferior status. This state of affairs, however, was not tolerated by the new leaders of 19th-century Europe, who believed in democracy and equal rights. The ghetto walls came down and Jews were granted equal status throughout western Europe. A few Jewish families such as the Rothschilds succeeded in amassing vast wealth in the new, industrializing Europe, and became highly visible to the European masses. The Rothschild family became powerful bankers, with branches in most European capitals. Their emergence to positions of power was taken, in many quarters, as proof of the invisible and international nature of the Jews—people who, it was alleged, owed no allegiance to any national authority.

The transformation of Europe from an agricultural to an industrial society in the years following the French Revolution of 1789 to 1793 was an unsettling and unpleasant experience for millions. Peasants became factory workers. A new elite rose to power and the hold of the modern state over its subjects and citizens was greatly strengthened in almost every way. Most of the major political movements of modern times, from Communism to nationalism, are rooted in this era. Although the Jews shared the trials and tribulations of the massive social upheaval, it appeared to some Europeans as if the Jews alone were the real beneficiaries of the process. After all, had they not received their political emancipation because of the Industrial Revolution? Were they not becoming prosperous as a result of it? Perhaps it was the Jews who were behind these changes, the Jews manipulating people and events for Jewish purposes. Those who still believed in the sinister nature of Jews and Judaism and who detested the changes that modernization was forcing on Europe concluded that the Jews were at fault. They began to spread their conclusions far and wide.

This was the origin of the Jewish conspiracy theory—a marriage between the medieval view of the Jew as a demon worshipper and doer of evil and the more modern notion of the Jew as plotter of economic depression, manipulator of governments and planner of wars and famines. The two became one and the same.[2]

Writings of various kinds associating the Jews with a conspiracy to control the world appeared often in 19th-century Europe. Jew haters usually linked the Jews with the Freemasons and Illuminati, even though neither group had any organizational, political or religious relationship to Jews. The Freemasons were and are a fraternal order pursuing liberal ends through charity and benevolence. Freemasons in Europe and the Americas were often found in the forefront of liberal revolutions because they believed in liberal principles. No reputable evidence of any international masonic conspiracies has ever been uncovered, much less linked to Jews.

The Illuminati, founded in 1776 by Adam Weishaupt (a non-Jew), was a society opposed to state authoritarianism and church authority. It disappeared very quickly and not much is known about it, except that the Bavarian branch of the group under Weishaupt was somewhat anti-Jewish. But no matter. The conspiracy was never concerned with reality. It bore no relationship to what Jews were really all about, to what they did, to what their aspirations were. It was a figment of the imagination from the start and still is.

The Jews of the conspiracy, like the medieval Jews who were said to poison wells and desecrate hosts, never existed and do not exist.

Of all the writings issued in the last century to prove the existence of the Jewish conspiracy, none was as influential or as important as *The Protocols of the Elders of Zion*. This book, almost certainly forged by an agent of the Czarist secret police living in Paris in the late 1890s, was purported to be made up of conversations, instructions and dialogues of the secret leaders of the world Jewish conspiracy. It supposedly summarized the progress of the conspiracy up to that point and laid out plans for the future. In this document Jews were linked with the downfall of the monarchies of Europe, the rise of liberal democracy, the disenfranchisement of Christianity and the spread of democracy and political liberty. It was all supposedly part of the Jews' plan to put the mob in charge, to create chaos and disorder prior to bringing about the rule of the Jewish conspiracy.

The book was actually plagiarized from a totally unrelated political satire published in France in 1865 by Maurice Joly, a liberal lawyer, entitled *A Dialogue in Hell Between Montesquieu and Machiavelli*. This satire was about French political life under Emperor Napoleon III and had nothing to do with Jews; it did not even mention them. But in the hands of a clever forger it became the ultimate proof of the Jewish conspiracy.[3] (No one knows why *A Dialogue in Hell* was used as the model for the forgery.)

The *Protocols* became the Bible of the Black Hundreds, a Czarist anti-Jewish organization responsible for everything from propaganda to pogroms. The document soon spread throughout western Europe and to America. The *Protocols* has been one of the best selling books of this century, and is still available around the world. *The Times* of London exposed *The Protocols* as a forgery in August 1921, but this exposé had little impact on its distribution. In the United States, for example, Henry Ford had it serialized in his *Dearborn Independent*. When the articles were reproduced as a book, entitled *The International Jew*, it sold half a million copies.

The Protocols has been called a "warrant for genocide" by Professor Norman Cohn because it was used by the Nazis in their ideological war against the European Jews which culminated in the Holocaust. The work has helped convince millions of non-Jews that the Jews carry the germ of conspiracy with them wherever they go—that each and every Jew is rooted to this plot, which has determined the course of history from far back in time to the present day. Whereas the Jews of the Middle Ages were accused of doing evil deeds from time to time—murdering Christian children or desecrating hosts—the "Elders of Zion" were portrayed as working every hour of every day of manipulating people and events to their own purposes. "Instead of muttering spells," Cohn points out, "these sorcerers place articles in the press; instead of poisoning wells, they plunge whole countries into slums and wars and revolutions."[4]

In the 19th century, writers such as Arthur de Gobineau, Christian Lassen and Paul de Lagarde had developed the idea that some races were superior to others; that racial "characteristics" were inherent and therefore unchanging; and that the Jews were at the bottom of the racial hierarchy. When these notions were combined with the belief that the Jews were also plotting daily to overthrow Christian civilization, the ideological justification for mass murder had been created. The Jews could not be assimilated or converted; wherever they were, there was "The Conspiracy." The solution? Annihilation.

This mode of thinking was linked to the attacks on Judaism exemplified by works such as *The Talmud Unmasked*. It is no coincidence that both were the product of Czarist Russia and both appeared in the 1890s. Czarist Russia was virtually without a rival as the foremost center of organized anti-Jewish hate at that time. Centuries of oppression of the peasants, and the rapid industrialization of urban Russia, had combined—in the late 19th century—with the frustrations of the heavily circumscribed intelligentsia to produce widespread unrest. Revolutionaries of various stripes were increasingly active as support for the absolute rule of the Czars ebbed. The Russian government, which had been anti-Jewish from the beginning of the 19th Century, used the Jews as a scapegoat, hoping to turn popular discontent towards these people and away from the government. In Russia anti-Semitism was part of state policy.

This was one reason why many Jews worked to topple the Czarist government and could be found in positions of leadership in Bolshevik regime, which took over in 1917. It also meant that the germs of extreme anti-Semitism were to be carried throughout Europe, wherever the anti-Bolshevik refugees settled after the Revolution. Some of the pro-Czarist émigrés blamed the Jews for the loss of their fortunes and power, and formed the nucleus for the spread of this particularly virulent strain of anti-Semitism. Their message was basically this: whatever may have been true about the Jews and God in pre-Christian times, Jews were now plotters who aimed to establish Communist rule everywhere and whose holy books (and in particular the Talmud) laid the basis for that plot. This meant that the Communists and the "international bankers" like the Rothschilds (who were Jewish) were both linked through the "Elders of Zion."

By the early 1970s, Jim Keegstra believed all of this and more. He had decided it was his duty, as a possessor of the truth, to pass it along to his students in order to show them what had really happened in the past, not what their purportedly Jewish-controlled texts told them had happened. On national television, Keegsta told Linden MacIntyre that Jews aim to enslave Christians, that the French Revolution was the product of the Jewish conspiracy and Napolean its servant, and that the United States Civil War was also caused by the Jews. It was the Jews who had assassinated Abraham Lincoln, Keegstra falsely claimed, because "John Wilkes Booth was of the Jewish religion."[5] Booth was in fact not Jewish.

Keegstra later told Nancy Millar of the *Calgary Herald* that Judaism, Communism, socialism and Freemasonry were "all related with the same ideological foundations." World War II had been planned by the Jewish conspiracy "to gain world control and force Jews to move to Israel."[6] He told Ross Henderson of the *Eckville Examiner* that the Jews were "responsible for the debts and the revolutions and everything else we have in the world today. There is no other. The Illuminati is behind it all."[7] (To Keegstra, the Illuminati and the Jews are synonymous.)

Nor was there a Holocaust, according to Keegstra. Jews were systematically rounded up and expelled by the Nazis and those who remained were put to forced labor. This supposedly resulted in the deaths of about 300,000 Jews, of whom only 20,000 or so were executed. The ruins of the Auschwitz-Birkenau death camp in Poland are not proof of anything, according to Keegstra, because "it was closed for ten years after the war" and "who knows what the Communists did with it."[8] Clearly anyone who, like Keegstra, believes that respected international organizations such as the Trilateral Commission, the Club of Rome and the International Monetary Fund[9] are all fronts of the Jewish conspiracy would have no trouble believing that the Holocaust was a hoax created by that same conspiracy to serve its own ends. Keegstra is ready and willing to advance his views publicly. He deeply believes them.

— II —

Jim Keegstra's anti-Semitism undoubtedly developed out of a combination of factors, including his early religious education and personal experience. But the views he holds now were molded by reading and studying a mountain of anti-Semitic literature. Reading was the way in which his youthful prejudice against Jews was turned into the complex and detailed schema that now exists inside his imagination. He began to reach his conclusions about the Jewish conspiracy in the late 1950s and early 1960s when he was already prejudiced against Jews and was clearly ready to believe the worst about them. He then devoted an

important part of his life to the study of that conspiracy,
amassing details, collecting books and pamphlets, absorbing the conclusions of others and expanding his own
ideas on the subject. There can be little doubt that
Douglasite Social Credit was his first introduction to such
ideas.

Jim Keegstra first learned about Social Credit as he
was growing up. His parents were strong Social Creditors
and Social Credit dominated the rural political scene in
Alberta. He considers Social Credit to be rooted in
"Christian principles, the importance of the individual,
maximum freedom and free enterprise" and claims to have
been a Social Creditor all his adult life.[10] In 1971 he
contested the Social Credit nomination for Red Deer in the
provincial election of that year. He was unsuccessful and
grew embittered at the provincial party (which was then in
its thirty-sixth and last year of power) because of the
"skullduggery" he believed had denied him the nomination. "The big shots said I was too Christian for them," he
later claimed. "I said Alberta Education had gone red."[11]

Spurned by the provincial party, Keegstra turned to
the federal wing and ran for them in the 1972, 1974 and
1983 general elections. He claims that Social Credit is "the
closest system to what the Scriptures enunciate" and that
although he is never likely to win, he runs "for those who
know the truth." Social Credit may be dead in the minds of
most people, he asserts, but "Christianity is as dead as a
doornail too."[12]

For Jim Keegstra, Social Credit is much more than a
political affiliation. It is the political embodiment of his
religious experiences and is closely tied to his views on
Christianity, the Jews and the Jewish conspiracy. Keegstra
claims that, by the time he finished high school in the early
1950s, he had read most of what Social Credit's founder,
C.H. Douglas, had written. Since Douglas had become a
raving anti-Semite and purveyor of the most extreme ideas
about the Jewish conspiracy by the early 1940s, it is clear
where Keegstra first learned about the Jewish conspiracy.

— III —

Social Credit came from England. C.H. Douglas had been an aircraft engineer during World War I. As he watched and studied modern production at work, he thought up the theory that he called Social Credit. Britain and much of the western world had experienced a severe Depression just prior to the war and many people feared that, as soon as the war ended, the bad economic times would return. Douglas concluded, from his study of modern production processes, that society was fully capable of producing all the goods that people could possible want. However, somehow many people were not able to obtain and consume those goods.

Douglas reasoned that—since production costs were always paid to someone in the form of wages, rents, commissions or salaries—all this money should be finding its way into the pockets of consumers, who would then be able to buy all the goods that were being produced. This, Douglas reasoned, was not happening because one of the major costs of production was finding its was back into the pockets of the consumers. This major cost was the cost of borrowing money—interest. Where was this money going? Into the bank accounts of financiers, who were growing rich because of the hard work and risks that other people were taking. Douglas, therefore, proposed to create a national dividend, which would be distributed by the government to replace the money being siphoned off into the pockets of the financiers. This process would give consumers enough money to buy all they needed, and it would undermine the power of the financiers over the economy. The proposed national dividend was called Social Credit.

Although Douglas was a pavement-bred Englishman, the theory was well suited to appeal to the farmers of western Canada. Their annual business cycle was heavily dependent on credit. They had come to think of bankers, railway magnates and eastern industrialists generally as opportunists who lived off the honest labor of farmers and workers. In 1923 Douglas was invited to Canada at the request of an Alberta Member of Parliament, to give evidence to the House of Commons Standing Committee on Banking and Commerce.

Social Credit rested on a foundation of conspiracy, and at first Douglas was circumspect in identifying the members of that conspiracy. From an early belief that if might have developed almost by accident, he soon graduated to assertions that the conspiracy resulted from "a very deeply laid and well developed plot of enslaving the industrial world to the German-American-Jewish financiers." By the late 1930s Douglas no longer mentioned any German-American element. He wrote only of Jews.

Nothing illustrates the lengths to which Douglas' anti-Jewish paranoia developed better than a series of articles published in England in early 1942 and later reprinted in pamphlet-form and entitled *The Big Idea*. It is Douglas' own version of *The Protocols* and *The Talmud Unmasked*, all in one. The main theme of this work is that the Jews had conspired to unleash the war and that both Germany and the Allies were serving the ends of "The Big Idea," Douglas' shorthand for the Jewish conspiracy.

In Douglas' words, World War II was "the war of the Old Testament against the New Testament, of anti-Christ against Christ." Two philosophies were "at death grips;" that of "world domination and the materialistic Messiah" and "individual freedom." This conspiracy of the Jews was only the latest in a long chain of events caused by them, stretching far back into history, according to Douglas. Their "shadow government" had brought about the Glorious Revolution in England, the American and French Revolutions and the Bolshevik Revolution, all of which had "tended to the advantage of Germany."

Douglas did not buy Nazi racial theory but he claimed that the Jews had a special "race consciousness" which, when combined with the ancient customs laid out in the Talmud (which Douglas claimed regarded "the non-Jew as cattle"), provided them with the resources to carry out their secret plans. Among other Douglas gems contained in the pamphlet were the following: "While all international financiers are not Jews, many are, and the observable policy of these Jews and Freemasonry is that of the Talmud;" "the most dangerous enemy of the British people has been a group of German-American Jews;" "Hitler [was] the grandson of an illegitimate daughter of Baron Rothschild of Vienna;" "Admiral Canaris, head of German military intelligence, was a Jew named Moses Meyerbeer." Douglas cautioned his readers not to be fooled by the apparent anti-Semitism of the Nazis because Hitler was, in reality, following a "Talmudic Jew policy and philosophy."[13] Such fantastic ravings seem beyond explanation.

Douglas based much of his Jewish conspiracy idea on the writings and research of Nesta Webster, daughter of a British Member of Parliament, mystic and hater of Jews, who published her work about the Jewish conspiracy in the early 1920s. Webster's *World Revolution; The Plot Against Christianity* was first published in 1921 and has since gone through at least six printings (Keegstra's copy was published in England in 1971). Webster wrote that the Jews were the main players in secret societies, and the Illuminati in particular, who aimed to form a world conspiracy bent on enslaving society.

Webster linked Jews with most of the "evil" events in European history and especially, through the Illuminati, with the French Revolution, the key to the Jewish plan. Keegstra told the court during his trial for wilful promotion of hatred against Jews that he had used Webster extensively in arriving at the conclusions that formed the basis of what he taught his students. Given his admiration of Douglas, and Douglas' dependence on Webster, the link is clear.

The Big Idea and other Douglas writings such as *Programme for the Third World War* closely followed the traditional lines of the Jewish conspiracy idea. They asserted that the Jews were manipulating world events and had been doing so for centuries, and that the Jews were fundamentally anti-Christian and took their cue from a Talmud that schooled them for the struggle against Christianity. These materials, and other similar writings by Douglas and by his followers, were widely available in the Alberta of the 1940s because they were distributed by an agency of the Alberta government, the Alberta Social Credit Board.

— IV —

Social Credit came to Alberta through William Aberhart, who introduced it into his religious broadcasts in the early 1930s and then led the Social Credit movement into government in the summer of 1935. Aberhart clearly had mixed feelings about Jews. He was a millennialist and as such the Jews played an important role in his religious thinking. They were second in importance only to Christians. He believed that God would judge nations according to how they had treated the Jews. He was a supporter of the Zionist movement, which he viewed as helping to fulfill the ancient prophecies about the return of the Jews to the Holy Land.

But Aberhart also accepted the idea that Christians were struggling against the anti-Christ, who was the illegitimate offspring of Satan and an apostate Jewish woman. And he clearly believed that Jews dominated international finance. Jewish business practices were a major cause of anti-Semitism, in Aberhart's opinion.

Aberhart's mixed attitude towards Jews was evident in a press statement issued in September 1938, after Douglas had attacked the Jews as a menace to western civilization because of their alleged control of trade. On the one hand, Aberhart claimed that the Social Credit movement was opposed to anti-Semitism and that the principles which his government followed made "no distinction between race or religion of any kind." But on the other hand Aberhart claimed that the Jews had brought much persecution on themselves by the "oppression" they had practised against others. This had been carried out, he asserted, by Jewish "money barons" acting in concert with the "Anglo-Saxon group of financiers."

Personally, I have little doubt that in working through Jews, the Jewish financial group has sacrificed its own people on the altar of its greed for power and this group is preeminently responsible for the poisonous anti-Semitism which is rampant in the world today.

Was Aberhart being a hypocrite in denouncing anti-Semitism while making the sort of statements he did? Howard Palmer, a Canadian historian who has studied intolerance in Alberta, thinks not. Palmer believes that Aberhart's religious views, his own sense of justice and his strong antipathy towards Douglas ensured that he would not be swept up in the Jewish conspiracy tide. Aberhart, Palmer points out, played no role in trying to keep Jewish refugees out of Canada in the 1930s. He also tried to muffle the most avowedly anti-Semitic members of the provincial Social Credit movement.[14]

From the start, Aberhart and Douglas did not get along. This personality conflict between the founder of Social Credit and the world's only Social Credit head of government was reflected in a division in the provincial movement and, to a lesser degree, the federal Social Credit party. Although Aberhart was elected in the summer of 1935, he did little to implement Douglas Social Credit doctrine, probably because he realized that it was not legal in Canada for a provincial government to try to control the money supply in any way.

In 1937 a backbench revolt largely engineered by Douglas followers forced Aberhart to act. The provincial government introduced a series of measures aimed at installing a Social Credit system. Almost all of these were declared to be unconstitutional. One that survived, however, was the Alberta Social Credit Act, which created the Social Credit Board. The body was responsible to the Cabinet and was charged with the introduction of the Social Credit system. Since this was later found to be an impossibility, the Social Credit Board became, in reality, a sort of Social Credit public relations and propaganda agency, which made annual reports to the provincial legislative assembly. Aberhart established the Board to keep the Douglasites happy and Douglas himself was asked to name a number of its members, ensuring that it would closely follow the Douglas line.

As Douglas became more and more vehement in his anti-Semitism, so too did the Alberta Social Credit Board, but with one difference. By the early 1940s Douglas was an increasingly isolated and embittered man, writing for a smaller and smaller audience of dedicated followers. The Alberta Social Credit Board was an official agency of a democratically elected government, financed by that government, and using the facilities of that government to spread its increasingly anti-Semitic message. Its members travelled the province lecturing on Social Credit. It reprinted and sold Douglas articles and pamphlets. It annually sent hundreds of thousands of pieces of literature across Canada and it submitted an annual report to the legislative assembly. The report to the legislature submitted in December 1943 closely followed the line Douglas had laid down in *The Big Idea:*

> If international finance and socialism are travelling in the same direction is it possible that socialism is promoted by the money power to hasten the completion of their plot for world domination? Not only is it possible, but there is a fund of evidence which leads to the inevitable conclusion that there is a plot, worldwide in scope, deliberately engineered by a small number of ruthless international financiers.

It was not long before Jewish and liberal circles in Alberta and elsewhere began to demand a stop to this type of anti-Semitic propaganda. [15]

Aberhart died in the summer of 1943 and his place was taken by Ernest Manning. Manning was not pleased with the anti-Semitic tinge which the Social Credit Board and followers of Douglas were giving to the government of

Alberta. In 1947 he purged the provincial party of the anti-Semites. The occasion was the appearance of the Social Credit Board's annual report of that year, which repeated the by-now standard attacks against Jews, but which also went on to question the validity of government based on secret ballot voting. Manning undoubtedly realized that in the new Alberta he was trying to create—conservative, measured and moderate—the hare-brained schemes of the Douglasites would be an acute embarrassment.

In February 1947, Imperial Oil had brought in Leduc No. 1, a gusher which was obviously going to transform Alberta from a province of poverty to one of plenty. The month after Leduc, Manning acted. The government passed a resolution repudiating "any statements or publications which are incompatible with the established British ideals of democratic freedom or which endorse, excuse or incite anti-Semitism or racial or religious intolerance in any form." Within the next year the Alberta Social Credit Board had been dissolved and the leading Douglasites had been purged from the Cabinet.[16]

Although Manning had rid the provincial party of its leading Jew-haters, the federal wing of Social Credit was beyond its reach. There, anti-Semitism continued to fester. Its leading exponent was Norman Jaques, M.P. for the Alberta riding of Wetaskiwin from 1935 until his death in 1949. Jaques seemed to devote most of his career to attacks on the Jews. In speeches delivered throughout the 1940s, he linked Zionism with the international financial conspiracy and Communism and charged that the Jewish aim to control Palestine was "the key to world control." At one point in 1943 Jaques tried to read portions of the *Protocols of the Elders of Zion* in the House of Commons. He was stopped by the Speaker, but this did not deter him in future efforts to vent his anti-Semitism in the heart of the Canadian governmental system.

In August 1946, for example, Jaques told the House of Commons that "all the terrible convulsions and troubles and upheavals in the world are the result of aliens seeking to impose their atheistic Oriental collectivism upon national cultures of individualism."[17] Jaques found a ready forum in *The Canadian Social Creditor* until Manning purged its young editor, John Patrick Gillese, in the 1947 shake-up. Although Jaques was the most openly and avowedly anti-Jewish of the federal Social Credit M.P.s, others were only more circumspect than he in pushing the anti-Jewish line. None was more so than the party leader throughout the late 1940s and early 1950s, Solon Low.

Jim Keegstra had little to do with the rise of Social Credit in Alberta. He was only in his mid-teens when the Manning purge silenced the anti-Semites in Edmonton. But there can be little doubt that the anti-Semitism which was so much a part of Social Credit had a significant impact on Keegstra and on many other Albertans. For more than a decade an official governmental agency poured its anti-Semitism into the Alberta political stream. Officials connected with the party, from Social Credit Board members to Members of Parliament, openly expressed the most virulent anti-Jewish views. When such views receive the official imprimatur of a government and highly visible political figures, they can become acceptable to many ordinary citizens. Despite the obvious fact that bigotry in general and anti-Semitism in particular can be found in all parts of Canada, there is a peculiar concentration of it in parts of rural Alberta to this very day. Most of it is a remnant from the days of Social Credit.

Not long after Keegstra was fired by the Lacombe County Board of Education, he was elected second vice president for Alberta of the national Social Credit Party. Party leader J. Martin Hattersley, an Edmonton lawyer and Anglican priest who has no sympathy for anti-Semitism, wasted little time in dismissing Keegstra from his post. Keegstra's sympathizers in the party rallied to his cause and sent a letter to Hattersley protesting the dismissal. Hattersley responded by threatening to fire two of the signatories from their posts. Within days Keegstra's membership was cancelled, along with that of Thomas Erhart of Calgary (second national vice president) and James Green, a regional supervisor. Green—who employed Keegstra at his

Bentley, Alberta, garage—was a founder of the Christian Defence League, set up to raise funds for Keegstra. Green and Erhart both endorse the Jewish conspiracy myths of Keegstra.

In the end, however, Hattersley lost. At a special executive meeting the dismissals and cancellations were overturned and Hattersley himself was forced to leave the party. Keegstra once again became vice president. There is not much left of the federal Social Credit Party in Canada or in Alberta today, but what there is seems to be as anti-Semitic as Douglas Social Credit ever was.*

— V —

By the time Keegstra began teaching in Eckville, he had come to believe strongly in the Jewish conspiracy notions that Douglas and others had propagated. But his "education" was only partially complete—there was still much left to learn, and the Canadian League of Rights provided him the opportunity.

The Canadian League of Rights is the brainchild of Ronald W. Gostick who, like Keegstra, learned his Social Credit views in the home of his parents. His mother, Edith Gostick, was elected for Socal Credit to the Alberta legislature in 1935 and later bacame provincial librarian. She and her husband were both strong Douglas supporters. Gostick himself appears to have started his public career traveling a lecture circuit in rural Alberta.

By 1947 Ronald W. Gostick had moved to Ontario, where he began to edit a semi-monthly, *The Voice of the Electors*. In April 1949, following the Manning purge of the Douglas supporters from the provincial Social Credit party, Gostick began publication of *The Social Credit,* which styled itself as "the official organ of the Canadian (Douglas) Social Credit Movement, a non-party organization neither connected with nor supporting any political party, Social

---

*The Social Credit Party of British Columbia has no relation to the Federal Social Credit Party to which Keegstra belongs.

Credit or otherwise." This newsletter printed the standard Douglas version of the Jewish conspiracy and declared itself determined to expose the "Communist-Zionist-Monopolist-Finance enemy of . . . Christian civilization."[18]

Note here the use of the term "Zionist" instead of Jewish. Following the Holocaust it became far less fashionable to attack Jews openly. Anti-Semites instead concentrated their fire on "Zionists." Zionists, after all, are supporters of a particular political philosophy—the need for Jews to have a state of their own. They are not defined by religion, ethnicity or culture. Anti-Semites are well aware, of course, that the vast majority of Jews are Zionists and that almost all Zionists are Jews. They claim, however, that it is not Jews or Judaism they speak of, but "Zionists." Even Norman Jaques spoke less about Jews and more about Zionists after Auschwitz had been exposed. Keegstra himself claims that it is "Zionist Jews" he speaks of.

The publication *The Social Credit* last appeared in December 1950. The following month a new Gostick-owned and edited publication appeared, *The Canadian Intelligence Service*. It originated (and originates still) in Flesherton, Ontario. The new monthly was somewhat different from Gostick's previous publication; it was clearly aimed at American audiences. Issue after issue hammered away at the Zionist-Communist-Financier conspiracy and its impact on American politics at home and United States policy abroad. Gostick's favorite targets were the United Nations, Israel, NATO, progressive education and the Voice of America. It was all standard McCarthyite fare with a large dose of anti-Semitism thrown in. Gostick claimed that the atomic spy rings which had been uncovered in Canada and the U.S. in the late 1940s and early 1950s had operated with the support of the Canadian and United States governments and that most of their members were Jews.[19]

Gostick's message had far-ranging appeal. By the mid-1950s he was in great demand among right-wing and anti-Semitic organizations in Canada and the United States as a speaker and publicist. He began to make overseas connections as well, especially in Australia and New Zealand. One of his collaborators is Eric D. Butler, an Australian and leader of the Australian League of Rights. Butler wrote *Censored History*, one of the texts Jim Keegstra used in his Eckville classroom. In 1967 Gostick launched *On Target*, a weekly. In 1968 he founded the Canadian League of Rights upon the readership he had built up with the *Canadian Intelligence Service* and *On Target*.

Today the Canadian League of Rights claims a membership/mailing list of 10,000 with headquarters in Flesherton, Ontario, and with branches in British Columbia, Alberta, Saskatchewan and Manitoba. The Alberta director is Eric Boswell of Brooks, who also runs a small bookshop devoted to the sale of titles recommended by the League. The League also operates the Institute of Economic Democracy, a Douglas propaganda outlet, which publishes *Enterprise*, a small newsletter, out of its Vancouver office. A recent issue of *Enterprise* claimed there are "many striking similarities between Judaism and Marxism," thus repeating a standard anti-Semitic canard.[20] Works by C.H. Douglas, including the virulently anti-Semitic *Programme for the Third World War*, are regularly offered for sale.

The anti-Jewish nature of the Canadian League of Rights and its various front organizations is directly reflected in the books which it promotes in its publications and regularly offers for sale at its meetings. *The Real Holocaust* by Malcolm Ross implies that Jews promote abortion because their hatred for Christianity. The cover of the book portrays an individual with long black beard and hooked nose (a stereotypical Jew such as that once used by the Nazi publication Der Stürmer) throwing a coffin into the ground.

The Zionists, by George W. Armstrong, is a review of *The Protocols*. Armstrong states in his introduction to it: "The Zionists of Wall Street are the financial backers of the Zionists of the world and of the Zionist state of Israel . . . [they] are anti-Christ . . . They are Communists. . . . Their motives are greed and power. They seek to acquire the wealth of the world and enslave the Gentiles."[21] This is also the theme of *The Talmud Unmasked*, which is sold at

League meetings. Other titles promoted by the League are *The Rulers of Russia*, which asserts that Communism was a Jewish development, and a number of works which seek to prove that Jews are the descendants of the Khazars. These works include *The Thirteenth Tribe*, *What Price Israel?*, *Iron Curtain over America* and *Israel's Five-Trillion-Dollar Secret*.

— VI —

It was natural that Jim Keegstra and the Canadian League of Rights would link up. The League grew out of Douglas Social Credit roots. It endorsed the Douglas view of the Jews and it promoted the Jewish conspiracy canard. Keegstra joined the Canadian League of Rights in the late 1960s while living in Medicine Hat and began to subscribe to *On Target* in 1968. He became an active member of the CLR, first meeting Gostick on one of his tours of the west in 1975, and even inviting Gostick to address a social studies class on constitutional reform at Eckville High.[22] Keegstra depended heavily on Gostick's publications and used the Canadian League of Rights as his main source for books and pamphlets about the Jewish conspiracy. What he did not obtain by mail directly from Flesherton he purchased from Eric Boswell's bookshop in Brooks, Alberta and from C.H. Douglas Social Credit Supplies, a mail order business run by Wallace M. Klinck and located in Sherwood Park, a suburb of Edmonton.

Klinck's 1983 order list offered a large selection of Social Credit material for sale, including most of the works of C.H. Douglas. On the list were the chief anti-Jewish works of modern times, such as *The Hoax of the Twentieth Century* by A.R. Butz (which claims that the Holocaust is a Jewish-perpetrated hoax), the *Protocols of the Elders of Zion*, *The Talmud Unmasked* and *Did Six Million Really Die?* by Richard Harwood, another standard Holocaust denial work.

Most of the titles Keegstra uses to bolster his arguments, and much of what he distributed in class, were on

Klinck's list. When questioned by reporters at the time of the Keegstra dismissal, Klinck admitted that most of his supplies came from the Canadian League of Rights in Flesherton, Ontario, and from Vancouver, and that he regularly attended League meetings. He denied being anti-Jewish, but asserted that the problems of the Western world grew out of a "Jewish financial system" operating in a Christian world.[23]

Gostick, not surprisingly, has become one of Keegstra's strongest supporters. He believes that the "Keegstra Affair" could "become a landmark or watershed in the struggle for freedom and the revival of genuine Christianity in Canada. . . ." Why? Because, Gostick maintains, Keegstra dared to challenge "this anti-Christian power in the public school system—the same anti-Christian power" which controls the western news media and which is also served by "well-meaning but blind and gullible 'ministers,' telling us that those who claim racial or spiritual descent from those who denied and crucified Christ [i.e., the Jews] are thereby a 'chosen' and exalted people."[24]

Gostick, as always, is circumspect in his attacks on the Jews, following the new style among anti-Semites. His real target, he claims, is Zionism and Israel, not the Jews. But the phraseology, the imagery, the methodology are as old as the ancient charges of well-poisoning, desecration of hosts, murdering of Christian children and worshipping of the devil.

The Jewish conspiracy is central to Jim Keegstra's life. He believes, and has believed for a long time, that this conspiracy is running the world and making the important day-to-day decisions about what people will do and what they will think. He believes that the conspiracy has come close to achieving its purposes: world domination and the suppression and eventual destruction of Christianity. He sees the power of that conspiracy in the world around him—in newspapers, magazines, movies and television. He is convinced that the conspiracy has succeeded in hiding itself by manufacturing the history which is written by scholars in its employ and which is, therefore, taught in schools and universities and contained on library shelves.

It follows that anyone who believes that the conspiracy must also believe that it would be powerful enough to accomplish virtually anything. The conspiracy would supposedly control the financial capitals of the world, Hollywood, the media, the Kremlin, most publishing houses and many churches. If the Jews create wars and revolutions and perpetrate hoaxes as all encompassing as the Holocaust, they are capable of anything. Censoring history, therefore, would not be difficult.

Keegstra believes that the Jews have succeeded in hoodwinking most of the modern-day Christian world into believing in the improvement of interfaith relations, the importance of the Jews for the fulfillment of Biblical prophecy and the Jewish roots of Christianity. Only a few people who really know the truth are capable of fighting back, and Keegstra strongly believes that he is one of them.

These thoughts motivate Jim Keegstra and drive him on, whether he is teaching adult Sunday School at Diamond Valley Full Gospel Church, fixing cars at Jim Green's garage in Bentley or standing in front of a classroom. There is a war on and Jim Keegstra has chosen sides. There was, and is, no room for objectivity, for distance between a teacher and his subject. For Jim Keegstra, the classroom was a key part of the battleground.

3

Keegstra in the Classroom

JIM KEEGSTRA BEGAN each semester of his grade nine and grade twelve social studies classes with lessons on the meaning of truth. He believes the educational system is based on "falsehood, censored history and false philosophy." It was, therefore, important for him to show his students how to recognize what is true and what is not. His students had probably never been exposed to this approach before and undoubtedly found the discussion stimulating and novel, even if some of them were at times confused by it.

Student notebooks faithfully reflected Keegstra's teachings. He began his lessons on truth by telling his students that facts are not, in themselves, true; they just *are*. Truth, on the other hand, describes a statement or explanation which could not be contradicted. If a supposedly true statement or explanation is contradicted by another statement or explanation, then one of the statements or explanations cannot possibly be true and both, in fact, could be false. Truth, according to Keegstra, depends on "making judgments [about the world] and taking them into the total witness of . . . experience." Keegstra's idea of truth was based on his religious faith. Christ, the creator of all facts, is truth and everything which is connected with

Christ is also truth. Human beings—finite—must search for truth and can find it in the word of God.

Keegstra taught his students that there are both false and proper tests for truth. Among the false (or inadequate) tests, in his view, are custom, tradition, consensus, subjective feelings, intuition and pragmatism. He claimed that truth does not depend on the opinions of others: "You can be the minority of one and still be the only one right if you went about your search for truth properly." How then to find truth? Basically, Keegstra claimed, in two ways. First, a truth cannot be contradicted. Second, it is systematically consistent with other truths. When both conditions are satisfied, Keegstra told his students, "a statement [or explanation] has a high probability of being the truth."

Keegstra's lessons on truth were the essence of his teaching.[1] When he appeared before the Board of Reference in March 1983 to appeal his dismissal, he claimed that he spent so much time teaching about truth because he wanted to give his students inquiring minds—get them to think and consider other points of view and to look at other values. He maintained that he was following the Alberta Social Studies Curriculum Guide in encouraging his students to test, falsify and substantiate generalizations in the history they were about to study.

In fact, Keegstra's lessons on truth were the start of, and were essential parts of, his teaching on the international Jewish conspiracy. When Keegstra taught his students about truth he taught them that there are only two ways of looking at the world and explaining history; a right, true and correct way rooted in "Christian" dogma and a wrong, untrue and incorrect way based on anti-Christian ideology. In his discussions of truth, Keegstra introduced his students to the simple world of black and white, right and wrong, true and untrue, Christian and anti-Christian, in which he himself believes. He taught his students: "You either have to serve God or Mammon."

Historians and other social scientists who study the course of human events and the human condition have long recognized that the world is very complex. The notion that it is a fundamentally simple place of direct cause and effect, or that a deity or deities directly determine human action, once formed the foundation of social and political thought in almost all societies. This is no longer the case. Modern society generally, and western democratic societies in particular, recognize that human affairs are rarely straightforward and that events usually have multiple causes. They recognize that reasonable human beings of good will may not agree on political, social or economic solutions to the problems that plague them.

The concept of the Loyal Opposition in the British and Canadian governmental systems is based on the idea that there is, or can be, more than one legitimate way to accomplish worthy goals. This idea is also reflected in the way historians approach the study of history. Two historians, working with the same historical materials and agreeing on basic facts, can arrive at two entirely different explanations for the same event.

Although historians do sometimes agree broadly about the causes of a particular war or the role of a certain person in the development of a society, they can also strongly disagree. This is because they recognize that the world is a complex place, and that it is impossible to reconstruct the past exactly as it happened. The best historians can hope to achieve is a reasonably accurate reconstruction in accord with recognized facts and built upon the available historical materials (the diaries, letters, memoirs, memories and so on).

This is a view of the world, and of history, with which Jim Keegstra fundamentally disagrees. For him there can be only one truth, one cause, one acceptable explanation and, more important, one good and one justice. If his students could be taught his definition of (and tests for) truth, they could be steered away from adopting the view he considers so dangerous—that of a world of competing truths, multiple justices and sometimes conflicting explanations and interpretations. More important, they could be made ready to accept what he was determined to introduce to them. This is his idea that a *single* explanation can be given to *all* the important events experienced by society for at least the last two centuries—that of a Jewish conspiracy to take over the world, destroy Christianity and establish "one world" government.

It is impossible to know how successful Keegstra was in trying to pass on his notions of truth. His students faithfully copied his teachings down in their notebooks. "A fact just is," one student wrote, and "facts are used to support truth." "Facts support truth but are not truth themselves" wrote another student. "Truth is absolute—it applies to everyone." "The human mind tries to arrange the signals it receives into a logical or coherent picture," wrote a third, "which forms the basis for a hypothesis which then becomes a theory." A theory, this student learned, "can predict" and "If no contradictions [to it] can be found, becomes law." A pattern emerges from these student notes: to Keegstra, history is as systematic, as verifiable and as predictable as any of the forces of nature studied by scientists.

— I —

Keegstra's discussion of truth taught his students the exact opposite lesson to that called for in the Alberta Social Studies Curriculum. In the years since Keegstra began teaching at Eckville High, three related social studies curricula have been used in Alberta schools. All of them were designed to teach students that the human condition is complex, that choices involving costs and benefits must usually be made when social directions are determined and that historical events usually have a multitude of causes.

The first of these three curricula was adopted in 1971, when more traditional programs of study such as history and geography were dropped. The new program deemphasized textbooks. It allowed students and teachers to spend as much as one-third of social studies class time in the pursuit of topics of their own choosing, and was based heavily on "values education." Educators hoped the new program would teach students to think about social issues and make value judgments based on their studies.[2]

Students in grade nine social studies, for example, were told to study questions such as, "How should [society] resolve conflict between individual and group control?" and "What institutions best ensure that human rights will be protected and to what extent should the individual sacrifice his rights for the benefit of society?" In resolving such issues, teachers were expected to show students how to use the methods of the social science disciplines (i.e., history, geography, economics, sociology, etc.) to arrive at informed value judgments.

The purpose of this approach was clearly stated in the handbook for social studies teachers, prepared by the provincial Department of Education: "In keeping with the basic tenets of democracy (and with optimism about the nature of man and the efficacy of democratic ideals), the new social studies invites free and open inquiry into the definition and application of individual and social values. Such inquiry will serve the humanistic goals of education . . . ."[3]

The new social studies did not work out well. Substantial revisions were introduced in 1978 and 1981. These shifted the focus of social studies back towards history. But the idea of values education was by no means scrapped. It was integrated into the study of history in an approach that de-emphasized the teaching of dates and events and stressed analysis of problems, mainly historical. In the 1981 version of the social studies curriculum, for example, one of the issues grade nine students were asked to study was, "What did many factory owners in 18th-century Britain and/or 19th-century U.S.A. seem to value most? What did the union leaders seem to value at this time?"

Such issues were selected "to acknowledge that the real world is neither 'all good' nor 'all bad.'" One of the major objectives of the program was to give students the opportunity to acquire characteristics of intellectual independence, sensitivity to their human and natural environments, moral maturity and effective participation in community affairs."[4]

A process of free inquiry was basic to these objectives. Principles were built into the social studies program that would take students from the identification of significant issues, to the gathering of information about those issues, to the development of research skills, through a process of synthesizing the information gathered and finally to the point where intelligent decisions could be made about the issues. Students were expected to make "sound judgments," and to use the authority of evidence to back up their conclusions.[5]

Jim Keegstra later claimed that he taught social studies according to this curriculum and that his lectures demonstrated the differences between the "Christian ideology and the Illuminati or collective ideology."[6] He maintained that he always made students aware of his own biases, that he told them the views he was putting forward in class were only his own theories and that it was important for them to examine all sides of the issues under study. Keegstra explained his distribution of anti-Semitic pamphlet material in class as a method of introducing his students to another side of the history in their textbooks: "If you have open and free intellectual enquiry, limitations can't be put on it," he told the press, "all points and theories should be brought forward."[7]

Keegstra succeeded in convincing some of his students, their parents and his colleagues and superiors that he was only trying to make his students think. Former Eckville High student Dana Kreil told Keegstra's preliminary hearing in June 1984 that Keegstra taught his students to be skeptical about everything they heard and read and to weigh the available facts before coming to their own conclusions. Former Eckville High principals Joe Lindberg and Ed Olsen also claimed to believe that Keegstra was only giving his classes a critical analysis of history.

But Robert David, the Lacombe County school superintendent, did not see it that way. When David first began to investigate the Eckville situation in December 1981, he concluded that what was actually going on in Keegstra's class was "straight indoctrination." Keegstra's testimony at the Board of Reference hearing confirms David's impressions. Keegstra was forced to admit, for example, that the notes he gave in class and the material he distributed represented only one point of view—his own. He claimed that other points of view were available to the students in newspapers, magazines and texbooks (including the recommended texts). However, he conceded that none of those sources made any mention of Illuminati or of a Jewish conspiracy. He told the Board of Reference that his library was always available to students who wanted to do further research into the Jewish conspiracy. But he then revealed that none of his books presented a reasoned argument against the Jewish conspiracy because he had never "been able to find one."[8]

Keegstra could not find books which present another side to the Jewish conspiracy question because he believed and believes that all "standard" history is censored. He told his students that their textbooks had been censored, that reference materials in libraries, such as encyclopedias, were censored and that his own materials were the only reliable resources available to them. He explained that this was because the "Illuminati" are destroying history by using their financial power to pressure publishers not to publish the truth. Financiers exercise that power through grants to authors and publishers, Keegstra explained to the Board of Reference: "publishers need money to keep publishing, and if a certain book comes out that's not liked by those who have the money, automatically that book is— can be, with monetary force, not published." And the historians themselves have been corrupted, according to Keegstra: "most official historians are forced into conformity by pressures from their peers or fear of losing their jobs or fear of being smeared in the . . . media," he told his trial in June 1985. Official historians "just play the game to keep their job."[9]

— II —

When the Keegstra affair burst upon the consciousness
of the nation, many observers concluded that the Alberta
Social Studies Curriculum was at least partly to blame for
the whole mess. The *Calgary Herald* published an editorial, which it headed "Re-think Social Studies," suggesting
that education officials should be having "second thoughts"
about social studies because of the lack of history contained
in the program and the interdisciplinary rather than
historical approach to current events. "The case for making
20th-century history compulsory couldn't be stronger," the
Herald concluded.[10] An even harsher judgement on the
social studies program was passed by *Alberta Report*
magazine, which also attacked the lack of history in
Alberta's high schools. In an editorial entitled "When there
is no curriculum what you get is Mr. Keegstra," publisher
Ted Byfield claimed that the Keegstra affair was dramatic
proof of what could happen when the Department of
Education abandoned all serious attempts to control curriculum in pursuit of its "values education" and "social
issues" oriented philosophy.[11]

The *Calgary Herald*, Byfield and others who blamed
the Eckville situation on the Social Studies Curriculum
were wrong. Firstly, Keegstra did not take an interdisciplinary approach to the study of social issues; he taught
modern history. The teaching of history in schools is no
guarantee against indoctrination, as the study of any
dictatorship shows. Secondly, whatever else Keegstra was
doing in the classroom, he certainly was not teaching the
Alberta Social Studies Curriculum. He was, in fact, dismissed for that very reason and for disobeying a lawful
instruction from the Lacombe County Board of Education
directing him to teach that prescribed curriculum.

Jim Keegstra did not cover the subjects he was
supposed to cover. He did not attempt to meet the aims and
objectives of the curriculum. And he did not try to foster

the skills in his students that he was supposed to teach them. If Keegstra had taught within the guidelines laid out by the curriculum, that would have been reason to attack it. He clearly did not. There may be many reasons why the Alberta Social Studies Curriculum should be revised, but the events in Eckville cannot be counted among them.

When Robert David was building the case for Keegstra's dismissal between December 1981 and December 1982, he consulted an Alberta Department of Education expert on the social studies curriculum, Francis A. Crowther. Crowther never actually observed Keegstra teaching in the classroom. However, he made a thorough examination of student notes, essays and exams which David had obtained from Keegstra's class. He also read through the two handouts—*Facts are Facts* and *Censored History*—which Keegstra had distributed to his students. Crowther told the Board of Reference that, in his opinion, "approximately 40 percent of the material . . . didn't appear to have any relationship whatsoever to the prescribed curriculum, and . . . wouldn't really be considered in any way as appropriate background." He did not think that more than 10 percent of the material he had examined "could be readily identified as within the strict parameters of the . . . curriculum."

But this was not all that was wrong with Keegstra's teaching of social studies in Crowther's opinion. There was no evidence in the notes, papers and exams that students had been "engaged in decision making" of the kind prescribed in the curriculum. There was also strong evidence of a "continued very negative" attitude towards Jews, which directly violated the curriculum objective of engendering respect towards others. Nor were Keegstra's teaching methods in keeping with the curriculum. Crowther maintained: "The building into the content . . . of this Illuminati association, and references to Khazar Jews . . . is quite inconsistent with the type of treatment of history that is included in any of the authorized resources for the social studies curriculum" and "there didn't seem to be any evidence that the spirit of inquiry had been acted upon."[12]

— III —

The spirit of free inquiry that was so much a part of the Alberta Social Studies Curriculum has no place in Jim Keegstra's world view. He has read voluminously and has probably studied more about modern history than the vast majority of social studies teachers. But there is a significant difference between the way Jim Keegstra researches his subject and the approach taken by historians, teachers and others who are truly dedicated to free inquiry. Keegstra does not do research to collect facts, which can then be formed into patterns of historical explanation. He searches for facts to confirm the hypothesis he arrived at long ago— that the Jews are conspiring to enslave the world. He accepts any facts or interpretations which, to him, confirm his thesis and he then weaves them into his hypothesis.

Anything which runs counter to his hypothesis is rejected because, to his way of thinking, it is not "truth." In fact, Keegstra believes that studies which reject or ignore his hypothesis are actually proof of it. Their silence or rejection can only result from the collaboration of authors and publishers with the conspiracy, he reasons. This was the system of knowledge, the way of thinking, that Keegstra imposed on his students.

In *Architects of Fear*, a recent study on conspiracy theories in American politics, journalist George Johnson gave a composite portrait of those men and women who are convinced that grand conspiracies of one sort or another underlie all important human events. The description fits Keegstra all too well.[13] Johnson begins his study by pointing out that the search for meaning and order in life is one of the most elevating of human activities, even though most of us know it is a quest that can never end. He calls this a "pluralistic view." Those who hold it are convinced that the world is a complex place, that there does not exist any single all-embracing explanation for everything, that knowledge is dynamic and that different people experience different realities and can have different, but legitimate points of view.

People who reject this view—the "absolutists"—have an extreme desire to find connections between events and to squeeze the world into the all-embracing systems in which they so strongly believe. When they discover some new fact or theory, it must fit the system, or else it is discarded as "untrue." These people see their way of life as an expression of absolute truth—theirs is the one true religion or the one true economic system or the one true national experience. Johnson points out that absolutists view the world in black and white terms.

This reflects what Keegstra told his students. That there are only two world views, that God and all things emanating from God are connected to one of these views and that human beings and everything resulting from human beings are basic to the other. Man, according to Keegstra, is either good or evil. There is nothing in between.[14] Keegstra's world, the world of the absolutists, is a far different place than the world of the pluralists, according to Johnson. Both are embodied in "systems of thought that are, by nature, almost mutually exclusive."

Johnson is careful to point out that the world of those who believe in conspiracies is not an arbitrary place. The "extremists" build their views according to "a coherent set of rules" and rationalize their fears "with superstructures so complex that they have a vocabulary and an internal logic— an architecture—of their own." These conspiracists look at the world as "a machine" with gears that mesh tightly: "there is no slack. Everything bad that happens is part of a plot. *There are no accidents* . . . wars, depressions, droughts, and plagues—happen according to plan." This, too, is what Keegstra taught his students.

— IV —

Once Jim Keegstra had introduced his students to his own ideas about truth, he began his introduction to modern history by giving them photocopies of two pamphlets from his personal library. Students were instructed to read and analyze these.[15] The pamphlets were *Censored History* by Eric D. Butler, leader of the Australian affiliate of the Canadian League of Rights and *Facts are Facts* by Benjamin Freedman, a self-styled Jewish convert to Christianity. These two tracts, taken together, presented an almost complete picture of Keegstra's beliefs about the Jews.

Facts are Facts was written in the form of a letter from Freedman to David Goldstein, who is presented as a Jewish convert to Catholicism eager to convince other Jews to join his newly adopted faith. Goldstein had apparently published an article pointing to the common roots of Judaism and Christianity. This prompted Freedman to write *Facts are Facts*—a vicious attack on Judaism—in order to convince Goldstein that increasing the number of converts would only increase the number of "latent traitors" inside Christianity.

Freedman's anti-Jewish diatribe follows rather conventional lines. He says Jesus was not a Jew but a *Judean*, and that the very word "Jew" did not "come into existence until the year 1775." The Talmud contains the most "vicious, libelous blasphemies of Jesus, of Christianity and the Christian faith by anyone, anywhere or [at] any time." Almost all modern day Jews are descended not from the ancient Hebrews but from the Khazar kingdom that existed in Asia in the 8th Century. Judaism and Christianity "are at the opposite extremes of the spiritual spectrum."

When Keegstra handed out *Facts are Facts* to his students, he attached to it a second, shorter anti-Jewish tract. This was written by Curtis B. Dall, former chairman of the Board of Policy of the Liberty Lobby, the American anti-Semitic organization founded by Willis A. Carto. Dall's tract combined a summary of Arthur Koestler's *The Thirteenth Tribe*, a book published in 1976 which repeated the Khazar story, and an appendix consisting of chunks taken from *The Talmud Unmasked*. Keegstra's students, most of whom had probably never met a Jew and who could not have known very much about Jews or Judaism, were thus forced to read an anti-Semitic handout which portrayed Jews as actively anti-Christian.

The *Facts are Facts* handout was concerned with the historical roots of Judaism, the Talmud and the relationship of Jews to Christianity in ancient times. *Censored History* was intended to continue the story into a more modern period. The latter claims that history has been censored to cover up the existence of a world Jewish conspiracy and to hide the activities of that conspiracy. It says international Jewish financiers are conspiring to bring about one world government. The Jews were at the heart of the Bolshevik Revolution, and Zionism and Communism are allies in the same cause. The Jews have no claim to Israel because most modern Jews are descended from Khazars and are not, therefore, Semitic. The Holocaust never happened and, in fact, the Zionists and the Nazis were active collaborators.

Keegstra obtained this pamphlet from the Canadian League of Rights and told his trial that he gave it to his students because it summarized his own point of view. "It had a lot of facts that were being censored in the mainstream history books that [they] needed to know to understand the conflicts in world history."[16]

Keegstra did not, of course, introduce the students to material that would give them an alternate view of Jews, Judaism or Zionism. Therefore his claim that he was only presenting the students with another point of view for them to consider rings completely hollow. Where was the *other* point of view? It was not available in Keegstra's class, nor in the texts (which did not cover any of these subjects because they were not part of the prescribed curriculum) nor in the library. By the early weeks of Keegstra's social studies classes, the process of indoctrination was well underway.

Keegstra believes, and taught his students, that the Jewish conspiracy is rooted in ancient times and began with the Babylonian conquest of Palestine. It was at that time, Keegstra taught, that a religious sect called Judaism was founded among the Hebrews. Thus although Christ was clearly a *Judean*, according to Keegstra, he was not a follower of the Jewish "sect." He, in fact, strongly opposed it and charged its followers with being sons of Satan. Keegstra believes that the followers of this Jewish "sect" were the Pharisees, who were also the originators of the Talmud and the founders of "rabbinical Judaism."

Keegstra told his students that the Talmud embodies the ideas, practices and plans of the Pharisee Jews and that it is an evil and fundamentally anti-Christian work. Keegstra had never studied a real volume of Talmud but completely accepted the basic view contained in books such as *The Talmud Unmasked, The Jewish Religion: Its Influence Today* and *Facts are Facts*. He taught his students that the Talmud led the Jews away from the Bible, that it promotes sexual perversion, slanders Christ and Christianity, calls upon Jews to steal from, and even murder, Christians and forms the basis for socialism and Communism. Judaism, by A.D. 500 had become, in Keegstra's view, a secretive, stealthy and amoral ideology which bore no relation at all to the faith of the ancient Hebrews.

Keegstra's teaching was designed not only to separate modern Judaism from the Old Testament. It was also aimed at separating modern Jews from the people whose early history is chronicled in the Old Testament. He therefore taught his students that by the 8th Century the Jews were disappearing almost everywhere and that they survived only because of the conversion of a tribe of "Mongolian Turks" known as the Khazars to the Jewish religion.

Since the true Semitic Jews were dying out in Europe at that time, Keegstra claimed, the Khazar Jews became dominant among European Jews and are the real ancestors of the Ashkenazic or European Jews of today. Semitic Jews did survive in the Middle East and North Africa, according to Keegstra, and are now called Sephardic Jews. However, it is the Khazars who have been in control of "anyone that believed in Judaism" since 1897—the year of the first World Zionist Congress.[17] And it is they, Keegstra taught, who turned Judaism into the atheistic, Communistic, Zionist ideology that forms the basis for the Jewish conspiracy.

There is a kernal of truth to what Keegstra taught about Khazars. A tribe of half-Mongolian people living between the Black and Caspian Seas did convert to Judaism in the 8th century, when the Khazar king decided to abandon paganism and adopt a monotheistic faith. This Jewish kingdom existed for several centuries. Although scholars are not certain when it disappeared completely, there are indications that it may have survived up to the time of the Tatar invasion in 1240. Some of the Khazar Jews then mingled with the Jews of the Byzantine Empire. Others remained Jews within the Principality of Moscow. Still others adopted Christianity.

At the time the Khazar kingdom existed, however, there were already large numbers of Jews living almost everywhere in Europe, from Spain to the Rhine River Valley. It is also by no means certain that all Khazars adopted Judaism because of the religious tolerance practised by the rulers of the kingdom. It is possible that Khazar Jews were among the first Jews in eastern Europe. But it is a well-known historical fact that the vast majority of the Jews who were later to be found in eastern Europe came from the Byzantine empire and from southern and western Europe. It was this latter group—driven east by the first Crusade and other persecutions of Jews in what later became Germany—who were the dominant cultural group establishing the foundations for the centuries of Jewish life in Poland and Russia that stretched into the 20th Century.

Keegstra taught that the "capture" of Judaism by the Khazars set the stage for what was, in his view, the central event of modern times. This was the founding on May 1, 1776, of a secret society known as the Illuminati by Adam Weishaupt. Keegstra believes that Jews were the driving force behind this society, which he claims was bent on world domination, and that the Jewish religion provided its basic ideology. To Keegstra the Illuminati were the instrument by which the Jews would carry out their plan to destroy Christianity and dominate the world.

His view of the Illuminati was based entirely on the work of authors such as Nesta Webster, who totally distorted the actual liberal aims of Weishaupt and his followers, and grossly exaggerated their importance in late

18th-century Europe. Keegstra told his students that the Illuminati plan contained five main points: the destruction of all monarchies; the destruction of all religions, especially Christianity; the abolition of marriage; the abolition of private property; and the abolition of all oaths of loyalty and allegiance to God, ruler and country. These aims, once accomplished, would allow the Jews to infiltrate and poison government, destroy the family structure, destroy moral bulwarks against the Jews (such as Christian morality) and enslave the peoples of the world. Keegstra blames all wars, revolutions, economic depressions and other humanly created catastrophes since 1776 on the Illuminati. He also believes that all the moral degeneration which he sees in current society, from pornography to divorce, can be traced to the Weishaupt plan.[18]

Keegstra taught his students that the Jewish-Illuminati conspiracy is the link which explains all of modern history. He said that the Jews had assassinated Abraham Lincoln and Franklin D. Roosevelt (who, in fact, died of natural causes). The Jews had carried out the Russian Revolution and started both World Wars. The Jews had created both Marxism and modern capitalist economics. The Jews had perpetrated the Holocaust hoax in order to ensure the founding of the State of Israel.

Keegstra told his trial in June 1985 that his job as a teacher was to show the cause and effect of what was happening in the world and this meant showing his students the Jewish connection in history.[19] When Superintendent Bob David investigated Keegstra's teaching of social studies prior to Keegstra's dismissal, he found that the Jewish conspiracy "had been the basis of the whole program." Although it is difficult to judge how much of this Keegstra was teaching in the early 1970s, it dominated his social studies classes by the end of the 1970s in the same way that it dominated his own thinking.

Keegstra told his Board of Reference hearing in March 1983 that "a student is never asked to believe what I believe, never." A mountain of evidence indicates otherwise—that he used the power to punish and reward possessed by every teacher to make sure his students parroted his theories and ideas. When Cindy Andrew used library material to research an essay on Catholicism for Keegstra's class in 1976, he refused to grade it. When Trudi Roth used sources other than those handed out by Keegstra for an essay on the Jews, he wrote in the margin: "your essay was to be based on what was in class also." Sherron Wolney told Keegstra's preliminary hearing in June 1984 that grades in Keegstra's classes depended on "how well you could regurgitate the stuff he said and throw it back at him." There was no point in doing independent research, she claimed, because "you got as good a mark or better if you took it from your notes." Michelle Desrosiers told a reporter in May 1983, that "if you wrote down what he wanted, you got good marks."

Dramatic proof of this emerged at Keegstra's preliminary hearing when essays and their grades were entered into evidence. One student received 75 percent for an essay in which she wrote: "If people would have been listening [to Hitler], he could have rid the world of Jews forever—it's funny how people never want to hear the truth." Another was given 85 percent for writing, "The Jews believe in violence and revolution to gain their end, while Christians believe in serving with compassion for each other. They live by the Bible and the Jews live by the Talmud, where evil acts are encouraged." A third student earned 65 percent for an essay which advocated genocide: "we must get rid of every living Jew so that we can live in peace and freedom."[20]

— V —

Keegstra's students learned their lessons well. When they began to tell the Board of Reference and Keegstra's preliminary hearing and trial what they had been taught, the full story began to emerge. It is clear that some of the many students who passed through Keegstra's classes over the years took all or most of what he said with a grain of salt and quickly learned to give him what he wanted in order to survive the process. It is also true, however, that many others believed him and believed in him. They interpreted his dismissal and prosecution as proof that he had run afoul of the Jewish conspiracy and was being punished for it. Their notes, essays and exam papers reflect what they were taught.

In an essay tracing "Judaism and its Role in Society from 1776-1918" a student claimed that "most Jews in the world today are strictly Jews by religion. This . . . makes the Jews very dangerous. . . . The Talmud . . . teaches the Jews to hate the Christians. They call Christians *Goyim* (dog) and say that the Christians are cursed."[21] Another student's notes reflected Keegstra's lurid description of events during the French Revolution: "The Jews controlled the Jacobins, who started the Feast of Reason. In it an innocent girl was slaughtered in the church of Notre Dame and her blood poured over a naked prostitute. Then they would cook the young girls and eat her flesh. When Jews hang a man or woman . . . they slit their stomachs and let the birds eat out of it."[22] One notebook contains this outline of recent history: The overthrow of the Czarist government was devised in 1897 at the World Zionist Congress meeting which also decided that "Russia must be destroyed and ruled by Israel" and that there must be a Jewish homeland in Palestine "so that [the Jews] can claim to be the chosen people . . . control the money system [and institute] one world government under the new world order."[23]

The notes, essays and exams reflect Keegstra's teachings about Jews and Judaism and show that a generation of students accepted his views about the international Jewish conspiracy in almost all its details. Keegstra's students came to believe that Jesus was not a Jew, that Judaism and Christianity are mortal enemies, that the Talmud is a perverted and evil book, that most modern Jews are not Jews at all but descendents of the Khazars and that the Jews have been slowly taking over the world by manipulating people and events all over the globe. They learned that the banking system, the media, Hollywood, the universities, most publishers, most of the churches and almost all political leaders are agents of the conspiracy. And they learned the very terminology of anti-Semitism, that Jews are "money thugs," "rug rats," "gutter rats," "Khazar Jews," "so-called Jews," "self-styled Jews," "Zionist Jews."

There are no Jews in Eckville and very few anywhere in rural Alberta. Almost all of the Jews of Alberta—some 10,000 people according to the 1981 Census Returns—live in Edmonton (4,200) and Calgary (5,500). Although a number of Jewish farm communities existed at the turn of the century, there are none today. Very few, if any, of Keegstra's students have ever seen a Jew.

This is one reason why teachings such as Keegstra's have such a devastating impact on a small community like Eckville. None of Keegstra's students had any daily contact with Jews. Since there were no Jews in Eckville, they could not do business with Jews. They could not enter their homes. They could not meet Jews their own age in the halls or classrooms of their school. They could not share their homework with Jews, go to dances with them, play baseball with them. Their teacher told them that Jews were evil, and they could not test that statement themselves, through their own everyday experiences.

It it impossible to know how much lasting harm Keegstra's years at Eckville High have done to the students who learned their history from him. Some have admitted that they still accept most or all of what he taught. Others have expressed an increasing skepticism. Still others claim they never believed him, but gave him what he wanted in order to graduate and perhaps go on to university. It is impossible to measure accurately what the long-term impact will be of Keegstra's indoctrination. However, it is clear that his students did not cover the material which they were expected to learn and which other Alberta students were covering. It is also clear that the values and methods of researching social studies problems which they should have been taught were not taught to them. If they escape a life of anti-Jewish bias, it will come only through self-education and a conscious effort to root out the lessons Keegstra taught.

Keegstra's students were at his mercy. Society placed them in his charge for him to educate. It expected him to act responsibly and fulfill the social and educational goals which society has established for its youth. That he did not do so is beyond argument. That he did bend his students to his own purposes is undeniable. Although Jim Keegstra was the chief perpetrator, he could not have succeeded without the passive help of an educational system which, whatever its purpose, protected him more than it protected his students. That is why he was able to teach what he did for so long without anyone blowing the whistle. When Jim Keegstra began to betray his trust as a teacher, the educational system failed to stop him. That system, in fact, gave him more than ten years of opportunity to take the unmolded minds of a generation of young Eckvillians and fill them with the stuff of Nazism.

4

The Alberta School System

WHEN JIM KEEGSTRA decided to use his classroom to fight the imagined international Jewish conspiracy, he violated the curriculum guidelines of the Province of Alberta. He violated the regulations on the teaching of controversial material laid down by the Lacombe County Board of Education and the standards of professional conduct established by the Alberta Teachers' Association. He betrayed the trust that society placed in him and in every teacher given the chance to mold young minds.

From the time Keegstra began to teach his own version of history to his students—about 1970 or 1971—they were victims of his deliberate campaign of indoctrination. As a teacher Keegstra held almost as much power over those students as their parents did at home. He could punish or reward, pass or fail, honor or ridicule in his efforts to shape the developing ideas, attitudes and prejudices of those who had been placed in his charge.

Keegstra's students were not sufficiently protected by their principal, by other teachers at the school or by the educational system itself. Until he was dismissed in December 1982, the system that was supposed to protect them from such a teacher operated instead to protect Jim

Keegstra. It allowed him to teach his paranoid views without interruption for at least ten years.

Jim Keegstra was considered by colleagues and superiors to be an effective and conscientious teacher. His teaching methods were somewhat informal, since he never used lecture notes or lesson plans. He knew his material so well that he could discuss his subject extemporaneously. He put notes on the board as he talked and interrupted his presentation to debate with students who disagreed with him or challenged his version of events. By most accounts, however, that did not happen very often because students learned that the key to good grades in Keegstra's classes was agreement with his interpretation of history; few disagreed with him. He was certain of himself and convinced that he alone possessed the truth. That certainty gave him calmness and control in his teachings, a very effective pedagogical tool.

A teacher's ability to show rebellious teenagers who is in charge is a valued characteristic in the educational system. Keegstra, it is clear, was always in firm command. Joseph Lindberg, principal of Eckville High School from 1970 to 1975 and a social studies teacher there at the time of Keegstra's dismissal, admired Keegstra's teaching abilities. He told the Board of Reference (which heard Keegstra's appeal of his dismissal) that Keegstra's "first qualification" as a teacher was his "command of discipline." Keegstra, in Lindberg's opinion, was able to keep "good order and without any psychological brutality." But it was not only discipline that Lindberg admired. He thought Keegstra had "a tremendous knowledge of his subject" and that students found his classes interesting.[1]

Edwin Olsen, who took over as principal in 1975, also admired Keegstra's ability to control his class and told the Board of Reference that Keegstra had done "a very thorough job" in preparing for his teaching. Olsen appreciated the special effort Keegstra made to be friendly to the students, to greet them in the morning, to discuss their problems with them and to be congenial to them.[2]

Olsen's high opinion of Keegstra does not seem to have

been affected by what went on in Keegstra's classes, even though he was well aware of it at least as far back as 1978, when his son took a course from Keegstra. People had complained to the vice-principal, John Taylor, but he told Keegstra's trial that he felt that Keegstra was a "forthright, honest man" who was always fair in dealing with students and other staff.[3]

Kenneth Bradshaw, a science and math teacher at Eckville High, told the same trial that Keegstra is "perhaps the most honest man I know."[4] These testimonials from colleagues and superiors show that *what* Keegstra taught was for them far less important than *how* he taught it. It is, therefore, not surprising that when Keegstra was fired in December 1982, Olsen was "personally surprised" at the dismissal, while most of the teachers at the school were "very upset" and "very shocked."

Some teachers at Eckville High School must have been aware of what Keegstra was teaching. Lindberg, for example, heard complaints about Keegstra at least as early as 1975 and told his own children not to take Keegstra's classes. Olsen heard similar complaints about Keegstra's biases after taking over Lindberg's position. Bradshaw testified at Keegstra's trial that he occasionally heard Keegstra's students make unflattering references to Jews. Taylor passed on to Olsen a complaint directed to him about Keegstra's teaching.[5]

Such incidents do not seem to have affected the teachers' high regard for Keegstra, either at the time he was teaching or since. It is no wonder that Keegstra was able to get away with what he did for so long. The silence of his colleagues aided and abetted Keegstra. They, too, betrayed the trust society place in them by putting their allegiance to their colleague, or their solidarity as teachers, ahead of their responsibility to the students of Eckville.

— I —

Keegstra began teaching in Eckville in 1968. Two years later he "started to get wakened up [politically]" and by

1971 he began to introduce his anti-Jewish views into his classes. It was not long before parents began to pick up the special slant that Keegstra gave to his lessons. Art and Dorothy Carritt remember their son Brian discussing the Holocaust after taking shop with Keegstra in 1971-72. Margaret Andrew was upset when her daughter Cindy took grade twelve social studies with Keegstra in 1976 and ran into trouble for using encyclopedia material in a history essay. Keegstra's red-pencilled comments in the margin of the paper left little doubt as to his views. Marxism was strong in Russia, he wrote, "because of the large Jewish population." A massacre of peasants in Russia in 1905 was caused by "British and Jewish perfidity" and staged by "three thousand Jews."[6]

But Keegstra, at this time, did not concentrate solely on the Jews. Catholics too came in for special treatment and it is apparent that his anti-Catholic teachings played an important role in early complaints about his biases. This was only natural in a town with a sizable Catholic minority and no Jews at all. There is no Catholic school system in Lacombe County. This meant that Catholic students in Eckville had to attend Eckville High School and take Jim Keegstra's classes. By all accounts, they had a hard time of it in the early 1970s.

Catholics and Catholicism are not Jim Keegstra's central preoccupation and do not form an important part of the international Jewish conspiracy that has seized his fancy. His anti-Catholicism is not fundamental to his world view in the way his anti-Judaism is. He does not see Catholics as deliberately serving the cause of anti-Christ or of plotting with the Jews to enslave mankind. His anti-Catholic biases are rooted instead in the more traditional Protestant rejection of Catholic teaching, especially Papal infallibility and the universal structure of the church. Such objections have marked Fundamentalist Protestantism through the centuries.

Lately the traditional objectives have been combined with the notion that the Catholic Church has become an unwitting dupe for Communism. (This claim has become even stronger since Pope John Paul II has been seated on the Throne of St. Peter.) Keegstra's Catholic students were made to suffer his taunts about the Church in front of their classmates. As a result some Catholic parents withdrew their children from Eckville High in the early 1970s.

After Keegstra was dismissed, many commentators pointed out that Eckville has no Jews. They claimed that Keegstra would not have been tolerated for long if there had been Jewish children in his classes, exposed to his biases, and prepared to complain to their parents. But for many years Eckville's Catholic children complained to their parents about his anti-Catholic biases and still Keegstra stayed and taught. In Eckville, Catholics are a minority. With a few notable exceptions, they appear to have been afraid to rock the boat. When one parent complained about Keegstra's anti-Catholic teaching to a priest in Sylvan Lake (there is no Catholic Church in Eckville), she was told not to be overly concerned. She was told that Keegstra was entitled to his opinions and that is was possible her child was overreacting.

— II —

Despite the complacency of many parents, the *laissez-faire* attitude of some of the teachers and the pressures to conform that exist in most small communities, a number of Eckville parents did resist the temptation to stay silent. They did try to do something about a popular man who was teaching bigotry to their children. But the two men who were principals of Eckville High School from 1970 until the time of his dismissal, Joseph Lindberg and Edwin Olsen, did not take any action against Keegstra.

Joe Lindberg graduated from the University of Saskatchewan with a Bachelor of Arts in 1947 and earned a diploma in education in Saskatchewan two years later. He has taught in Saskatchewan and Alberta for almost thirty years and was principal of a half-dozen schools. He came to Eckville as principal in 1970 and held that position for five years before transferring to a school in Blackfalds, also in

Lacombe County, for one year in 1976. When he returned to Eckville High in 1977, he specialized in social studies. As principal he had been called upon to handle the earliest complaints about Jim Keegstra, some of which were directed to him by Art and Dorothy Carritt.

Art Carritt was born in Bentley, Alberta, in 1921. He remembers that his parents, members of the United Church of Canada, stopped attending Sunday services at Rainey Creek United Church in the 1930s because two or three church members would stand in the church foyer every Sunday morning and denounce the Jews. Art's father thought highly of those Jews he met in the Lacombe area when they came to his farm to buy poultry, eggs, animal hides and horse hair. He felt they always paid a fair price. When they took goods on consignment because they did not have money to pay for them, they always returned to pay their debts. Art himself had many contacts with Jews while serving in the army in World War II. Like his father before him, he never cared for talk of anti-Semitism or bigotry of any kind.

When Keegstra began to give one Catholic student a hard time in class in the early 1970s, the Carritts' son Brian spoke up to defend him. He was put out of class for his trouble. That was when Art and his wife Dorothy first went to Joe Lindberg to complain. Lindberg, according to Carritt, took a "shoulder-shrugging attitude" and told them that the episode was "just their child's opinion."[7]

Lindberg appears to have been somewhat ambivalent about Keegstra. He clearly did nothing about the Carritt complaint and when "a girl who professed to have Jewish ancestry" also approached him about Keegstra, he told her that social studies was not compulsory and that she should not take it. He later told the press that although Keegstra's lessons were "one-sided," he did not "see anything wrong with this because [the grade 12 students] saw that bias and therefore weren't led into traps."[8]

However, Lindberg was concerned enough about stories of anti-Russian and anti-liberal bias in Keegstra's classes to instruct his daughters not to take Keegstra's courses, because he did not want them learning a view of events radically different from his own. And although Lindberg appeared as a character witness on behalf of Keegstra at Keegstra's trial, he admitted that he tried in 1975 to stop Keegstra from teaching grade twelve social studies. At that time he reached an agreement with Keegstra, whereby Keegstra would stick to shop courses. However, he never followed through on the agreement because he was concerned about making waves and causing the community dissatisfaction.[9] Before anything further came of this, Lindberg left to teach for a year in Blackfalds. When he returned to Eckville, Keegstra was still in his old position under a new principal, Ed Olsen.

Obviously Lindberg was concerned enough about the situation to suggest that Keegstra stop teaching social studies. However, he did not press the subject further with the Lacombe County Board of Education, the Alberta Department of Education or the Alberta Teachers' Association. Lindberg explained this by citing his own fear of making waves, but it is clear that there were other contributing circumstances. He never personally visited Keegstra's class and was not aware of the extent of Keegstra's biases. He later admitted that he did not know Keegstra had been "soft on Adolf Hitler and the Nazis or that students were being taught the Holocaust . . . was a hoax.[10] In fact, he trusted Keegstra. He was sure Keegstra had control of his class and "respect for personality," and this was of the utmost importance. He also liked and respected Jim Keegstra, and thought of him as an umpeccably honest man "renowned for his generosity" and as a good Christian.

Lindberg told Keegstra's trial that he knew Keegstra had entertained people of different religious and racial backgrounds in his home. "I'm familiar with Albert the Eskimo and Jerry the Indian," he stated, in reference to two non-whites who are supposed to have been Keegstra's guests. But he had "never met Bob the Jew," whom he had seen "driving around in [Keegstra's] car."[11] Joe Lindberg seems to have thought of Jim Keegstra as a good and likeable man, a pillar of the community who happened to have a few political and perhaps religious quirks that showed up in the classroom from time to time. Given Lindberg's admiration for Keegstra's abilities as a teacher and his ignorance of all that was transpiring in Keegstra's classroom, it is no wonder that Keegstra continued to teach at Eckville High up to 1975. What is truly amazing is that Lindberg even contemplated action.

The same cannot be said for Edwin Olsen, principal of Eckville High School since 1975. Olsen, who holds a Master of Educational Administration degree from the University of Alberta in addition to his Bachelor of Education degree, started his teaching career in the County of Lacombe in 1963. He was named vice-principal of Eckville High in 1965 and kept that position until Lindberg left and he took over. He, like Lindberg, began to field complaints about Keegstra as early as 1976, but did little or nothing about them. Art Carritt thought of Olsen as "totally complacent." It is possible that Olsen had no idea of the specific content of Keegstra's social studies classes until 1978, when his son took a course from Keegstra.

When Olsen did discover the full truth, he remained nonchalant. He told the CBC's Linden MacIntyre, after the dismissal, that he did not believe Keegstra meant to generate hate or that he succeeded in generating hate. He told Keegstra's trial that he did not think the complaints he had received before 1981 were serious.

When one parent complained to Olsen about Keegstra's views on Jews, he asked Keegstra to clarify to his class that he had not meant to suggest that all Jews were bad, but only those who adhered to the evil doctrines about which Keegstra was concerned. When asked for his reactions to the allegations that Keegstra's views were anti-Semitic, Olsen told a reporter just after Keegstra's dismissal: "If I were semitic, I don't know how I would look at it. Not being semitic, you know, to me, I don't have feelings one way or the other when I read it. If you look for the thing being anti-Semitic, I think you could find it there."[12] Olsen seems to believe that Keegstra's students did not suffer any bad effects from their social studies classes and that Keegstra was and is a tolerant man.

Olsen found it easy to brush off most of the complaints he received about Keegstra. However, one parent, Margaret Andrew, was more persistent than most. Andrew, a non-practising Catholic, had settled with her husband in Eckville in 1971. All five Andrew children were exposed to Keegstra's teachings, beginning with daughter Cindy's grade nine social studies class in 1973. But it was not until 1976, when Cindy took grade twelve social studies, that Andrew noticed the strong biases being taught by Keegstra.

Andrew had been upset when Keegstra wrote anti-Jewish comments on her daughter's essay on Russian history, but this soon proved to be only the beginning. In one lecture on religion and ideology, Keegstra attacked Catholicism, claiming that it was not really a religion at all but a humanly created ideology. Cindy was determined to prove her teacher wrong and did research for an essay on Catholicism. Keegstra returned the paper without a grade and told her the books she had used had been censored. Cindy threw the essay in the garbage and vowed thenceforth to give Keegstra what he wanted in order to get good grades.

Margaret Andrew was even more upset when she learned Keegstra had told his class that the Irish Republican Army, which fought for Irish independence early in this century, had been a Communist organization and that the troubles in Ireland had been fomented by German Jews. Andrew, whose father had been in the I.R.A. before coming to Canada in the early 1920s, was insulted by this. She sought a meeting with Keegstra to set him straight. He agreed to meet her, but insisted that he was right and she was wrong. She found him difficult to deal with, and received the strong impression that he believed she could not know much of anything because she was only a mother and housewife. Andrew left the meeting feeling that Keegstra was totally unrepentant and was convinced that he alone knew the truth.

Andrew kept the 1976 incident fixed firmly in her memory. In the fall of 1978, when her daughter Darcy was about to begin grade twelve social studies with Keegstra, she decided to try to do something about him. Margaret Andrew knew she would need corroboration from other students who had taken classes with Keegstra, especially non-Catholics. She called other parents. Two of them agreed to help her out. Andrew then phoned Frank Flanagan, superintendent of the Lacombe County Board of Education, to make her complaint. He told her to put it in writing. She did, and he then went to her house to meet with her and the two other parents.

There Andrew asked Flanagan if what Keegstra was teaching was part of the curriculum. This was always her central concern, because she knew that children of a small rural high school would be at a distinct disadvantage in life if they were not taught the same subject matter, and thus assessed over the same course of study, as all other children in Alberta. Flanagan admitted that Keegstra's teachings about Communists, German Jews and Ireland were not part of the Alberta Social Studies Curriculum and agreed to raise the matter with Keegstra. [13]

Flanagan spoke to Keegstra at least once and told him to stop expressing his anti-Catholic views in the classroom. Keegstra at first insisted on a meeting with Andrew and Flanagan but then backed down and apparently assured Flanagan that he would stick to the curriculum. Flanagan later told *Alberta Report* magazine that he "was perfectly satisfied that [Keegstra] was cognizant of the things he was teaching and they were modified." [14]

Flanagan issued no written instructions to Keegstra over the matter and did not enter a report of the incident in Keegstra's file. He was apparently satisfied that he had settled things, as was Olsen. But neither man ever followed up. Keegstra's teaching materials were not examined; his teaching of social studies was not monitored; the notes, essays and exams of his students were not checked. In the school, Olsen continued to treat Keegstra with kid gloves even though he was aware by the end of the 1978 school year of what was going on in Keegstra's class. By that time Olsen's own son had completed Keegstra's social studies course. Olsen's and Flanagan's inaction thus gave Keegstra four more years of opportunity to indoctrinate his students.

Olsen's attitude towards Keegstra may in part be explained by the pressures of living and working in a small community. He and Keegstra were colleagues and Keegstra was a pillar of the community. Keegstra was, by 1978, mayor of the town. Flanagan, however, is another matter. He was not Keegstra's neighbor or colleague. As superintendent of the school system in Lacombe County, he was charged with the responsibility to get to the root of matters such as this. That he did not do so is a matter of record. Both he and Olsen are unwilling to discuss their role in the Keegstra affair.

— III —

Although Flanagan was ultimately responsible for keeping tabs on Keegstra, Olsen and Lindberg were the men on the spot. They were in daily contact with the teachers at Eckville High, including Keegstra, and in a position to evaluate the gossip, rumors and complaints that flow daily from students and staff in any school. Both men have been condemned for doing nothing about Keegstra and both deny any responsibility. Legally, they are right. They were not responsible for checking up on Keegstra, for evaluating him or for reporting him to Flanagan or anyone else.

The Alberta School Act is the foundation of elementary and secondary education in the province. It says virtually nothing about the role and duties of a school principal in Alberta. Section 93 of the Act specifies that a school board "shall designate one teacher to be the principal of each school" but does not list the powers, duties or responsibilities of that principal. At the same time the School Act allows principals to join the Alberta Teachers' Association, which is both professional association and teachers' union to all Alberta teachers. It is clear, therefore, that the principal is supposed to be in charge of the school but it is unclear how that responsibility is to be discharged. And there is no obligation placed on the principal to represent the employer—the school board—in dealing with the teachers.

The Alberta School Act is designed to give the greatest amount of autonomy possible to school boards in administering their schools.[15] They act on behalf of the Minister of Education, who delegates important responsibilities to those boards. The theory behind this is that the boards are in a much better position to gauge local needs, values and aspirations than is the Minister in Edmonton. The boards are also locally elected, and responsible to the ratepayers in each jurisdiction. If the ratepayers are not happy with the decisions made by their school boards, it is expected that they will deal with those boards when local elections take place.

One of the responsibilities delegated to school boards is that of determining the role and duties of the principal. This means that principals in one jurisdiction can have duties assigned to them by their school board that are much more extensive than the duties assumed by principals in a neighboring jurisdiction. It is generally true that school boards in large urban centers place more authority on, and demand more of, their principals than do those in small jurisdictions such as Lacombe County (which has approximately 3,500 students and 200 teachers scattered across an area about thirty by a hundred kilometres). It is also true, however, that city school boards have far more support personnel to help principals keep things in line.

Lacombe County did not ask much of its principals until 1981 when Bob David, who took over from Flanagan in 1979, began laying out administrative guidelines for principals, requiring them to evaluate and report on their teachers and conduct seminars, study sessions and retreats to train them in teacher evaluation.[16] (Such requirements, it must be noted, run counter to the long-range goals of the Alberta Teachers' Association, which hold that "reporting on the competence of individual teachers in the school is not a routine function of a principal."[17])

Sandra Weidner—who was chairperson of the Lacombe County Board of Education at the time Keegstra was dismissed, and who was instrumental in that dismissal—has admitted that neither Lindberg nor Olsen was obliged to evaluate Keegstra's teaching or to report on him, and that Olsen was "doing what [the Board] asked him to do as a principal."[18] (Weidner only joined the Board in the fall of 1980.)

David supports Weidner's views and points out that Olsen never received training in teacher evaluation prior to 1981, was not given clear instructions by the Board and had a full teaching load himself. At the time David took over, the Board had "no clear policy on a principal's duty."[19] David began to institute the changes before he became aware of the trouble at Eckville High School. They were part of a general tightening-up on what had obviously been a loosely administered system in the county.

Ed Olsen had no legal responsibility to evaluate or report on Keegstra prior to 1981, but what about his moral responsibility? He himself said it best when he was called to the stand to testify in March 1983 during the Board of Reference inquiry into the Keegstra dismissal. His questioner was S.D. Hillier, Keegstra's lawyer at the hearing:

> *Question:* Is it the general responsibility of the principal [in Lacombe County] to deal with these problems as the first line of authority?
> *Answer:* Yes.
> *Q:* And the superintendent's office would become involved if it was not resolved at the local level, but only after that step was taken?
> *A:* Usually, yes.
> *Q:* And what about with respect to parents complaints, is it usual that they go through the school or through the head office?
> *A:* In most cases they would go through the school first.
> *Q:* And is that a general policy or understanding within the County?

A: I don't know that it's written policy, but it's sort of an understanding.

Q: What's the rationale for that then?

A: If you have local problems, usually they're best dealt with at a local level, and usually that's the easiest place to solve them.[20]

— IV —

In the summer of 1985 Dave King, Alberta's Minister of Education, admitted that there was "very little reliable evidence" of what was going on in the classrooms of the province.[21] Since then King and the provincial government have left no stone unturned in their efforts to restore accountability to teaching practices and curriculum. King himself has run afoul of the Alberta Teachers' Association with some of his suggestions for change.

Although there is some evidence that King was contemplating changes to the system of certification and evaluation of Alberta teachers at least as far back as 1979, it is clear that the Keegstra affair provided a major reason for change and the opportunity to speed things up. If the 1970s can be categorized as the decade of "do your own thing" in the classrooms of Alberta, it is clear that the 1980s will be the decade of accountability.

Most institutions in North American society were affected by the post-World War II baby boom and by the rapid changes to social and political institutions that the young boomers demanded during the era of 1960s radical-ism. Education was no exception. By the late 1960s and early 1970s two factors were combining to loosen govern-mental control over the quality of teaching and instruction in Alberta: the baby boom and prosperity. Alberta, in one way, was no different from anywhere else in North America during this period. The babies born to the many young families established after World War II began to work their way through the school system in the early to mid-1950s. By the late 1950s and early 1960s, there were too few schools, classrooms, teachers and administrators to accommodate them.

Alberta was also affected by the prosperity created thanks to the expansion of petroleum exploration and extraction. People began to pour into the province, adding to the already existing pressures on the educational system. For many school jurisdictions in Alberta in the late 1960s and early 1970s, it was a tough enough job providing classes with teachers. Evaluating all those teachers on an ongoing basis seems to have been out of the question. Besides, evaluation smacked in some way of too much authority in an age when doing the democratic thing and allowing almost everyone free reign regarding what to teach was the order of the day.

In 1971 the government abolished the regular inspections of schools by provincial Department of Education Inspectors. Such inspections had once been a hallmark of the education system. Now representatives of the Minister of Education would no longer poke around schools, sit in on classes, evaluate teachers and report directly to the Department of Education. From 1971 on, evaluation of teachers, regular or not, was left completely up to the boards of education. Some jurisdictions introduced a regular system of evaluation and reporting. Others did not. Again, the large urban systems, with their more sophisticated administrative structures and larger staff, were in a far better position to conduct regular evaluations than were smaller rural school districts such as Lacombe County. Evaluation there was largely a matter of trust until superintendent David began to put evaluation guidelines in place in June 1981, three months before he was aware of the Keegstra troubles.

The Alberta government is now tightening up the situation considerably. School boards have been told that effective evaluation procedures must be adopted by all boards, although evaluation will still be left up to them.[22] If such requirements had been in place in 1971 when provincial school inspection was discontinued, Keegstra would no doubt have been caught much more quickly.

The making of a teacher in Alberta begins in an undergraduate Faculty of Education. Alberta, like most Canadian provinces, long ago abandoned the requirement that teachers first earn a Bachelor of Arts or Science degree and then pursue a Bachelor of Education degree for an addition year or two after graduation. The emphasis now is on teacher training, not on undergraduate education in the liberal arts. It is considered more important to teach teachers to *teach* than it is to teach them traditional subjects. They are of course required to take a number of liberal arts courses in the pursuit of the B.Ed. degree.

After graduation from the University of Alberta or the University of Calgary (or an equivalent institution elsewhere), the prospective teacher must apply to the Department of Education in Edmonton for an Interim Professional Certificate (a temporary license to teach.) This will almost certainly be granted if the application is supported by the candidate's Faculty of Education. The temporary license allows the prospective teacher three years to prove competency. During this period, the relevant board of education is supposed to conduct a number of in-class evaluations of the candidate using different inspectors. (The Department of Education has not established a minimum standard for these classroom visits.)

If the board is satisfied that the prospective teacher is competent and recommends to the Department of Education that the teacher be given a permanent license, a Permanent Professional Certificate is granted. As long as it is valid, this certificate will allow the teacher to teach anywhere in the province. The Minister of Education is the only authority empowered to cancel or suspend the certificate. Cancellation or suspension is almost always done at the suggestion of the Alberta Teachers' Assocation.

Once a teacher has been hired by a school board and has taught for one year, tenure must be granted by the board if the board intends to continue to employ that teacher. Tenure then forms part of the contract of employment between the teacher and the board. It is not transferrable should the teacher leave to work in another jurisdiction. Tenure is designed to protect a teacher from dismissal for the expression of unpopular views. However, it is, in fact, little more than an agreement by the board to continue to employ the teacher unless the board believes it has a good reason for dismissal.

In Alberta, as in most other provinces, dismissal procedures are spelled out in the School Act. They are not very specific. A board can fire a teacher by giving the teacher a notice of termination at least thirty days prior to the date of dismissal. Section 89(2) of the Alberta School Act states that the notice of termination "shall specify the reasons for the termination" and warns the board to "act reasonably."

A study of teacher dismissals in Canada done by A.K. Harrison (who represented Keegstra during his dismissal proceedings) shows that most teachers fired in Alberta were dismissed because their positions were eliminated or because of incompetence, misconduct or insubordination.[23] Harrison's figures show that, from 1970 to 1979, Alberta boards of reference—the last court of appeal for a dismissed teacher—handled only ten cases of dismissal for cause (incompetence, misconduct or insubordination). In eight of those ten cases, dismissals were overturned and the teachers reinstated. There are currently over 26,000 teachers in Alberta. It is clear that some teachers do not bother to appeal dismissals to boards of reference because they do not have good cases. But it is probably fair to conclude from the few cases appealed to the boards of reference that in fact very few teachers were dismissed during this period.

It should not be easy to fire teachers. Those who are entrusted with the education of young minds must have security of position, a reasonable living standard and freedom to express themselves within the curriculum guidelines established for them by the Departments of Education. The job they do *is* that important. But at the same time society must be assured, if it is to grant permanent licenses to teach, that teachers continue to do their jobs properly once they have been accepted into the system. This can only be achieved through continuing evaluation.

What happened in the 1970s was that a system evolved in which teachers were granted permanent certificates and tenure within the first three years of their careers and could then escape effective evaluation of their performance for long years at a stretch. Society had, in effect, lost control over what went on in the classroom by not requiring regular in-class evaluation and reports on teachers. Jim Keegstra was a legacy of the age of "do your own thing" in the educational system.

— V —

Dismissal and the cancellation of a Permanent Professional Certificate are matters spelled out by the School Act as being within the jurisdiction of the school board and the minister. However, discipline of teachers in Alberta has been placed by law in the hands of the Alberta Teachers' Association (ATA). The ATA is a self-governing professional body which derives its powers from the Alberta Teaching Profession Act. Section 5(1) of that act specifies that no one can teach in Alberta who is not an "active member" of the Association. Should the ATA revoke a teacher's membership, therefore, it would effectively end a teacher's career in a classroom in almost every school in the province. Usually, such revocation is followed by the revocation of the Permanent Professional Certificate by the Minister of Education.

The Teaching Profession Act gives the ATA power to discipline its members and establishes a discipline committee, procedures for the governance of that committee and a Teaching Profession Appeal Board to act as a court of last resort.

The ATA's discipline committee must first receive a written complaint about a teacher before it can investigate his or her conduct. The committee received no complaints against Keegstra until well after his dismissal had been upheld by the board of reference in the spring of 1983. In the period 1955 to 1983 the ATA's discipline committee heard only 143 charges and conducted only 116 hearings even though approximately 150,000 teachers were employed in the province over that 25-year span.[24] The major teacher 'crimes' were contract jumping, criminal convictions and improper criticism of colleagues.

This last 'offence' stems from one of the provisions of the ATA's Code of Ethics which states: "The teacher does not criticize the professional competence or professional reputation of a colleague except to proper officials and then only in confidence and after the colleague has been informed of the criticism." This clause was cited many times in the aftermath of the Keegstra dismissal as one of the reasons why Keegstra was not found out sooner. However, it clearly placed no ethical roadblock in the way of anyone who taught at Eckville High who might have wished to lay a complaint about Keegstra to the discipline committee of the ATA. It was not the ATA Code of Ethics which was at fault, but the siege mentality which pervades so many levels of the educational system from kindergarten to university. This way of thinking prompts many educators to place the protection of colleagues before responsibility to students or the general public.

The ATA was the target of much criticism after Keegstra's dismissal. Some of it was more than justified. But much of the criticism was also misplaced because the ATA was not responsible for certifying Keegstra, giving him tenure, evaluating his performance in the classroom or prompting Lindberg, Olsen or Flanagan to do virtually nothing about him. The ATA's official involvement in the Keegstra matter began only after the Lacombe County Board of Education had started to consider dismissing Keegstra. Unions are not popular in Canadian society today and unions of teachers seem even less popular than most. As such, the ATA presented a fat target for many critics of the educational system who were unable or unwilling to closely examine more basic flaws.

A Trust Betrayed

— VI —

When Ed Olsen and Frank Flanagan failed to stop
Keegstra in 1978, they gave him almost four more years to
teach Eckville students that the Jews are trying to enslave
them and destroy western civilization. Keegstra took full
advantage of the time. He toned down his anti-Catholic
teaching after the Andrew complaint in 1978 but put more
anti-Jewish material into his courses. There were, after all,
no Jewish students in Eckville whose parents might give
him a hard time.

Jim Keegstra had been teaching his own brand of
history for at least six or seven years at that stage. He had
encountered almost no opposition from colleagues or superiors. He had side-stepped what little negative reaction had
been expressed by students or parents and he had escaped
unscathed from the intervention of the County school
superintendent. He probably became bolder as he got away
with more. His anti-Jewish teaching soon dominated his
social studies course. It ceased to be an investigation of
modern history and became, instead, the forum for Keegstra's paranoid ideas about a Jewish conspiracy. By the fall of
1978, Jim Keegstra had invented his own curriculum,
centered on that conspiracy.

5

Dismissal

BOB DAVID WAS NERVOUS and upset the morning of December 8, 1982, as he drove from his office in Lacombe to Eckville High School.

He was about to fire Jim Keegstra. David had been working as a school administrator for eight years—from 1974 to 1979 as assistant superintendent in Edson, Alberta, and since 1979 as superintendent in Lacombe. However, this was the first time he had had to hand a letter of dismissal to a teacher.

The day before, the Lacombe County Board of Education had met behind closed doors for six hours, following complaints by Susan Maddox, an Eckville nurse, that her son Paul was being taught political and religious bigotry in Keegstra's grade nine social studies class. The Board had first encountered Jim Keegstra at the beginning of 1982, after David had investigated complaints about him lodged in mid-December 1981. At that time they had instructed Keegstra to revamp his social studies course and get back to the curriculum. But when Maddox brought forward her complaints, it was obvious Keegstra had not complied. The Board then decided to dismiss him. After the December 7, 1982, meeting David had phoned Keegstra to tell him he had been dismissed and would receive the letter of termination the next morning. David then phoned Ed Olsen, repeated the news and instructed Olsen to find a substitute teacher as soon as possible.

By the time David arrived at the school on the morning of December 8, Keegstra was waiting for him in Olsen's office. Olsen was visibly upset; David could see that his face was ashen. After David handed Keegstra the letter, Olsen told him that the teaching staff had assembled in the staffroom and wanted to have some explanation for the dismissal. David was not anxious to confront the staff. When he entered the staffroom, pandemonium broke out as the teachers vented their anger against him and the Board.

David just stood there as Keegstra's colleagues shouted questions at him: "Does this mean we have to show you our lessons before we teach them from now on? Does this mean that teachers have no academic freedom whatever in this country?" A young teacher declared, "If this is the way this school system is going to treat teachers, there is no way I'm going to participate any further in this volunteer program." He then threw his looseleaf binder on the desk in front of David with a loud bang.[1]

— I —

Robert K. David, the man who finally did something about Jim Keegstra, was born in Edmonton in 1943 and educated at the University of Alberta. He began his teaching career with the Edmonton Public School Board in the late 1960s, before moving into school administration and completing a Master's degree in Educational Administration. From the time he took over from Frank Flanagan in Lacombe in 1979, he busied himself revamping and tightening procedural and administrative guidelines and regulations in the County school system. David introduced new rules for teaching controversial material. He brought in new guidelines for teacher evaluation. He initiated regulations defining the authority of Lacombe County principals. He arranged workshops and retreats to familiarize the principals with their new duties.

Bob David is a naturally exuberant, even excitable, man. He is completely dedicated to his job and determined to do things by the book in a straight, no-nonsense manner. His education, his teaching and his years as assistant superintendent had prepared him well for the job in Lacombe County. However, nothing had prepared him for Jim Keegstra.

When Frank Flanagan turned the superintendent's office over to David in 1979, he mentioned nothing about the problems which had arisen over Keegstra's teaching in the fall of 1978. David had no idea anything was amiss at Eckville High School until the first week of school in 1981. That was when he received a telephone call from Brenda Bartholomew, editor of the *Eckville Examiner*, asking him to meet with a group of parents who were concerned about the way Keegstra taught social studies.

David told Bartholomew he would not attend any such meeting unless Keegstra and Olsen were present. It was then agreed that the meeting would include them and that Bartholomew would set it up for Friday, September 4. When David drove to the school on the day of the meeting, he learned it had been cancelled (he never discovered why). Olsen and Keegstra told him they were not sure why the meeting had been arranged, except perhaps that some parents were concerned because Keegstra was a demanding teacher and his program of study might be too difficult for their children.[2]

On December 15, David received another telephone call about Jim Keegstra, this time from Kevin McEntee, a member of the Lacombe County School Board. McEntee had settled in Eckville in 1980, when he was hired as business manager of the local hospital. He was subsequently elected to the School Board.

It was not long before McEntee began to hear rumors about Keegstra. By December 1981, he had heard enough to prompt him to call David and pass along parental complaints about an essay assignment in social studies 30 (grade twelve social studies). David did not react immediately but promised McEntee that he would look into the matter. Two days later he received another telephone call about Keegstra from K.E. Ackerman, a parent, who read David a few comments Keegstra had written in the margin of his son's essay. David was concerned by what he heard. The next day, December 18, he drove to Eckville to investigate.

When David arrived at Eckville High School the morning of December 18, he met with Keegstra and Olsen and told them about the complaints. He asked to look at a student essay. Keegstra handed him "Judaism and its role in society from 1776-1918" by Danny Desrosiers. As David worked his way through the closely packed scrawl, he began to realize the enormity of what lay behind the complaints and rumors he had heard. "Judaism is a religious cult that claims to trace its origin to Abraham," Desrosiers had written. "But most Jews in the world today are strictly Jews by religion. This mixture makes the Jews very dangerous." David read on, carefully absorbing the essay's contents. When he finished, he asked Keegstra if the essay reflected his teaching. Keegstra confirmed that it did and that it had been based almost exclusively on Desrosier's class notes. David was appalled.

A heated discussion followed about the aims and contents of the curriculum and Keegstra's teaching of it. Keegstra told David that he should do more research into modern history and that the courses David had taken in university (David had majored in history) were not adequate for an understanding of modern events. He brought out *Censored History* and *Facts are Facts* and tried to convince David to read them. David lost his temper for a moment when Keegstra refused to demur. He told Keegstra point blank that his job was to teach the curriculum and that the type of material covered in the essay and in the pamphlets was not acceptable.

He then asked to see a number of Keegstra's students and was introduced to three of them. They told David that they believed Jews were behind all international disasters, were allied with Communism and were conspiring to control the world. They had learned this from Keegstra.

When David completed his discussions with the students, he again talked to Keegstra. He told him to begin to teach the prescribed curriculum and suggested that the Board would probably be interested to hear of the matter. Keegstra replied that he would be pleased to present his position to the Board of Education at any time.[3]

David returned to his office and dictated a long letter to Keegstra, summing up his findings and reviewing his instructions. This was where his actions differed radically from those of his predecessor. Flanagan had handled the Andrew complaint informally and had been content to leave it at that. David was determined to put matters on the record.

In his letter David reminded Keegstra about the complaints that had been made in 1978 (David undoubtedly checked Keegstra's file on returning from the school). He told the social studies teacher that his discussions at the school that day had led him to conclude that Keegstra had a "highly biased" view of history and that he was "teaching these biased and prejudiced views as if they were confirmed by historical fact." This was "simply not acceptable," was "not in keeping with the constraints of the curriculum," and "must cease."

David stressed that he was not issuing this "directive" to muzzle Keegstra's academic freedom or limit his "intellectual integrity" but instead to "insist that all sides of a historical question . . . be presented in as unbiased a way as possible, so that students [could] judge contradictory points for themselves." In other words, the Jewish conspiracy theory was "not [to] be taught as if it were fact instead of just another view of history." David told Keegstra that the matter would be brought to the attention of the School Board and that Keegstra should consider David's directive as a "lawful order of the Board." (See Appendix Document 1.)

David did not instruct Keegstra not to discuss the Jewish conspiracy theory in his classes. He made clear, however, that he was to mention it only in explaining to his students that there are those who believe such a conspiracy exists. Keegstra was also to tell his students that others deny the existence of any such conspiracy. David believed, and still believes, that this approach would have served the purposes of the curriculum. It would have placed both sides of the issue before the students and allowed them to form their own conclusions, based on their own research, as well as the material presented to them in class. But Keegstra could not do this. He does not believe there is another side to the question. He is convinced of the truth of the Jewish conspiracy and he was determined to pass his views on to his students.

He did not modify his teaching in response to David's letter, either in his grade twelve social studies course (which ended at the end of January 1982) or in the grade nine social studies course (which was continuing at that time). David was well aware, after his investigations on December 18, that he was dealing with a fanatically anti-Jewish teacher. However, he also knew that Keegstra had a right to his prejudices as long as he kept them out of the classroom. David was convinced that Keegstra could be forced to do this if he could be forced to stick to the Alberta Social Studies Curriculum.[5]

— II —

David needed the Board's approval for his directive. He included a copy of it and a typed version of the Desrosiers essay in the mail-outs to the Board members for the January 12, 1982 meeting. Sandra Weidner received hers in the mail on December 21. Weidner was born and raised in Alberta and had moved to Lacombe with her first husband in 1969. (He was killed in a car crash in 1970.) She had attended the University of Calgary and completed a two-year education program before teaching school in Bentley and Lacombe. When she married a local car dealer, she quit teaching and became active in service clubs and recreation organizations. For a time she served on the board of St. Andrew's United Church in Lacombe. In the fall of 1980 Weidner was elected by acclamation to the Lacombe County Board of Education.

Sandra Weidner was shocked when she read the Desrosiers essay and David's letter to Keegstra. She called Kevin McEntee to find out as much as she could about Keegstra. Weidner hardly slept that night and the next morning hurried over to David's office to discuss Keegstra with him as soon as he came in. She told him that his letter was inadequate; Keegstra should be fired as quickly as possible. She wanted a special meeting of the Board to deal with the case.

Bob David was pleased with Weidner's response. He had been worried that the Board might think he had overreacted. But he also knew how difficult it was to fire a teacher and that special care must be taken to follow proper procedures and due process. He pointed this out to Weidner and reminded her that other Board members might not agree with her. Since the regular Board meeting was only a little more than three weeks away, and the Christmas holidays were about to begin, it was better, he suggested, to wait for that meeting. Weidner agreed.[6]

When the Board met on January 12, David's letter was discussed *in camera* and at length. Not everyone was as shocked as Weidner had been. There were only three or four, including Weidner and McEntee, who wanted to fire Keegstra right away even though David's December 18 letter was unanimously approved. Most of the Board members were more cautious and doubted whether Keegstra could be dismissed on the basis of what David had discovered. They decided, instead, to direct David "to continue to monitor the situation" and to call Keegstra in for a termination hearing at their February meeting.

The Board suggested that David get legal advice. After consulting Judith Anderson, the Board's solicitor (who also acted for the Alberta School Trustees Association), David wrote to Keegstra, telling him that the Board would be considering the possible termination of his contract at its February 9 meeting on the grounds that he had failed to comply with the Alberta Social Studies Curriculum. David charged that Keegstra was "teaching . . . discriminatory theories as fact" and had failed to "modify sufficiently" his teaching content to "reflect the desires of the Board of Education, its officers, and the local community."[7] (See Appendix Document 2.) Keegstra was "comletely shocked" that the Board was considering his dismissal and contacted the Alberta Teachers' Association.[8]

— III —

When the telephone rang in the members' services office of the Alberta Teachers' Association in Edmonton on January 26, 1982, Keith Harrison answered. There have been times since when he wished he hadn't.

Harrison was born in Manitoba and educated at the University of Manitoba (receiving a Bachelor of Science and a teaching certificate there) and the University of Alberta (where he completed a Bachelor of Education, Master of Education and, in 1980, a Ph.D. in Educational Administration). After many years as a teacher and principal—he was principal of Lacombe Junior High School from 1966 to 1970—he concentrated on ATA work and ended up in the members' services department specializing in handling dismissal cases. His Ph.D. thesis was entitled "Procedures and Reasons for Termination of Teacher Contracts in Canada." Harrison is undoubtedly one of the country's experts on the subject. He is a careful, precise and even-tempered man. He is soft spoken, but gives the impression of having an iron will.

Keegstra telephoned Harrison on January 26. He outlined the situation and told him about the two letters he had received from David and about the February 9 Board meeting. He asked Harrison to help him. The two men arranged to meet for lunch at the Juniper Lodge, near Lacombe, on the day of the Board meeting. Over the phone Harrison suggested that Keegstra get letters of support from the principal and others in Eckville. He also asked Keegstra to send him photocopies of the two letters from David. Keegstra did this, but did not send Harrison a copy of the Desrosiers essay.

When Keegstra met Harrison on February 9, Harrison had not seen the Desrosiers essay or any other material from Keegstra's students.[9] Keegstra brought along letters of support from Olsen, Craig Taylor (the vice-principal), several members of the Eckville town council and letters from former students. Whatever Harrison may have thought about David's December 18 letter to Keegstra (which detailed David's findings about Keegstra's teaching of the Jewish conspiracy theory), he decided to handle this case in the same way he had treated all the other dismissals with which he had been involved. He decided to give Keegstra the best advice and the strongest representation possible. In his view the matter seemed to rest on a single complaint and this was more than balanced by the many letters of support Keegstra had collected.

Bob David had interviewed only three students. He had not gone into Keegstra's classroom and he had not conducted an ongoing evaluation of Keegstra. It was, Harrison reasoned, premature to be discussing dismissal. Harrison suggested to Keegstra, and Keegstra agreed, that they propose to the Board that a social studies consultant from the Alberta Department of Education be brought in for an independent evaluation of Keegstra's lessons to either confirm or refute the charges David had made. If the charges were confirmed, Keegstra would resign. Harrison was thinking about the end of June as a deadline for the evaluation.[10]

Harrison's suggestion reflected conclusions he had reached in his Ph.D. thesis. At one time the Alberta Teachers' Association could ask the Department of Education to have a look at a teacher's performance in the classroom. However, that practice had been discontinued in the mid-1970s. Harrison wanted it reinstated. He suggested, in his dissertation, that an outside evaluator be brought in whenever a board was considering the dismissal of a teacher for incompetence. But in this case, David had already made an assessment on the basis of student notes and essays, interviews with three students and interviews with Keegstra himself. Had the Board accepted Harrison's suggestion, their action would have shown a lack of confidence in Bob David.

The *in camera* termination hearing was held following the Board's regular business meeting. Keegstra was ushered into the room accompanied by Harrison and carrying a small pile of books, pamphlets and diagrams. Harrison spoke first. He claimed that David had overreacted in responding to a single telephone complaint from one parent. He passed around the letters of support Keegstra had brought in, and he made his proposal regarding bringing in an outside evaluator.

Then Keegstra spoke. For the next hour or more, he taught the Board his Jewish conspiracy theory. He kept many of the Board members spellbound as he led them through the world of Adam Weishaupt and the Illuminati, and tried to show them that he was justified in teaching what he did. Keegstra claimed that what he taught offset the socialism the students had learned from previous teachers. He told the Board that they had been duped by the conspirators and had been filled full of censored history. He offered to make any of his materials available to Board members who wanted to learn the truth. At all times, however, he claimed that he had not taught his students that the Jewish conspiracy was a proven fact, only that it was his personal theory of history.

Keegstra made a deep impression on his listeners. David later wrote that Keegstra's presentation "was most convincing," while Weidner remembers a Board member remarking to her after the meeting that she wished she had had a teacher like that herself. Although Keegstra's presentation was not direct evidence of what was going on in his classroom, there could no longer be any doubt in the minds of the Board or Keith Harrison that the social studies teacher was strongly committed to the notion of a Jewish conspiracy. This was not enough, however, to warrant his dismissal because Keegstra claimed to be teaching it as a theory only and not as fact. As David later observed: "We don't control what people believe, but we do control what they teach in our classrooms, and if they are teaching things that we don't approve of we can direct that they cease. . . ."11

After Keegstra left the meeting, the Board debated the matter at great length and sought the advice of solicitor Judith Anderson, who was present. Although David pressed for Keegstra's dismissal, Anderson urged caution and most of the Board agreed. Keegstra's history lesson had confirmed David's allegations, but there was still little direct evidence of what was transpiring in the classroom. Keegstra had not received much warning of the possible termination after the December 18 letter. Besides, grade twelve social studies had ended at the end of January. Apparently no one was aware at this point that Keegstra's grade nine social studies classes were somewhat simplified carbon copies of his grade twelve classes.

The Ackerman and McEntee complaints, and David's December 18 investigation, had all centered on grade twelve (in fact Keegstra was teaching grade nine social studies at that very time).

The Board decided not to dismiss Keegstra at that point, but directed David to write him a letter, in consultation with Anderson, which clearly set out the Board's expectations. David did so, presented it to the Board for approval on March 9 and mailed it the same day. (See Appendix Document 3.) The letter was very specific:

> . . . the Board of Education wants you to clearly understand that your teaching practices, as reviewed with the Board at our February 9th meeting and referred to in my letter of December 18th, are not acceptable and are not to continue in the future. Specifically, the Board of Education directs:
>
> 1. That in your teaching of Social Studies, you comply with the *Alberta Social Studies Curriculum* guide . . .

2. You must not teach discriminatory theories as if they were fact. This is particularly applicable to the Jewish conspiracy theory of history . . . [This too, is in keeping with the intent of the Social Studies Curriculum Guide] . . . If you do not comply with the directives in this letter, the Board will again consider the possible termination of your contract of employment.

Keegstra was asked for written assurances that he would follow the directives "at all times in the future."[12]

The letter of March 9, 1982, laid the groundwork for a possible termination of Keegstra's contract. David knew how difficult it was to take action against a teacher and he also knew that it was the Board's responsibility, and not his own, to make the final decision. But it was his responsibility to ensure that the steps the Board took were both lawful and proper. It was also his responsibility to begin documenting the case. This had now been accomplished. Keegstra had been lawfully warned and had been given time to correct his ways. What could be fairer than that? At the same time David took care to collect student notebooks from the grade twelve social studies class which had ended at the end of January. All this took place within less than three months after the first complaints about Keegstra had been directed to David.

Keegstra's reply to David's March 9 letter did not satisfy the Board. He claimed he had been teaching "in accordance to [the Social Studies] guide" and assured the Board that he would "continue to teach in accordance to the . . . guide" in future.[13] (See Appendix Document 4.) This was hardly what the Board wanted to hear. The members directed David to write Keegstra that his letter was "not entirely satisfactory" and that if further complaints reached the Board, they would be investigated. David wrote on April 7, telling Keegstra that it was the position of the Board that he was "not teaching in accordance with [the social studies] guide" and it was "their directive that [he] change" so that his teaching would conform "to the intent of the curriculum."[14] (See Appendix Document 5.) This was the fourth such letter Keegstra had received. The Board had more than fulfilled its responsibility to act in a fair and lawful manner.

— IV —

By January 1982, Margaret Andrew had lost patience with Jim Keegstra's teaching. She was not aware of the complaints that had been made to R. K. David in December, or of the *in camera* Board discussion that took place on January 9. However, she was more than aware of the anti-Jewish attitudes that her children had picked up in Keegstra's classes. The 1980-81 school year had been the worst yet. Her daughter Corinna had taken grade twelve social studies from Keegstra, while her twin sons Brad and Blair took his grade nine social studies class.

For months dinner conversation in the Andrew home was dominated by talk of "gutter rat" Jews, as the young people repeated the latest lessons from Keegstra's classes. When Brad and Blair would repeat Keegstra's explanations for historical events, Margaret would challenge them to do independent research in the school library. The reply was always the same: Keegstra had told them the books had been censored by the conspirators. For a time Margaret and her husband considered leaving Eckville because of the situation, or having the children bussed to school in Lacombe. But Margaret did not want to leave. She decided to stay and fight instead. Her aim was to have Keegstra removed before the fall of 1983, when Brad and Blair would encounter him in grade twelve.[15]

On January 12, 1982, Margaret Andrew sent Bob David a package of student notes from daughters Cindy and Corinna (grade twelve) and son Blair (grade nine). This would have been the first tangible evidence that the problems David had uncovered in Keegstra's grade twelve classes were also occurring in grade nine. However David failed to notice, perhaps because there were no noticeable differences between the notebooks. No mention was made at subsequent Board meetings that grade nine might also be a problem area. When no action was taken as a result of Andrew's sending of the notes—she was not, of course, aware of any of the *in camera* discussions the Board had held February 9, March 9 or April 7—she drew up a petition:

> We the undersigned feel Jim Keegstra should not be allowed to teach Jr. Sr. High classes, for reasons listed below:
> 1. Attitude toward the Jews; all Jews are gutter rats. Only good Jew is a dead one.
> 2. Teaching pertaining to the Second World War; six million Jews were not killed . . .
> 3. Attitude toward Catholics . . . the Pope is a dangerous man.
> 4. Attitude toward the Black race; they are very inferior.
> 5. Anyone buying a Russian tractor is Communist inspired.

The petition pointed out that the problem arose in grade nine and twelve social studies and also in grade nine science.[16] It was kept at the Andrew home and Marg and some of her friends contacted other parents and asked them to sign it. By early May she had collected sixty signatures from parents and students and a few from other Eckville residents who had no direct contact with Keegstra. It was presented to the School Board by Marg Andrew and Rod Daniels, another parent, on May 11, 1982.

Although the petition might have served as warning that Keegstra's grade nine social studies was just as much a problem as grade twelve, the Board essentially dismissed it as more evidence of what they already knew. The wording of the petition, as well as its form, made it essentially useless as a document to use in building a case against Keegstra. It was, however, an indication that at least some parents were concerned enough about Keegstra to sign a petition. Not everyone in Eckville was complacent about him. Not everyone was behind him.

The petition prompted the Board to pass a resolution directing David to "conduct a further investigation" into Keegstra's teaching. On May 17 Earl A. Clark, David's deputy, visited Eckville High to look in on Keegstra's grade nine science and social studies classes. He took the opportunity, while in the social studies class, to examine the notebooks of one of the students and noticed frequent mention of "Khazar Jews," which he believed to be "derogatory." He also read notes indicating "that the Czars of Russia would have accomplished many needed reforms except for these Jews." He noticed that the term "money thugs" was used in several places. Clark was "puzzled about some of the information this student [had] picked up" but generally reported Keegstra "to be quite a forceful tacher" who kept "excellent control of his class."[17]

Clark's report, which clearly indicated that all was not right in Keegstra's grade nine social studies class, was sent to David, with a copy to Olsen. It rang no bells in the superintendent's office, although it was an indirect indication that Keegstra was still in open defiance of the Board's directives.

— V —

David responded to Andrew's petition the day after the Board meeting in May. He informed her of the Board's motion, but Andrew was not kept apprised of the progress of the investigation of Keegstra's teachings. Indeed, it would have been highly irregular for David to do so. By the end of May, therefore, Marg Andrew was growing increasingly impatient and felt herself to be involved in a lonely and frustrating campaign. On May 26 she even phoned Harrison to find out what the ATA was doing, but he refused to discuss the matter with her. In early June she wrote to Dave King, Alberta's Minister of Education.

Andrew's letter to King was a two-and-a-half page detailed exposition of the recent career and teachings of Jim

Keegstra. She stressed her concerns about Keegstra's failure to follow the curriculum and his "derogatory statements about the Jews" and listed some of the details of the 'history' her children had picked up in Keegstra's classes since 1976. She asked for King's immediate attention to this matter.[18] Several days after mailing her letter, Andrew received a reply from the Department of Education telling her that her letter would be "placed before the Minister at the earliest opportunity" and that she could "expect a further response in the near future."[19] That response did not arrive for four months.

In mid-July, the Department of Education finally acted on Andrew's letter to King. It sent Clayton Allen, an official with the Red Deer regional office of the Department, to investigate. Allen went to Eckville, interviewed Andrew and took some of the notebooks in Andrew's possession. He tried to contact Keegstra by telephone but could not reach him. Allen later claimed that the purpose of his investigation was to find out if the Board was handling the complaint properly: "The people who hire him are the people who have to fire him."

Allen apparently reported back to King that Keegstra "wasn't doing what he was supposed to be doing," but that the Lacombe Board was handling the problem correctly. Allen arrived at this conclusion, however, without conferring with David, Earl Clark or Sandra Weidner. He also did not visit the Lacombe School Board offices to examine the growing file of documentation on Keegstra. Following standard procedure, Allen filed his report directly with the Department of Education. Neither David nor anyone else connected with the Lacombe County Board ever saw it.

Andrew finally heard from the Department of Education in mid-October—at least two months after Allen's report must have been filed. King wrote that "bigotry and parading falsehood as truth" have no place in Alberta's classrooms but that the locally elected Board was responsible for the operation of the schools. The results of the Department's investigation indicated that the Board was "making an effort to deal with the situation" and King was "confident that its efforts [would] result in positive action."[20] (See Appendix Document 7.) By the time Andrew received this letter, Susan Maddox had already set in motion the events that led directly to Keegstra's dismissal.

— VI —

Susan Maddox lives with her husband on a farm near Eckville and works as a nurse in the Eckville Hospital. Her son Paul entered grade nine at Eckville High School in September 1982 and was assigned to two of Keegstra's classes, science and social studies. Not long after the school year began, Paul returned home and told his mom that Keegstra had discussed creation and evolution at great length in his science class and said that evolution was a Communist notion. Maddox was disturbed by this but did not think much about it until Paul asked for help in preparing for a social studies test at the end of September. When she went through Paul's notebook, she discovered just what brand of 'history' Keegstra had been teaching.

At the first opportunity Maddox spoke to McEntee, who was business manager at the hospital. She asked about the rumors she had heard over the previous year concerning complaints directed at Keegstra. McEntee, told her there had indeed been a complaint and that the School Board had looked into it. Maddox then told McEntee she had a complaint of her own, and asked him what to do. McEntee suggested she first see Keegstra. Then, if she received no satisfaction, he suggested she go to Olsen and possibly also to the Board.

Maddox, however, had been checking Paul's notebook daily and was becoming increasingly alarmed by what he was being taught. She had no desire to work her way slowly through the system. She therefore called Bob David on October 7. He, too, suggested that she begin by going through channels but assured her that, if she received no satisfaction that way, he would be prepared to follow through as long as she put her complaint in writing and documented it as carefully as possible. He also warned her that she would probably have to appear before the School Board and possibly also the Board of Reference. David happened to be at Eckville High on another matter later that day. He told Keegstra and Olsen that he had received a complaint and that a meeting would be set up shortly.

Susan Maddox did not want to meet with Keegstra and Olsen, at least not yet. She knew that the School Board would be meeting on October 12 and was determined to put her complaint before the Board in time for the meeting. After her conversation with David, she spent hours at the Red Deer College library looking into the 'facts' that Keegstra had been teaching her child. On October 11 she sat down and wrote a two page, single-spaced letter detailing what Keegstra had taught Paul in his science and social studies classes and pointing out the material she considered objectionable. To this she attached a photocopy of Paul's notebook containing dictated and blackboard notes from the start of the school year up to October 8.

Maddox carefully numbered the objectionable material in the notebook with a red pen and referred to those numbers in making her comments about Keegstra's views and his gross historical inaccuracies. She and her husband had "always taught [their] children to accept people regardless of race, color or creed and to judge each on his individual merits," she wrote. This was why she found Keegstra's "racial and religious bigotry and prejudice intolerable." She charged that ninety percent of what Keegstra taught was "indoctrination" and she appealed to David to "dismiss Mr. Keegstra from teaching classes in which our children will be enrolled."[21] After completing the letter, Susan Maddox delivered it to Bob David. (See Appendix Document 6.)

The Maddox letter was the prime topic of discussion at the Board meeting the next day. It was clear evidence that Keegstra was still teaching material he had been ordered to discard and that he was also doing so in grade nine. This was another violation of curriculum guidelines which, naturally enough, specified different programs of study at the different grade levels. The Board, therefore, gave

David an informal directive to pursue the matter further by contacting Keegstra and the Board's solicitors in preparation for the establishment of a termination hearing.

In the days that followed, David was kept busy by the Keegstra matter. He had kept students' notebooks, exams and essays from the previous semester's grade twelve social studies class in his office. He now compared them carefully with the grade nine material he had received from Maddox. He found it virtually the same.

David spoke to Richard McNally, a lawyer who temporarily replaced Judith Anderson, to get advice about the best possible way to proceed. He also spoke to Frank A. Crowther, a social studies expert with the Alberta Department of Education, to seek Crowther's opinion on the suitability of Keegstra's lectures. He asked Crowther to have an informal look at the Maddox letter and notebook. Crowther replied that he would get back to David shortly.

Maddox herself was not through with Keegstra or Eckville High School. On Friday, October 15, she went to the school to talk with Keegstra and Olsen. She told them she had decided to pull her son Paul out of Keegstra's social studies class and have him take the course by correspondence. Keegstra accused her of "taking a slanted point of view" and when she denied this he loaned her photocopies of *Censored History, Facts are Facts* and a new pamphlet he had just obtained, *The Rulers of Russia*. Maddox quickly mailed copies of all three to David noting, "I believe you will find much of the [grade nine social studies] notes are based on these three publications."[22] (See Appendix Document 8.) Neither Keegstra nor Olsen was able to convince Maddox to leave Paul in Keegstra's class.

David's preparations for the termination hearing began to move along quickly by the third week of October. On October 20 he called Crowther, who told him he was willing to help as long as David formally requested it in writing and specified that the Lacombe County Board of Education had not given Keegstra permission to teach what he was teaching either as part of the curriculum or in the free-time portion of class time that social studies teachers were allowed.[23] David mailed such a letter the following day, and also notified Crowther that the special termination hearing would be held November 22.

That day David also wrote to Keegstra, to the trustees, and to McNally, Olsen and Maddox. He told them about the November 22 meeting and invited them to attend. The letter to Keegstra specified three reasons for the termination hearing: Keegstra's failure to comply with the Alberta Social Studies Curriculum; his failure to "modify sufficiently" his teaching content to "reflect the desires of members of the local community and the Board of Education" as communicated to him by David; and his refusal to comply with the directives given him in David's letter of March 9, 1982.[24] (See Appendix Document 9.) David also visited Keegstra's grade nine social studies class on October 28— after he had notified Keegstra of the termination hearing— but found nothing amiss. He noted "good teaching and management skills were demonstrated during the time of my visit and good discipline was maintained."[25] But then, classroom management had never been Keegstra's problem.

— VII —

When Keegstra received David's notice of the November 22 termination hearing, he contacted Keith Harrison for advice and to invite Harrison to help him present his case to the School Board. Harrison had been exposed to Keegstra's views by this time and had seen the Desrosiers essay at the February 9 Board meeting, but he had not seen the Maddox notebook. He no longer remembers precisely what his reaction was to Keegstra's views, but he is still clear about where he thought the weight of evidence lay at that time. This new termination hearing was still the result of a single complaint, just as the last one had been. Therefore the picture in his mind was of "two pieces of negative information . . . and lots of positive information as well." This included letters of support and a positive classroom evaluation made by David himself on October 28 and a second positive evaluation done by Ed Olsen on November 5, 1982.[26] Keith Harrison called David, asked for a postponement of the hearing until December 7 (he was to present a paper at a conference in San Francisco) and discussed the grounds on which David based his termination notice to Keegstra. When he finished speaking to David, he put his queries concerning the notice in writing and asked David what evidence he had for his charge that Keegstra was not teaching the curriculum.[27]

David agreed to postpone the hearing until December 7. He notified the parties concerned but he was somewhat angered by Harrison's approach. The excitable David and the taciturn Harrison had not gotten along well from the start. Harrison thought David was acting too quickly; David could not believe that Harrison did not understand what was at issue. He told Harrison that the evidence of Keegstra's wrongdoing was contained in "student notebooks, student assignments, handouts, background reading material provided by the teacher and recommended to students, examinations, and a review of these materials by an expert in curriculum."

Here David was referring to Crowther, who would not attend the December 7 hearing due to illness, but who sent a two-and-a-half-page report on Keegstra's grade twelve social studies class which left no doubt that he did not consider Keegstra's handouts, or the lessons he taught as reflected in the student notes and essays, in keeping with curriculum.[28] (Harrison did not get to see this evaluation until the beginning of the December 7 meeting.) In preparation for the meeting, David also asked his deputy, Earl A. Clark, to evaluate Keegstra's teaching practices in grade nine social studies and science.

The hearing into the termination of Jim Keegstra's contract was called to order at one o'clock in the afternoon on Monday, December 7, 1982.[29] The entire Board was in attendance with Sandra Weidner in the chair (it is a rotating position and she had assumed it several weeks before). Bob David and his deputy, Earl Clark, were there. Richard McNally attended as legal advisor to the Board. Harrison attended to help present Keegstra's position. It was to be a long and exhausting meeting.

The afternoon's events began with a presentation by Keith Harrison. He repeated his earlier proposal that the Board bring in an outside evaluator and suggested that Keegstra's freedom of speech in the classroom was being interfered with. He claimed that the Board was acting too drastically because it had only one letter of complaint. He thought that "perhaps [they] were being unreasonable."

Harrison was followed by Keegstra, who explained once again what he had been teaching in his social studies classes. In Weidner's opinion, Keegstra merely confirmed that "he had not changed in the substance of what he was teaching from what he had taught the previous winter." He claimed that he had always taught properly and had always complied with the curriculum. When Keegstra finished addressing the Board, he and Harrison stayed until all the other witnesses had made presentations. They were given the right to ask questions for clarification.

After Keegstra spoke, Maddox appeared to tell the story of why she had withdrawn Paul from Keegstra's classes. Then Clark gave the Board his opinion about Keegstra's teaching. This paralleled the written reports he had prepared at David's behest. Clark concluded that Keegstra had strayed from the prescribed curriculum. Olsen then spoke, followed by vice-principal Taylor and George Friesen, a Keegstra character witness. At about four-thirty, the presentations were completed and Harrison and Keegstra left.

The Board then deliberated until eight in the evening, with a one-hour supper break at six. Keegstra had almost no support, with the exception of Bill Zuidhof, an old Social Creditor who found Keegstra's presentation quite convincing and maintained that "some Jews are involved in this conspiracy." One other trustee was against dismissal because he apparently did not have the heart to dismiss anyone, no matter the provocation. The other twelve voted to fire Keegstra as of December 31 for his failure to comply with their previous directives.[30] (See Appendix Document 10.)

Susan Maddox, the woman who had done so much to bring Keegstra down, regretted the dismissal. She told the press that she would "probably have preferred that he was transferred to another school and taught shop."[31] But that probably would not have stopped Jim Keegstra. For Keegstra, the forum was and is incidental. He believes he has a duty to carry on his struggle as he sees it and this to him is a higher duty than any he might owe a particular school board or principal. The prime duty of the Lacombe County Board, however, was to solve its problems, not transfer them.

— VIII —

Bob David returned to his desk late on December 7, picked up the phone and made the fateful call that ended Jim Keegstra's teaching career. As the chief officer of the Board, it was his responsibility to tell Keegstra about the dismissal and deliver the letter the next day. In a way, it was also his responsibility to take the misplaced wrath and anger of Keegstra's colleagues. Keegstra, after all, would probably not have been fired if it had not been for David.

David was severely criticized by at least one educational expert for not acting quickly enough after he discovered what had been going on in Eckville.[32] David certainly did make mistakes from time to time. But, after all, he had never handled a situation like this before because no one in Alberta had been forced to deal with anything similar in living memory, if ever. There were no precedents for David to check, no experts to consult. He was forced to cope with the situation virtually alone. He could not have done it without the support of Sandra Weidner, Kevin McEntee and Earl Clarke and without the help of Margaret Andrew and Susan Maddox. But he was the point man. And although it is the Board which hires and fires, not the superintendent, they will almost always seek

advice and guidance from their principal officer, which they
did in this case.

David knew just how hard it is to dismiss a teacher. He
knew how carefully the file had to be built so that the
charges would stick and the action would be sustained. He
started, from the very beginning, to put it all in writing and
to inform his Board of what was taking place. David's
actions contrast sharply with those of his predecessor. On
December 7, 1982, someone finally blew the whistle on Jim
Keegstra.

6

The ATA's Dilemma

ALTHOUGH THE LACOMBE COUNTY Board of Education had fired Jim Keegstra, he still had one hope left: to appeal to a Board of Reference which had the power to reinstate him. Keegstra had two weeks to file an appeal with the Minister of Education. If he did so, such a Board of Reference would be set up automatically. Keegstra filed his appeal on December 14. He alleged that he had not been given sufficient notice of his termination hearing, that the Board of Education had not acted reasonably, that the Board's grounds for the dismissal were inadequate and that he was not guilty of the reasons for termination given in the Board's December 7 letter to him.

The Department of Education responded to the appeal by establishing a Board of Reference, presided over by Justice Elizabeth McFadyen, to sit in Edmonton on March 22 to 25, 1983. In Alberta, Boards of Reference are quasi-judicial bodies with the power to hear sworn testimony. Both the appellant and the respondent are entitled to be represented by legal counsel. These boards have almost unlimited power to issue orders ranging from full reinstatement with damages to upholding the dismissal.

From almost the moment Keegstra learned of his dismissal until the Board of Reference hearing concluded at the end of March, Keegstra had the help and financial support of the Alberta Teachers' Association. This touched off a torrent of criticism unprecedented in the recent history of the ATA. It came from journalists, school officials, parents and even teachers.

— I —

The Lacombe County Board of Education began to prepare for the Board of Reference hearings shortly after the termination. Bob David worked closely with the Board's legal representatives, advising them about the effectiveness of potential witnesses and the availability of evidence exhibits. F.A. Crowther, who had been unable to attend the December 7 Board meeting due to illness, agreed to testify on behalf of the Board. So did Susan Maddox, Margaret Andrew, Sandra Weidner and several others who had been close to the events of 1982. David, of course, was to be the chief witness.

The only hitch in the Board's preparations arose from the absence of Judith Anderson from the province. Anderson had been the Board's legal advisor on the Keegstra matter from the start, but was on sabbatical leave in Ottawa. When the Board failed to gain a postponement of the hearing, they arranged to be represented by Richard McNally, one of Anderson's colleagues. McNally had been present to advise the Board of December 7.

Keegstra too was to be represented by legal counsel, paid for by the ATA. The day following Keegstra's dismissal, Harrison told Bob Warwick, a reporter for the *Calgary Herald*, that the Association would support Keegstra's appeal. It was the most controversial single act the ATA committed in the Keegstra matter. Harrison maintained, when the Board of Reference hearings ended, that "it was a simple matter of fairness." Everyone is innocent until proven guilty, he told the press, and it was ATA policy to handle all teachers' legal fees in cases involving their work. "We don't necessarily agree with what he said or did but if we didn't support him why should anyone be part of our

Association? We are supposed to advise, assist and protect teachers. It's not up to us to prejudge the case."[1]

Harrison helped Steve Hillier, Keegstra's lawyer, prepare the case. At one point, he went with Hillier to Eckville to interview possible witnesses for Keegstra. Harrison did not, however, appear as a witness at the hearing.[2]

— II —

Keegstra's Board of Reference hearing opened in Edmonton on Tuesday morning, March 22, 1983, and continued until Monday, March 28. Although there had been a growing number of news stories about the dismissal of the teacher who had taught that the Holocaust was a hoax, the hearing revealed for the first time the full details and extent of Keegstra's teaching. The Board of Education case was based on the reasons for its decision to fire Keegstra and on the need to prove that it had done so through due process. This process involved giving Keegstra an order which the Board was legally entitled to give and which he deliberately refused to follow.

Bob David took the stand first to give a detailed account of the events leading up to the decision to fire Keegstra. David was followed by Frank Crowther, who explained the philosophy underlying the Alberta Social Studies Curriculum. Crowther reiterated the opinion he had presented in writing to the Locombe County Board of Education: that Keegstra had wandered far from the curriculum guidelines both in his methods of teaching and in the content of his lectures. Other Board of Education witnesses were Earl Clark, Susan and Paul Maddox, Ed Olsen, Margaret Andrew and Sandra Weidner.

Hearing all these witnesses took a little more than two days and allowed McNally an opportunity to introduce thrity-two exhibits into evidence. They included correspondence between Keegstra and the Board, notes, examination papers and essays taken from Keegstra's classes, as well as pamphlets Keegstra used in his lectures including *Censored History* and *Facts are Facts*.

Keegstra's case was based on several arguments. He had not been given sufficient supervision and assistance. An expert should have been called in to evaluate Keegstra and perhaps give him 'in-service' training. The dismissal was a violation of his right to express his own opinions in class. One of Keegstra's witnesses, Dr. F.O. Schreiber, a social studies consultant with the Edmonton Regional Office of the Alberta Department of Education, appeared to criticize David and the Lacombe County Board. He suggested that they had not conducted a prolonged evaluation of Keegstra's classroom performance.

The highlight of Keegstra's case was his own appearance on the stand. On Thursday, March 24, he began hours of testimony that stretched into the next day. The courtroom was packed as Keegstra claimed over and over that he had tried to make his students think. He had tried to present another side to history and to force students to do their own research and seek out their own facts. He claimed that he had presented the idea of a Jewish conspiracy as his own theory, not as fact. He said that he had always made clear to his students that he believed only a small number of Jews are involved in the conspiracy. Keegstra drew a picture of his classes as exercises in free inquiry, with students and teacher freely exchanging ideas. The students, Keegstra maintained, were never asked to believe what he believed.

Keegstra's evidence-in-chief took most of the morning; the cross-examination took all afternoon and part of the next day. McNally skillfully drew Keegstra out. The cross-examination was like the peeling away of the layers of an onion, since Keegstra was clearly reluctant to discuss his ideas in too much detail at first. McNally kept at it, however. He questioned Keegstra about various passages in the student notebooks until Keegstra began to spew out a complete description of the Jewish conspiracy he believed in.

Keegstra began to describe how Jews were behind all international catastrophes and major upheavals such as the French and Bolshevik Revolutions and the Industrial

Revolution. He described the link between the Jews, the Illuminati and Marxism. He claimed that Israel is a nation of atheists, that Christ was not a Jew and that Jews are working for the overthrow of legitimate government and the creation of a "one world government." By the time Keegstra stepped down, the Board of Reference, the press and the country could no longer have any question of what Keegstra believed.

Keegstra's beliefs were only part of the picture. The most important question was whether he had taken these beliefs into the classroom and taught them as facts in the face of a direct order not to do so. McNally, in his summation, claimed that the student notebooks, exams and essays showed clearly that Keegstra had done exactly this. But McNally's argument was not only an administrative one. It was a moral argument as well:

> It must be remembered . . . that the audience to which Mr. Keegstra played was a captive audience of young and impressionable minds. Even grade twelve students are not as mature as might be thought, when dealing with such value laden material as presented by Mr. Keegstra.
>
> The possibility for harm to grade nine students exposed to such teachings is even more manifest, and the prospect of students being exposed to such teachings twice in their school careers, is truly frightening.
>
> The minds of students and their personalities are society's raw materials with which the future is fashioned. To have a doctrine of hate taught to students is not only a betrayal of the trust and respect accorded teachers, but is a betrayal of the hopes of society for a better future.[3]

The Board adjourned on Monday, March 28. Justice McFadyen gave her ruling on April 14. She found that although Keegstra claimed to have been presenting the Jewish conspiracy as a theory only, the evidence clearly indicated that he taught it as fact and that he continued to do so even after having received a directive to cease. In this, Keegstra had refused to comply with "the lawful and reasonable direction of his employer" and with "the Alberta Social Studies Curriculum." Keegstra's appeal was dismissed; the termination of his contract was allowed to stand.[4]

— III —

Once the Keegstra case had been dealt with by the Board of Reference, a flood of comment and criticism was unleashed. Much of this was directed towards the Alberta Teachers' Association and resulted from the words and deeds of ATA itself. The controversy arose over two issues: the ATA's provision of legal help to Keegstra and the length of time it took for the ATA to strip him of ATA membership.

The day following the announcement of the Board of Reference result, the press approached the ATA for comment. Charles Connors, then head of the Member Services Department of the Association and Harrison's superior, told reporters that the ATA could not appeal the Keegstra dismissal any further because the Board of Reference was the end of the line. He added that the ATA had been "barraged with calls from people asking why it defended Mr. Keegstra."

On April 15, Harrison told the press that the evidence presented to the Board of Reference was too sketchy to determine whether or not Keegstra should have been fired and that he still had "a real problem in trying to determine what went on in Mr. Keegstra's classroom." Harrison now had much more to work with than the Desrosiers essay and the Maddox notebook because the Board of Education had produced a whole pile of evidence at the Board of Reference. Despite all this Harrison told reporters that "the only evidence [against Keegstra] were notes, essay papers and exam papers. Nobody went in class and monitored it over a long period of time."

As to the question of why the ATA had defended

Keegstra, Harrison explained that the ATA gave such assistance "in most cases" although in a "very few cases" it did not.[5] He was, in effect, claiming that ATA support was virtually automatic in cases such as this.

The official position of the ATA appeared in a press release issued on April 20, 1983. This was after the Board of Reference hearings had been concluded and public criticism of the Association for paying Keegstra's legal fees had started to mount.

> For the last forty years, The Alberta
> Teachers' Association has provided legal assis-
> tance to teachers in Board of Reference cases.
> This ensures that all teachers have . . . due
> process of . . . law. . . . The Association's legal
> services are withheld only when the teacher's
> conduct has previously been the subject of an
> Association investigation that has proven grounds
> for non-support. In short, the teacher has a right
> to the "day in court," and the Association has an
> obligation to ensure that legal services are avail-
> able so that the teacher's right is not abridged by
> lack of adequate defence. In the case of Keegstra,
> all this proceeded as it should.[6]

The ATA pointed out that this did not mean it condoned or would defend "the teaching of content which, as alleged, Mr. Keegstra taught" and that the organization was against "both racism and stereotyping."

Despite this statement, ATA legal representation is in fact not automatic. A careful reading of this press release and of Harrison's April 15, 1983 statement to the press shows that the Alberta Teachers' Association *can* withhold its support under certain circumstances. This question was raised in an interview conducted for this book in March, 1985, when Harrison was asked if ATA legal representation is automatic. He replied: "I think it's fair to say it's automatic unless Provincial Executive Council [the ATA's executive and administrative body] says no." It would depend, he said, on the facts of the case.[7]

The process would normally work like this: A teacher would be dismissed and would appeal the dismissal to the Department of Education, which would set up a Board of Reference. The teacher would seek and would be granted representation by the ATA's lawyers. The ATA would help the lawyers and would pay their fees. But if the Provincial Executive Council intervened in this almost automatic process and decided that the ATA should not support the teacher, then no support would be given. The Council would intervene only to deny ATA support if the case was brought to its attention and if it had a compelling reason to withold support.[8]

Harrison's announcement to the press December 8, that the ATA would support Keegstra's appeal, came less than twenty-four hours after the Lacombe County Board of Education had made its decision to fire Keegstra. Since the Provincial Executive Council consists of twenty members from all over Alberta, there was not enough time between the dismissal and Harrison's announcement for the Counil to have met to consider the Keegstra case. It is possible that Harrison conducted a telephone survey of the Council before making his announcement. However, it is highly unlikely that so important a decision could have been made in so informal a manner. In fact, there has never been any indication that the Provincial Executive Council deliberated on the matter at all.

The ATA press release and Harrison's statement of April 15 produced still more criticism of the ATA. One of the more thoughtful observations on the matter was made by *Edmonton Journal* columnist R. Glenn Martin. Martin agreed that Keegstra was entitled to due process in his dismissal. The columnist was ready to concede that the ATA may have had to defend Keegstra. But he drew a parallel between the ATA's defence of Keegstra and the defence, by the American Civil Liberties Union, of the right of U.S. Nazis to demonstrate in a Chicago suburb. In that case the ACLU made clear from the start that it was not condoning the racial attitudes of those it was defending. It simply wanted to protect their constitutional rights. The ATA, Martin wrote, "showed none of ACLU's sensitivity in distancing itself firmly and promptly from some of the most dreadful doctrines ever devised."[9]

The indignation directed towards the ATA reached a peak following the broadcast of the CBC documentary "Lessons in Hate" on The Journal the night of May 2. Although reporter Linden MacIntyre had interviewed Harrison for about twenty minutes in preparation for the program, he used only one forty-second clip. It showed McIntyre interviewing Harrison at the ATA offices in Edmonton:

> *MacIntyre:* You were present at the first . . . hearing before the board, I believe.
> *Harrison:* Yes, I was.
> *MacIntyre:* And you heard Mr. Keegstra pretty well . . . confirm what people suspected about what he taught. It wasn't a simple case of students' notes. He tried to proselytize the board to his way of seeing things. Didn't that affect you any?
> *Harrison:* No, it really didn't. I guess I'm a fairly tolerant person and I'm able to accept different points of view. And I thought that Mr. Keegstra was putting forth a different point of view and that he was certainly entitled to do that.[10]

The complete interview had focused on the rules of natural justice as applied in dismissal cases, the ATA's involvement and the procedures by which legal assistance had been provided to Keegstra. The short clip actually telecast appeared to have Harrison state that Keegstra had a right to teach the Jewish conspiracy as a fact of history. But in fact Harrison had not said this, and it would have been inconsistent of him to have done so. He had always maintained that no one really knew what went on in the classroom. He had not claimed that Keegstra had a right to teach his own views in class as if they were fact. The public's perception, however, was that Harrison was defending Keegstra's right to teach his students about a Jewish conspiracy.

When the broadcast was put together with Harrison's earlier comments, it brought forth a storm of criticism from concerned Canadians of all types, including teachers. The Calgary Public School local of the ATA felt moved to issue a statement of its own on the historical reality of the Holocaust. Local president Stephen Brown expressed a "level of annoyance" with the ATA executive for not coming out with "even a mildly worded" statement on racism after Keegstra was fired.[11]

The mounting criticism prompted the ATA to issue a second press release on bigotry on May 16. This time ATA president Art Cowley was explicit about the ATA's position:

> The Alberta Teachers' Association abhors bigotry in every form. . . . It believes that the teaching of material that distorts and misrepresents history or presents views that are racially and religiously prejudiced is totally unacceptable.

What can account for the words and actions of the ATA? The Association took the same position that Harrison had taken from the very start of his involvement; there was no conclusive proof of what Keegstra had taught to his students and, therefore, charges against him were only allegation. The evidence, in their view, was too skimpy. The ATA was willing to condemn bigotry in general but it did not, at that juncture, issue any condemnations of Keegstra.

Some observers accused the ATA of harboring a trade union mentality, giving rise to the view that teachers must be defended to the last and all costs against their employers. There is much to this. From the very start, Harrison displayed a tendency to view Keegstra's case as he would have any other. A teacher was being dismissed for failure to adhere to an employer's directive. In Harrison's view that directive had been issued without conclusive proof that the teacher had done anything wrong. But why did Harrison insist that there was no conclusive proof even after the Board of Reference had made its findings? Why did the ATA's press release of April 20 refer to "allegations" that Keegstra had taught this or that, even though the Board of Reference had decided that those "allegations" were true, and thus much more than just allegations?

The answer must, in part, lie in the "we-they" mentality that can creep into teacher unionism. It is a mentality which is necessary and effective for raising teacher standards of living but which impairs judgment in matters such as the Keegstra case. In continuing to insist that there was no conclusive proof of what had happened in Keegstra's class despite all the evidence that had piled up by this time, Harrison and the ATA were implying that David and the Lacombe County Board of Education were not competent to know what had happened in the classroom. This may be the reason why Harrison insisted that an impartial observer be brought in, and why the ATA sought, and seeks, the right to evaluate teachers.

Employers, the ATA seems to be saying, are *ipso facto* prejudiced because they are on one side of the fence, while the teachers' association and its members are on the other. If they are indeed saying this, it follows that any evidence presented by the employer in a case such as this would be considered tainted by the ATA. Susan Maddox certainly got this impression: "Most of us don't see the ATA as a professional association. It is a union, a militant union."[12] The ATA treated Keegstra as an auto worker who had been drilling holes in the wrong place.

— IV —

The Board of Reference had upheld Keegstra's dismissal. However, Keegstra still had a Permanent Professional Certificate and could teach school anywhere in Alberta. On Monday, April 18, Alberta New Democratic Party legislative assembly member Ray Martin, a former teacher, asked Education Minister Dave King in the legislature what action was being taken to remove Keegstra's license to teach. King replied that it was a well-established practice that this was done only on the ATA's recommendation. However, he admitted that he had the final say in the matter:

> We are faced here with a situation in which there appears to be more than enough justification for the certificate to be removed by the minister of his own volition. The question is, how might this be done without relying upon the recommendation of the Alberta Teachers' Association? That is under consideration. [13]

Outside the legislature, Martin criticized King for waiting too long to curtail and condemn Keegstra's teachings, but maintained that the ATA had been forced to provide Keegstra with a legal defence. In response to this exchange ATA associate executive secretary Dr. Nicholas Hrynyk told the press that the ATA had no comment since there was "a legal procedure that must be followed" in revoking a teacher's license. [14]

Although the Department of Education Act of Alberta gives the minister sole authority to revoke a teaching license, King chose to wait for a recommendation from the ATA. It is possible that he was guarding the delegated right of the ATA to recommend a course of action to the minister. But it is also possible that he was waiting to see how long it would take the ATA to act, while the public screamed from the sidelines. This would have been a good way to soften the ATA up for the changes in the educational system that King appears to have been considering since 1979. These included: tightening accountability, redesigning curriculum, sharpening up certification and evalution procedures. The ATA might have been expected to oppose these changes. Whatever the reason for King's waiting, he did not let the ATA off the hook. It was forced to act by itself.

ATA disciplinary procedures cannot be put into effect

until the Association receives a written complaint about the conduct of one of its members. Eventually such a complaint about Keegstra was lodged with the ATA and the Association's disciplinary committee took up the case. A closed hearing was held for two days at the beginning of October 1983. The committee recommended that Keegstra's teaching certificate be suspended (not revoked) and that he be stripped of ATA membership.[15] Keegstra was informed of the decision on Saturday, October 8. Two days later King announced that he would revoke Keegstra's license. He was clearly not pleased that it had taken the ATA so long to make a recommendation and told the press that "nobody deserves to stand in uncertainty for as long as has been the case in this situation."[16]

The last act in this part of the Keegstra drama was played out in early 1984, when Keegstra appealed the ATA's decision to strip him of his membership to the Teaching Profession Appeal Board. Rudy Penner, the lawyer who represented Keegstra at the quasi-judicial hearing, claimed that the content of Keegstra's lessons had never been proven false. Penner, a former teacher, argued that there was nothing in the Teaching Profession Act or in the ATA bylaws which made it a violation of the Association's rules to teach material likely to promote prejudice towards Jews. Therefore, Penner said, Keegstra was not guilty of an offense against the Association.[17] Despite this convoluted reasoning, the Board upheld the revocation of Keegstra's membership. Keegstra, already without a license to teach, was cut off from the ATA.

Under the current laws of Alberta, Keegstra is still eligible to teach in certain types of private schools. However, there are moves afoot to outlaw these unregulated schools, which receive no provincial funding and no Department of Education supervision. At present, no one knows how many Jim Keegstras might be teaching in those schools.

7

Early Warnings, Cautious Responses

ON MAY 11, 1982 reporter Ross Henderson of the *Eckville Examiner* was covering the regular monthly meeting of the Lacombe County Board of Education. This was part of his routine duties as the sole reporter and photographer for the small-town weekly, and he expected no more than the usual business of school financing, teacher training programs and other nitty-gritty matters that normally filled school board time. At the lunch break the Board members filed out of the room, leaving Henderson and *Lacombe Globe* reporter George Lee behind. As Henderson and Lee walked towards the door they spied a document inadvertently left exposed on the table. It was the petition organized by Margaret Andrew and signed by other Eckville residents, accusing Jim Keegstra of teaching anti-Catholic and anti-Jewish bigotry in the classroom.

Both Henderson and Lee, who were just beginning their journalism careers, were delighted with their find. The 26-year-old Henderson had recently joined the *Examiner* following a job as a sports writer in Grande Prairie. Lee had been a reporter with the *Globe* since 1980, when he was 22 years old. "Finally," Henderson thought to himself, "something is going to happen."[1]

122

But nothing did. Although J. A. Parry, the publisher of the *Examiner*, was appalled when Henderson talked to him about the petition, the reporter was told by one of his superiors to hold the story until something more concrete developed. Lee, who had already heard about the Eckville mayor's anti-Jewish views, took a similarly cautious approach. He considered it a story of interest mainly to Eckvillians.

Several months after this, around November, Henderson mentioned the board room discovery to Bob Warwick, who staffed the *Calgary Herald's* bureau in Olds, a town south of Red Deer. Warwick already had a dozen years of professional journalistic experience, and his instincts told him that this was a story of significance. Teachers don't get fired very often, he thought. This one may be worth pursuing.

Warwick rushed out to Eckville, interviewed Keegstra for about twenty minutes in the presence of Vice-Principal J. Craig Taylor and talked to more than a dozen students and parents. The whole exercise left Warwick confused. Teachers at the school seemed to be "paranoid" and wouldn't talk about Keegstra. Some seemed to support Keegstra's right to teach his own view of history. Some students thought Keegstra was the "salt of the earth," while others said that he was making anti-Catholic and anti-Semitic statements in class.

Having received mixed signals from those with whom he spoke, Warwick was uncertain that he had enough concrete information to document an article. So he drove over to Lacombe to speak with Bob David. David was determined not to give the story publicity until the School Board made a definitive decision on the matter. He refused to confirm what Warwick had learned. Warwick felt he had no alternative but to wait for the results of the December School Board meeting.[2]

Henderson, Lee and Warwick were all present in Lacombe on December 7, 1982 when Bob David emerged from behind closed doors to announce that Jim Keegstra had been fired. But all three had missed the opportunity for a scoop. This was not due to any desire to cover up the events in Eckville or to protect Jim Keegstra. They simply did not understand the enormity of what they had uncovered. Keegstra's career was indeed difficult to understand. There were too many unanswered questions at that time. Was he teaching a "point of view," or was he teaching anti-Semitism? Henderson, Lee and Warwick were not certain exactly what had been going on in the classroom. Their editors did not know then that the bits of information that had leaked out were the tip of an iceberg that would only be uncovered slowly in the months and even years ahead.[3]

Since the reporters did not know what they were dealing with, they did not know how to respond. Thus the chance slipped by to expose Keegstra bofore he was dismissed. And even when he was fired and the affair became public, the full implications were not immediately clear. Even the Jewish community—the target of Keegstra's hate—was initially unprepared to grasp the enormity of what had happened in Eckville.

— I —

Ross Henderson and George Lee first learned of complaints about Keegstra's teaching in May 1982, but an effort had been made to alert the Jewish community in Alberta several months earlier. At the end of December 1981, in preparation for the January meeting of the Lacombe School Board, Bob David sent a packet of material to Board members. It included a copy of his December 18 directive to Keegstra instructing him to change the content of his teaching. It also included a student essay written for one of Keegstra's classes.

One Board member was aghast: "I could not believe that a kid in our school system could write that kind of essay. What the hell was going on?" The shock was magnified when it appeared that not everyone privy to the information felt such a deep sense of outrage. So in January, the Board member gave the confidential material to a friend with connections in the Calgary Jewish community. That friend soon made contact with Harry Shatz, the Executive Director of the Calgary Jewish Community Council, the representative body of the organized Jewish community in Calgary. Shatz recommended that the Lacombe caller photocopy the material and send it to Jewish community leaders in Edmonton. The information had no access to a photocopier and the material was never sent.[4] Thus an opportunity to expose Keegstra faded away.

Nevertheless the Keegstra affair continued to fester behind the closed doors of the Lacombe County Board of Education as Bob David gathered his evidence and the Board prepared for its showdown with the Eckville teacher. In late fall 1982, the Lacombe informant was on the telephone to Shatz once again. There was now more solid evidence, including several student essays. This time photocopying would be no problem. Shatz was now acutely interested and from this point exam papers, essays, class notes and press clippings began to flow to Calgary.

Shatz showed the material he had received to Fay Schwartz, the Council's Community Relations Committee head, and later they sat down with Council President Gert Cohos to assess it. Around December 1982, Shatz shipped the material thousands of kilometers away to the Canadian Jewish Congress in Toronto.[5] This organization, founded in 1919 as the "parliament and voice of Canadian Jewry," claimed to be the "official representative before all levels of government on matters affecting the status and welfare of Jews in Canada." In reality it represented more on paper than in fact. Its presence in Alberta, and in much of western Canada, was weak.[6]

Shatz decided to give the material to Congress anyway, because he believed that it had a committee of legal advisers knowledgeable about such matters and thought that "there was no sense duplicating" their work in Calgary.

He did not immediately contact the Edmonton Jewish Federation, the representative body of Edmonton's organized Jewish community, even though the communities are each only about two hundred kilometers from Eckville.

Ties between the Council in Calgary and the Federation in Edmonton were not close. Perhaps, too, Shatz and the other Calgary Jewish leaders failed—like Henderson, Lee and Warwick—to fully grasp what was happening in Keegstra's classes.

In any case, it was not until about the third week in January that Shatz called Hillel Boroditsky, Executive Director of the Edmonton Jewish Federation, to tell him. Boroditsky jotted down the information on a note pad: "Teacher Fired in Lacombe. Hearing in Edmonton on March 20th. ATA defending Teacher to reverse Town's decision to fire him." And under that, Boroditsky wrote: person "has evidence," with the name and phone number of the Lacombe informant.[7]

In Toronto, Ben Kayfetz, the veteran Executive Director of the Canadian Jewish Congress' Community Relations Committee, was shocked by the material sent from Calgary. "I have never seen such systematic anti-Semitism in pedagogic form regurgitated by pupils," Kayfetz wrote to Shatz on January 18. At the end of the letter he wondered if there was "any liaison with the Edmonton community to formulate a common policy for the Alberta Jewish community." He hoped this policy would be formulated under the auspices of the Canadian Jewish Congress.[8]

But there was no such policy in either Calgary or Edmonton, nor was there to be one during those crowded, densely packed months of activity which were to follow. One example of the type of contact that did take place between officials of the two Jewish communities occurred on February 13, at the Chateau Airport Hotel in Calgary. During a Western Regional Conference of the United Israel Appeal of Canada, Shatz handed Boroditsky a Safeway shopping bag, stuffed with the material from Lacombe. Not surprisingly, Boroditsky felt that the whole matter had been dumped—both literally and figuratively—into the lap of the Edmonton Jewish community.[9]

Alberta's Jews were shocked and dismayed by what was happening in Eckville. Yet, like the press, they learned only slowly about the full implications of the Keegstra affair.

News was spotty at first, and press reports tended to concentrate on the Holocaust denial aspect of Keegstra's teachings. There was great uncertainty in the Jewish community about how much support Keegstra had, and fear that he represented a resurgence of the sort of virulent anti-Semitism that had been commonplace in Alberta in the 1930s. Some Jews thought there were many Jew-haters in rural Alberta who had been waiting to make a comeback. This fear sometimes produced caution: if the Jews responded too loudly, perhaps attacks on Jews would increase.

But other Jews took a different, less cautious approach. They tended to draw an historical parallel to the situation that had faced Canadian Jews in the 1930s when the Government of Canada had refused to open the doors to German Jewish refugees. At that time a quiet and measured response had produced no results, and tens of thousands of Jews who might have been saved were murdered.

These different approaches meant that Jewish reaction to Keegstra was largely disunited and almost always *ad hoc*. It was, as well, shaped by the historical development of the Alberta Jewish community and the personal outlook of various community leaders.

— II —

The first Jews to permanently settle in Calgary and in Edmonton came from the same areas in Eastern Europe and at about the same time (1888 and 1891). In Calgary and in Edmonton, Jews established many of the same organizations, some of which even had the same name. With significant shared roots of this type, Jews living in the two large Alberta centers would have been expected to have close fraternal relations. But like the two cities' populations in general, the Jews of Calgary and Edmonton considered each other more as rivals than as family.[10]

A different pattern of character development had been significantly influenced by immigration trends. The Russian

Jews who settled in Calgary stood out as a distinct ethnic and religious group in a city composed largely of Western European, American and British immigrants. In Edmonton, on the other hand, the Jews were only one of several minorities who had come to Canada from Eastern Europe. The varied ethnic composition of Edmonton seems to have encouraged the Jews there to feel more comfortable in the larger community and to be more outward-looking and involved in social and political activities. There was less inclination to be overly concerned about how others might view the Jewish community, and less fear of community activism.

During the 1970s—the years of Alberta's financial and demographic "big boom"—Edmonton Jews began to reach out to the non-Jewish community. This effort gained momentum in 1980, when Mark Silverberg, a 32-year-old Winnipeg-born lawyer, suspended his practice to become the Assistant Director of the Edmonton Jewish Community Council. Central to Silverberg's outlook was his belief that the Jewish community must build coalitions with other ethnic groups in Edmonton, and that it must always be striving to find and develop new leaders.

Mark Silverberg was in Edmonton for only two years, but he left his mark in the form of an aggressive, confident and outward-reaching style of community relations leadership. And he left a disciple—Herb Katz.[11]

During 1983, when the Alberta media wanted to know what Jews were thinking about Jim Keegstra, what their position was on hate literature or what they thought about the Lougheed government or virtually any other related topic, they invariably first thought of, and usually first turned to, Herb Katz. In a period of great intensity and emotion, he *was* the Jewish community.

Some thought the tall, good-looking man with the thick black moustache was reckless, and he was usually blunt and fearless in his criticisms. "We are pretty disappointed that we have got no response from the premier [of Alberta] in the face of this blatant display of anti-Semitism," he once remarked. He called those who made anti-Semitic statements "a lunatic fringe," and he added, "I want them to know that we're going to fight. I want them to know that every time they say these [anti-Semitic] things, it's going to cost them." Those whom he confronted he offended. He was the "ultimate in vanity, conceit and arrogance" to Wally Klinck, a one-time supplier of anti-Semitic literature in Alberta, who maintained he was being persecuted by Katz. [12]

Born in Montreal in 1947, Katz always felt that he was Jewish, even though (like his parents and grandparents) he had no Jewish schooling or formal affiliation with the organized Jewish community. The main Jewish influence on his life—as for so many Jews raised in Montreal—came from the streets of the Côte St-Luc area in which he was raised. "You could grow up, and sort of know that you were [Jewish]. You didn't have to work very hard at it," he recalled. "The informal cultural aspects came through." [13]

After graduating from Sir George Williams University with an Honors B.A. in English literature in 1968, Katz lived in Israel for awhile. He later pursued graduate studies at the University of Calgary, and moved to Edmonton in 1979, where he started a machine tool importing business.

A phone call from Mark Silverberg inviting Katz to become involved in community work came two years after he had settled in Edmonton. By April 1982 Herb Katz had become the head of the Jewish Community Relations Council. Katz was chosen for his activist views. He was, essentially, an outsider to the Jewish community, unfamiliar with its structures and a stranger to most of its leaders.

Within a few months he was presented with his first major challenge. Israel's invasion of Lebanon on June 6, and its aftermath, stirred up Jews throughout the world in a way no event had in the past decade. It also seemed to serve as an excuse for obsessive media attacks on Israel, some of which were interpreted by Jews as being anti-Semitic. Like his counterparts elsewhere, Katz needed to explain and to justify Israel's invasion both to Jews and to non-Jews.

As 1982 drew to a close, Edmonton Jews continued to be disturbed by the media's perceived antagonism to Israel.

They were also beginning to fear that "the smell of anti-Semitism is once again in the air." At the office of the Jewish Federation (the re-named and re-structured Community Council), a telephone registry to record anti-Semitic actions was established.[14]

— III —

When Herb Katz first read about the teacher from Eckville who was fired for defying a School Board's directives, the incident did not make much of an impression on him. There had been no attack on Israel; there had been no denial of Jewish suffering in history. This seemed to be a local issue.

Katz and Hillel Boroditsky, another newcomer who had come to Edmonton from Winnipeg in 1980, discussed it at the Federation office around the end of January. "I hope this doesn't become public. Who needs it?" Boroditsky thought to himself. It seemed, then, to be the "same old stuff" being generated by "a small number of kooks." There was a similar reaction in Calgary.

But this attitude soon changed. As more news stories were published about Keegstra and his teachings, and more solid evidence turned up in the form of student essays, exams and notebooks, Katz and Boroditsky became increasingly alarmed and determined to do something. But what? No one appeared to be providing any direction. So far the Alberta government was silent. There was no leadership from the Canadian Jewish Congress which was itself confused about what had happened and what should be done. And Calgary's Jewish leaders seemed content to watch and wait for the outcome of the Board of Reference hearings.

At this point, Katz and Boroditsky decided that as much publicity as possible should be brought to bear on Keegstra and the events that had taken place in Eckville. They *wanted* Canadians to know what had happened in all its fantastic detail. They determined to speak out.

Although the full implications of the Keegstra firing

were not apparent, the case was beginning to have some disturbing associations for Katz. He had recently read *None is Too Many,* by Irving Abella and Harold Troper. This book documents the successful efforts of the Canadian government to keep Jews out of this country during World War II. Katz felt ashamed of his country, and of the Canadian Jewish leaders of the time who, he felt, did not intervene enough. And he also recalled reading accusations of complicity against the Jewish leaders in the *Judenräte* (Jewish councils) in Europe during the Holocaust.

The lessons of history were clear to Katz. Anti-Semitism in Alberta could not be met by silence or by the fear of the powerless. Katz was determined "to fight tooth and nail" against those who attacked his people.

The first effort was successful. At the end of February, Katz phoned Stephen Weatherbe, of *Alberta Report,* to voice his concern that anti-Semitism was becoming respectable in Alberta. At first, Weatherbe was not interested in the story, or in Jim Keegstra. "You've got some jerk in Eckville, in your own backyard, and you don't even care," Katz said to him. Weatherbe reconsidered. An article entitled "Alberta's Jews see proliferating signs of the old conspiracy theory" appeared in the weekly magazine's March 14, 1983 edition.

The press and Alberta's Jews had been given early warnings that something disturbing was happening in Eckville, but the news met with caution. No one really knew what was happening. No one realized how long Keegstra had been teaching anti-Jewish material, or how fundamentally he had affected the students in his charge. The press at first seemed to poke around the edges, treating it as a local issue or as an educational matter alone. The Jews were horrified but did not know how best to react. It was only when Katz and Boroditsky decided to "go public" that a Jewish response began to emerge. They helped convert the press to the understanding that the Keegstra affair was one of the most important stories in recent times. None of this might have happened so fast were it not for Katz and Boroditsky: the one an outsider, the other a newcomer, to the Edmonton Jewish community. "I didn't understand a lot of the complexities of the community," Katz later recalled. "Essentially, I was acting for a Jewish community whom I didn't know, and they didn't know me, and when I looked at the Jewish community, all I saw was me and I saw Hillel, and there was nobody else . . . So I just acted on my own, and I acted and reacted straight for myself. Things were going so fast there was no way it could be controlled."[15]

8

The Stiles Affair

SOONER OR LATER, most journalism students learn about the "Afghanistan syndrome"—a phrase coined by the late H.L. Mencken, one of the giants of American journalism. Mencken wrote that it would always be easy for newspaper people to write hard-hitting editorials about the state of Afghanistan but much harder to take on the local water works commissioner or school board chairman. And yet it is the local story that most directly serves the interests of the readers. As the Keegstra story began to break in the spring of 1983, the press in Alberta played a major role in keeping the story alive. Few people did more in this regard than the young reporter for the *Eckville Examiner*, Ross Henderson.

The *Eckville Examiner* is a small weekly newspaper, with a circulation of only about a thousand. It is housed in a small office in Art Carritt's frame gas station-store-office in the center of Eckville. The paper is not locally owned or printed, but it relies almost exclusively on the town for its advertising revenue. Henderson wrote news stories and took photographs; J.A. Parry of Rimbey, Alberta, published the paper and wrote the editorials. The *Examiner* was not profitable, and Parry did not appear to Henderson to take much interest in it, according to Henderson.

Henderson took the job in Eckville fresh out of

journalism school. He knew he would get a variety of experience working on a small town paper, covering everything from high school dances to town council meetings. Although he lived down the road from Eckville, in Sylvan Lake, he liked the town. However, he found that he could not warm to its mayor, Jim Keegstra. To Henderson, Keegstra was more than a little arrogant. He also took notice when Keegstra's sons received local youth grants handed out by the town administration, and that Keegstra himself was first in line when the town decided to give away some trees to local residents. These were not major incidents, but to Henderson they tarnished the image of Jim Keegstra as the upright mayor and teacher.

Henderson missed the opportunity to expose the Keegstra story in May 1982 after the chance sighting of a petition at a Lacombe County School Board meeting. But once the story broke he was relentless in tracking it down and writing it up in the *Examiner*. He interviewed students and parents, conducted a poll on the attitudes of Eckville residents and pieced much of the story together by the end of May 1983. He was convinced Keegstra was a racist, and he felt a professional obligation to expose him.

— I —

North of Eckville, in Edmonton, Herb Katz was also trying to expose Keegstra. Katz was convinced that silence would play into the hands of the bigots. The full glare of publicity would expose their doctrines and alert decent people to the dangers in their midst. So he continued to make contact with local media reporters at CBC radio, the *Edmonton Journal*, the *Edmonton Sun*, with Robert Lee of the *Red Deer Advocate* and with Ross Henderson.[1] Lee and Henderson knew the importance of the story, but the rest of the media still treated the Keegstra dismissal as a local issue.

When Howard Starkman, the President of the Jewish Federation of Edmonton, went to Ottawa to attend the annual national meeting of the Canada-Israel Committee just prior to the Board of Reference hearings, he found that David Kilgour, MP for Edmonton Strathcona, was unfamiliar with the matter. Bob Warwick, of the *Calgary Herald's* Olds Bureau, had suggested to his editor that he go to Edmonton to report on the proceedings. Warwick's offer was not accepted, and the paper relied on Canadian Press reporting. The only Alberta dailies to cover the hearing were the *Edmonton Journal*, the *Edmonton Sun* and the *Red Deer Advocate*. None of the three Toronto dailies—the *Toronto Star*, *Toronto Sun* or *The Globe & Mail*—sent reporters to the hearing.[2]

Although publicity was one way to expose what had happened in Eckville, it could also produce a circus-like atmosphere. That became apparent when Mel Lastman, the flamboyant 49-year-old mayor of North York—one of the cities making up the Metropolitan Toronto area—announced on April 11 that he was prepared to come to Eckville to tell students there "about racism and hatred and how wrong it is." Katz and Boroditsky were strongly opposed to the trip and were quick to make their feelings known. "Lastman doesn't speak for the Jewish community of Edmonton, Toronto or Canada," stated Katz, at this point still calling the Keegstra affair "a local problem." To him, Lastman's offer to straighten things out in far-off Alberta encapsulated "the whole eastern Jewish establishment." He wanted an issue in Alberta to be dealt with by Albertans.

Reporters seemed to feast on this disagreement between Lastman and Katz, and the two were soon arguing about the proposed trip through the media.

Lastman never did get to Eckville. In May, he told the press that he had never really intended to go; he only wanted to draw attention to what was happening there.[3]

Katz's concern about the "eastern Jewish establishment" was not without foundation. In a disparaging Yiddish pun, some Toronto Jewish leaders liked to refer to Eckville as *Eck-velt*—"the edge of the world"—as if to suggest that Keegstra's ideas could surface only in a far-off Alberta town. The national media—headquartered in Toronto—at first treated the Keegstra affair as a local issue. It was a curiosity, something that might have been expected out in "red-neck" Alberta, but without important implications for the rest of the country. It seemed, too, that the entire matter was being resolved.

There was satisfaction when Keegstra's firing was upheld, but at the Jewish Federation office in Edmonton, Herb Katz and Hillel Boroditsky knew there were still many unanswered questions. How had Keegstra managed to teach for so many years without attracting attention? Why did the Alberta Teachers' Association seem to be defending him? What damage had he done to the youth of Eckville, and how could it be rectified? Would Canadians tolerate such outbursts against minorities in their society?

In editorials and feature stories, Alberta newspapers asked these same questions and posited solutions. In the legislature Education Minister Dave King called Keegstra's teaching "unacceptable," and Marlene Antonio, head of the Alberta Human Rights Commission, announced that Keegstra's source material would be studied. In Eckville, Dick Hoeksma, Keegstra's replacement, was told to counter his predecessor's world-conspiracy teachings. Martin Hattersley, the president of the Alberta branch of the federal Social Credit Party, ordered Keegstra to resign his position as a vice-president of the party.[4]

As April drew to a close, the Keegstra affair was sliding into oblivion.

— II —

Stephen Stiles, Conservative MLA of Olds-Didsbury, had attended law school at the University of Calgary in the 1970s. An Edmonton lawyer who had been Stiles' classmate phoned the *Edmonton Journal* one day in April 1983, telling them they might be interested in talking to Stiles. He recalled that Stiles had told his law school class that there was no such thing as the Holocaust.

"I don't think that that's quite correct," Stiles replied, when the *Journal's* Cheryl Cohen interviewed him on

Tuesday, April 19. Nor did Stiles know whether his views were similar to those of Keegstra, since he maintained that he was not familiar with what Keegstra had been teaching.

Edmonton Journal: Well, you didn't mention whether or not you thought that there was a Holocaust or not during the Second World War.

Stiles: Well, what was the Holocaust? I mean, the Holocaust is the name of a movie. It sold and made a lot of money for the people who produced it.

Journal: Do you believe that millions of Jewish people were actually killed or . . .

Stiles: I think millions of people died during the Second World War and of that number a large number were Jewish people, yes.

Journal: Do you think that the Jewish people—say in Germany—were particularly persecuted and rounded up and massacred?

Stiles: I'm not really aware of that happening, no. I don't have any evidence to the effect that that happened. There've been a lot of, as I say, commercial productions. . . .

Journal: So perhaps you're saying that a lot of this has been blown out of proportion to what it might actually have been?

Stiles: Well, unless you really have the facts on this it's not very easy to say one way or the other, but ... .

Journal: Are you saying there are few facts?

Stiles: Well, I think what has happened here is that over the passage of time it has become very profitable to exaggerate perhaps what occurred, in films and books and magazine articles, and it seems that if you can come up with something that's really atrocious it's more likely to earn you— what do you call it when a writer gets paid?

Journal: Royalty or whatever?

Stiles: Or whatever. OK. So are we being

exposed to a great deal of popular myth perhaps? I
realize that the Jewish people are very touchy
about this and they have probably a lot of
documentation, but as I say it's become very
profitable to exploit this. And frankly I'm not
unsympathetic to the horrors that were suffered
by families during the Second World War but they
were suffered by all people in Europe—not just
the Jewish people. . . . it appears to me it's
become very profitable for some people to exploit
what appears to be a very popular subject in terms
of money, making money.

Journal: In your view then, Jewish people
were not persecuted, say under Hitler?

Stiles: I'm not saying that. I'm just saying . . .

Journal: That's what I'm trying to ask.

Stiles: I'm saying that I haven't seen anything
in terms of documentary evidence to prove to me
that they were necessarily persecuted. I'm not
saying they weren't or they were. I'm just saying I
haven't seen anything that I would say is hard
evidence of their having been persecuted.[5]

When excerpts from the *Journal* interview were
published in Alberta newspapers on Wednesday, April 20,
there was shock and disbelief. "What evidence do you
need?" asked an Edmonton MLA rhetorically. "I don't think
there's any doubt whatsoever that there was persecution of
Jews during the Second World War," said a Red Deer
MLA. The head of the Canadian Human Rights Commission (who happened to be in Edmonton) was appalled. The
late Grant Notley, then NDP leader of the Opposition in
the Alberta Legislature, called on the government to
combat "these repugnant doctrines" by initiating a public
information campaign through the provincial human rights
commission.

Neil Crawford, the Alberta Government House
Leader and Attorney General, was incredulous: "I can't

believe that anyone would make the statement that there wasn't mass murder, that there wasn't a Holocaust." But he also told reporters that after meeting with Stiles, the MLA had indicated to him that some of his statements had been omitted from the *Journal.* Crawford claimed that Stiles' words were "vastly over-publicized" and "probably misunderstood." The man was not an anti-Semite. And even if Stiles' statements had been accurately printed, he would "certainly not" be expelled from the seventy-five-member Conservative caucus. "The caucus doesn't operate that way," Crawford stated. The Attorney General noted, however, that his office would be studying the Board of Reference transcripts to determine if Keegstra would be charged with promoting hate.[6]

Jewish spokesmen were dumbfounded by the Stiles interview. "If he doesn't have evidence about the atrocities, then he must not read books," Jim Diamond, the Assistant Director of the National Community Relations Committee of the Canadian Jewish Congress in Toronto, told the *Red Deer Advocate*. "Either that, or he has been dead for 40 years. The whole thing is so absurd it's hardly worth commenting about."

The afternoon that the story broke, Herb Katz was convinced that Stiles was an "insignificant backbencher" appealing to a sympathetic constituency in middle Alberta. Several hours later, however, Katz's mood was not so benign. A flood of angry calls to the Edmonton Jewish Federation office convinced him that he had misjudged the significance of the Stiles interview.[7]

The following morning, in anticipation of being contacted by the media (but without consulting anyone), Katz went in early to his business and prepared a statement on behalf of the Edmonton Jewish community. By 8:30, he was telling reporters that the Alberta government must make its position known. It was wrong, he said, for the government to maintain its "stupid invisibility." He called on Premier Lougheed to expel Stiles from the Tory caucus to show that the Alberta government would not tolerate anti-Semitism in the province.[8]

On April 21 the *Edmonton Journal* was filled with stories about Stiles. Since the accuracy of the newspaper's initial report had been questioned, a transcript of the taped interview was printed. It clearly showed that there had been no misrepresentation of the Olds-Didsbury MLA.

Reactions to Stiles' statements were covered in two news stories, including one on the front page ("Stiles's views stir up a storm"). Columnist Don Braid chastised the government for its inability to take a moral stand, while an editorial noted that there were signs of "frightening anti-Jewish sentiments in Alberta."

At the same time that many readers of the *Journal* and *Calgary Herald* were noting Neil Crawford's assertion that the Conservative caucus does not discuss the personal views of MLAs, the caucus was in fact meeting to discuss Stiles' remarks.[9] After telephone communications with Peter Lougheed (who was in Vancouver for private discussions with business people), a seven-sentence statement was drafted and read by Stiles when the Legislature met that afternoon, April 21.

"I apologize to Alberta's Jewish community and others who naturally have been gravely upset by the quotations in which I appear to have cast doubt on the reality of the horrors suffered by themselves and their kinsmen during the period of Nazi repression in Europe," Stiles said. He did that because he had "no doubt that horrible atrocities were committed principally, but not exclusively, against the Jewish people." He also regretted that he had "left the implication that such events should be forgotten"—the exact opposite, he maintained, of what he actually believed.

Then Crawford stood up and read a three-sentence comment. "The Premier, myself, and all other members of the government caucus wish to completely disassociate ourselves from the views which were expressed outside the House by the Hon. Member from Olds-Didsbury," Crawford said, as Stiles sat isolated in the far corner of the government back-benches. "It is our belief that there is no doubt that mass murder and genocide occurred in Europe during World War II and that the Jewish people were tragically persecuted."[10]

This seemed to be a sincere repudiation on the part of Stiles and the government. But there were two problems. On his way out of the chamber, Stiles told reporters that what he had just said involved no change in his previously stated views. "My statement today is my position now and it has been in the past. It has never changed. That has been my position throughout."[11] In addition, the government's action—sincere as it may have been— did little to convince observers that the Stiles affair was over. "It becomes more obvious every day that the teacher's [Keegstra's] dangerous views are widespread in Alberta," wrote *Edmonton Journal* columnist Don Braid. And many people agreed with him.[12]

The Stiles apology, far from calming the Jews of Alberta, further enraged them. "His apology had no relation whatsoever to what he said yesterday, in his interview [printed in the *Edmonton Journal*] . . . . he's just trying to get off the hook," Hillel Boroditsky said. "We want him kicked out of the party."

— III —

The Stiles episode threw new fuel on the smoldering coals of the Keegstra affair. Here was a member of the caucus of Alberta's governing Conservative Party openly questioning the Holocaust. If he did not hesitate to express his views publicly, just how widespread were they?

The Jews of Alberta became even more alarmed. They were determined to do something, although there was still no unanimity about just how to respond. The national press began to wake up to the wider implications of the affair, even though there was no direct connection between Keegstra and Stiles. The press in Alberta, led by the *Edmonton Journal*, redoubled its efforts to find answers to the key questions that had still not been resolved and to force the Alberta government to take effective action.

In Edmonton, Boroditsky and Katz orchestrated an extraordinary, full-scale emergency response from the Jewish community. A major strategy session with some Jewish community leaders and a meeting with Art Cowley, President of the ATA, were both set for Friday, April 22. Lougheed's office was contacted to arrange for a meeting. The Jewish Federation asked several lawyers to examine legal actions which might be taken. At the same time, it initiated an *ad hoc* Eckville Outreach Program. The date of the Federation's presentation to the Alberta Human Rights Commission was confirmed for May 4, and Katz was expecting a response to his request for a brief meeting with Dave King, the Minister of Education. "In this regard," Katz pointedly wrote, "we look forward to learning of the Minister's intentions in the matter of the revocation of the teaching certification of Mr. James Keegstra. In addition, we should appreciate the Minister's views on the distribution of responsibilities for substantive options available in correcting the damage wrought by Mr. Keegstra's teachings."[13]

The situation was now fluid and dynamic, and things were happening very quickly. Those involved could feel the force of the events pushing them ahead, and they realized that an internal dynamism might allow those events to get out of hand. These were dazzling, volatile and frightening days.

Howard Starkman, the president of the Jewish Federation, believed that Edmonton Jews were so wrought up over the Keegstra and Stiles affairs that the community was like a ticking timebomb. Up until the Stiles interview, Starkman had been kept informed of developments by Boroditsky, who had also served as the intermediary between Katz and Starkman. But after the Stiles story broke, the Federation president (though occupying a voluntary position) began to be directly involved. He became convinced that the community "had to act and act decisively." He foresaw that judgements would be rendered on the Federation's response. Jews would see it as a test of the viability of the newly created Federation structure, and as a means of assessing the attitude of elected government officials to a small minority group.

Non-Jews would take the conduct of the Federation officials as a measure of the Jewish community itself.

Starkman consulted with other friends and colleagues, and found them to be equally concerned. It was in this mood of fear and outrage that nine men met in the comfortable downtown boardroom of the Shoctor, Hill law firm at noon on April 22 to discuss approaching Lougheed about the Keegstra and Stiles matters. Besides Starkman, Boroditsky and Katz, the Federation president had also called in Joe Shoctor, the influential Edmonton lawyer and Jewish community leader; Aaron Shtabsky, a personal friend, colleague and a member of the Federation Board of Directors; Irv Kipnes, a prominent businessman and another Board member; Peter Owen, a lawyer who had come to Canada after fleeing Germany in 1939; Mel Hurtig, the Edmonton book publisher; and Dr. Myer Horowitz, the president of the University of Alberta.

This was the first meeting organized by the Jewish Federation to respond to the crisis situation. Up until that Friday, it had been Katz and Boroditsky who had dealt with the media and formulated positions. Indeed, had it been up to Katz, there would have been no such gathering. "I thought we would shoot it out" with the Lougheed government "like a naval engagement, at a distance," Katz thought to himself. But regardless of Katz's feelings, this meeting had not been called to repudiate his work or that of Boroditsky. In fact, Starkman—though he was aware of some criticism within the Jewish community of Katz's outspoken statements to the media—had supported Katz all along.

Most of those present knew Lougheed, or knew someone who was close to him. They decided to tell the Premier and his colleagues of the Jewish community's strong feelings. On the list of Cabinet ministers to be contacted were Lou Hyndman, the provincial Treasurer; Neil Crawford, the Attorney General; David Russell, Minister of Hospitals; Julian Koziak, Minister of Municipal Affairs; and Marvin Moore, Minister of Transportation. Owen and Horowitz warned the others that Lougheed

didn't like to be told what to do, and would get his back up
if that were attempted. Thus it was agreed that the
tentatively planned press conference on the Stiles affair
would be postponed. Give Lougheed a chance to do
something, Shtabsky urged. Use the opportunity of a
meeting with him to push for an inquiry into the scope of
this "problem," added Shoctor. No decision was taken as to
who should be in the delegation seeing Lougheed. Shtabsky did not want "traditional lobbyists" to be present.[14]
Most of those at the meeting seemed to assume they would
have Lougheed's strong support.

— IV —

While the Jewish community was mobilizing, the
press in Alberta continued its coverage. In the case of
Stephen Hume, the young editor of the *Edmonton Journal*,
it had taken a phone call from a prominent Edmontonian to
help crystallize his thinking.

Why was the newspaper picking on Keegstra? the
caller asked. It was doing no more than reporting on a
series of events, Hume replied. As the conversation
continued, Hume sensed "a lot of sub-vocal innuendo" and
"a sinister undertone" in the caller's voice. When Hume
hung up the phone, he had the sudden recognition that the
Eckville teacher was not alone. "There is an underlying
body of opinion in Alberta that seems to give credence to
some of the things that Keegstra and his ilk are saying,"
Hume thought to himself.

Though shocked by the call, and disturbed later by the
Stiles affair, Hume never doubted the type of response
which he had to make. It was precisely because he was a
confirmed advocate of freedom of expression that he also
felt an obligation to speak out against "this type of virulent
view." "I believe there is a fundamental obligation to
challenge opinions that are wrong. And what [Keegstra]
said was wrong. And what he was propagating was a lie."
For this reason, both Hume and the *Journal's* editorial
board became committed not only to covering the Keegstra

affair, but to combatting what they felt were the implications of the story. The paper would later receive an award for its hard-hitting coverage.

While the 36-year-old editor acted out of conviction, his aggressive moral posture had benefited from experience. Not from the experience of having known or socially mixed with Jews. That was not the case at all, for he had only very limited associations with them. It was, rather, from having been sensitized during his youth to ways in which public apathy can lead to institutionalized discrimination. Raised in British Columbia, Hume was appalled at the way in which Native people were treated there. He also studied the historical record and learned how racism against Asians in the province had become embedded in parliamentary statutes.

Hume was also influenced by the reaction of the local Jewish community. Though the *Journal* had been accused of being insensitive to issues related to Israel, this did not prevent Hume from being struck by the Jewish community's "passionate response" throughout the Keegstra and Stiles affairs. For the media, Hume felt, this established the "integrity of the issue." The Keegstra affair and its implications thus became a story which had to be covered.

And that is exactly what Hume and his colleagues on the editorial board of the *Journal* did. In a series of outstanding signed feature articles—on the implications of the Eckville affair, on the moral obligation to combat hate mongering and on why it is important to remember the Holocaust—the remarkable editor educated his readers and urged them to moral activism. "Freedom of expression," he wrote,

> means we share an obligation as individuals and institutions to exercise our own right to speak out strongly—and instantly—against these diseased attitudes when we encounter them. We are also a democracy, and that means we defend our minorities. We don't achieve that by averting our eyes from attacks on them and citing the attackers'

right to free speech as justification for our inaction. . . . Too many of us look the other way. Too many of us are only sensitive when it is our own interests that are under attack. Too many of us are complacent in our comfortable majority.

Hume's editorials, the unsigned ones by the *Journal's* editorial board, features by Don Braid, Ron Collister and George Oake, and the reporting of Cheryl Cohen, Cathy Lord, Agnes Buttner and others, made for an impressive journalistic product. Background feature articles added an educational dimension to the newspaper's campaign. They were devoted to interviews with Jewish Holocaust survivors and veterans of World War II, to the reaction of professional historians to the "Holocaust hoax" mythology and to the coverage of the Holocaust in school textbooks. A number of these editorials and articles were used in courses on human rights in the Faculty of Education at the University of Alberta. A professor of social studies there even recommended Hume for a Pulitzer Prize.[15]

Unlike other Alberta dailies, in 1983 the *Journal* was published in two editions. Because new information was invariably added in the afternoon paper to a story which may have appeared in the morning edition, this meant that in its coverage of the Keegstra and Stiles affairs, the *Journal* reporting was extensive and up-to-date. It was a hard example to follow, but there was notable enterprising reporting in other Alberta publications, such as *Alberta Report* magazine and the *Red Deer Advocate*.

The same was true with the coverage of Ross Henderson of the *Eckville Examiner*. Henderson assiduously pursued the story, in spite of the dilemma of most weekly newspapers in small communities—how to respond to controversial situations.

Although newspapers dedicated significant space to a story which they knew would sell papers, not all were characterized by a drive and devotion to providing high-minded professional journalism.

In May, the *Calgary Sun*, a sensationalist tabloid, ran

the headline " 'Holocaust a lie,' " in inch-high letters, across
a full-page article on Keegstra. A large photo showed the
Eckville teacher smilng in an easy chair, reading an issue of
Holocaust News with the headline " 'Holocaust' Story an
Evil Hoax." In a Sunday edition, the *Edmonton Sun*
published one article in which a professor of history at the
University of Alberta stated that "the basic facts of the
Holocaust are beyond doubt,' and another article in which
Keegstra claimed that six million Jews could not possibly
have been murdered during the war. In yet a third
instance, this time in the *Lethbridge Herald,* an anony-
mous letter writer was allotted thirty-four column inches to
detail the "Holocaust as hoax" and Jewish world-conspiracy
myths. Sometimes even a serious paper lost its perspective,
as occurred when a *Calgary Herald* story was headlined:
"City Jews insist Holocaust real," as though this were not a
documented fact. [16]

To an extent, the treatment was predictable: the
serious journalistic publications approached a sensitive
issue in a professional manner; the others gave it the same
sensational treatment which some of their material receives. More often than not, the press coverage of the
Keegstra affair was thorough and objective, while editorial
and feature comment reflected disapproval and rejection of
the Eckville mayor and his teachings. In this way, the press
added to its traditional role of disseminator of information
an additional one of moral guide and persuader.

In the area of analysis, however, the journalists were
less successful. Though aware of the anti-Semitic streak in
Social Credit theory and politics, almost no attention was
given to the pathological myths and fantasies on which
Keegstra's thought is based. That is not surprising, for even
many historians are unfamiliar with those arcane, subterra-
nean ideas which first came to prominence in medieval
Christian Europe. Unaware of that context, journalists
reflected the common sense knowledge of the moment.
They adopted the phraseology of Justice McFadyen and
others, who referred to Keegstra's "theory of history." The
inability to distinguish between theory and myth resulted

in the injection of issues such as freedom of expression, which were irrelevant to this case.

After the statements of Stephen Stiles, the press also began to confuse Keegstra's teachings with the published remarks of the Alberta MLA. Stiles was a Holocaust denier; Keegstra's focus was on spreading paranoid myths about a Jewish world-conspiracy. The two may be, but are not necessarily, related. Only during the Red Deer trial did the public finally learn about the nature of Keegstra's thinking.[17]

For more than a million Canadians living outside of Alberta, their first knowledge of Jim Keegstra came not from the print but from the electronic media. On May 2, 1983, when CBC television broadcast "Lessons in Hate" during its popular evening news program, "The Journal," viewers saw all of the main personalities in the drama. They heard Jim Keegstra air his views, and they listened as they were challenged by the producer and interviewer, Linden MacIntyre. It was, as Don Braid of the *Edmonton Journal* wrote, a "powerful, alarming piece"—too alarming, as it turned out, for some people. In the House of Commons, Liberal MP David Smith was critical of the CBC for allowing Keegstra's "ridiculous allegations" to be broadcast across the country. In Montreal, similar complaints were coming to the local Canadian Jewish Congress office from the Hadassah-WIZO organization, a women's charitable fund-raising group. Ben Kayfetz, however, was convinced that "The Journal" program was "a matter of legitimate news which required full treatment."[18] In fact, this program probably did more than any other single event to finally focus national attention on Keegstra.

The Jim Keegstra story had begun in Eckville, and it might well have ended there. But by May 1983 it had assumed a wider significance. The story would not go away, because a politician seemed to align himself with some of the teacher's views. Stephen Stiles' musings prompted many Canadians to begin to believe that Keegstra and his myths were undermining the social structures which had been built up over the years to sustain a harmonious

Canadian society. What Keegstra represented, therefore, had to be confronted. Although the Jews were convinced that this was not only a "Jewish issue," they were in the forefront in meeting the challenge. They were soon to find out that they did not stand alone.

9

A Month of Turmoil

"KATZ DEMANDS PREMIER speak up on race hatred." So proclaimed the three-column-wide headline on the front page of the morning edition of the *Edmonton Journal* on May 9, 1983. No exclamation point was needed to suggest to readers the seemingly reckless audacity implicit in those words.

Who was this "Katz" who issued orders to Peter Lougheed of Alberta—that leader who had served as Premier for nearly a dozen years and who ran the Legislature as if it were his own personal fiefdom? If Katz had a complaint, why didn't he direct it through the proper channels? Why was the province's largest-circulation daily giving such prominence to this demand? Politics just wasn't conducted this way in Alberta, and Jews, certainly, did not tell heads of government what to do.

Katz later maintained that the *Journal* reporter had actually misconstrued what he had said, and that he had never issued an ultimatum. Yet it was irrelevant what impression Katz may have intended to convey. Feelings had been running high in Alberta during the spring of 1983. It was a period of passion, and the Jews, in particular, were "shaken by passion."[1]

One story behind the *Journal* headline is about the

Jews of Alberta, and how they had become increasingly alarmed as they sensed an outburst of anti-Semitic activity in the province. It seemed that Jim Keegstra was not alone. It seemed that, notwithstanding his dismissal from Eckville High, he had a serious following in the province.

Another story is about the Alberta community itself. Within that community, the newspaper editors and reporters stood from the start in the front ranks with the Jews. There were, as well, those in the community who hesitated to get involved, and those who did not respond at all.

— I —

Newspapers took their cue from their communities. Voices of criticism and condemnation were heard in editorial boardrooms. In Edmonton, a decision was made by Jewish community leaders to publicize the Keegstra affair through the media. In Calgary, there was no such decision, and the city's major daily, the *Calgary Herald,* reflected this. Its coverage was initially low-key. It provided its readers with information, but there was no "initiative" journalism until later.

The *Herald* was at first uncertain how to treat the actions of "one crazy teacher." It was also viewing the story from the perspective of a newspaper that is part of the large Southam chain (as is the *Edmonton Journal*). It is part of Southam policy that its publications are to be local in outlook. The Board of Reference hearing, the ATA and the Legislative Assembly—the events related to them all took place in Edmonton. At this point, it was natural for the *Herald* to react to the Keegstra story in geographical terms.

The *Herald* also thought that it reflected the reaction of the Jewish community itself. Kevin Peterson, the paper's managing editor, had the impression from his social contacts with Jews that they felt it was unfortunate that newspaper space had to be devoted to the Eckville teacher. Additionally, the *Herald* was never formally approached by local Jewish leaders about its over-all coverage of the affair.

Although Peterson was surprised that the local Jewish community "was as muted as it was," this attitude seemed to confirm the propriety of the *Herald's* handling of the story.[2]

However, the paper soon began to receive indications that all was not well with its coverage. In April, it published an article on Keegstra by freelance writer Nancy Millar. That article consisted mainly of verbatim responses by Keegstra to Millar's questions. There was no commentary. Letters and phone calls came in to the *Herald*.

The turning point in the *Herald's* coverage followed an editorial in the independent Calgary newspaper, *The Jewish Star*. In its first coverage of the Keegstra and Stiles affairs on April 29, the paper carried three brief editorials: "Dear Peter," "Dear Patrick," "Dear Sam." The first called on Lougheed to eject Stephen Stiles from the Conservative caucus; the last urged the head of the local B'nai Brith lodge to hire a full-time person to staff a League for Human Rights office in Calgary. The second one, addressed to J. Patrick O'Callaghan, the *Herald's* publisher, severely chastised the paper for its coverage of the Keegstra affair, comparing it unfavorably with that of the *Edmonton Journal*. "This is as if the *Herald* were saying, 'The case was a local one relevant mainly to Edmontonians,'" the editorial stated. In addition, the two *Herald* features relating to Keegstra, both by Millar, were placed in the religion section. "We find all of this rather odd, don't you?" the editorial concluded.

When a City Desk reporter brought O'Callaghan the editorial on May 3, he immediately drafted a scathing reply. The editorial, he wrote, made accusations which were "offensive, totally uncalled for, not substantiated by the evidence, [and] an outrage to a newspaper that has a proud record of speaking out on the subject of racism and oppression."

At the same time, Peterson himself was beginning to feel the need to "tune up" the paper's news coverage. *The Star* editorial convinced him that this was the correct thing to do, because Keegstra "was striking deeper roots inside the community than we had thought."

Nonetheless, though agreeing with the sentiments of the editorial, Peterson saw it as a "low blow." He believed it incorrectly suggested that the *Herald* had intentionally underplayed the story for some ulterior reason. In addition, *The Star* was unaware of the dual irony inherent in its comparison of the two Southam chain newspapers. The editorial was faulting them for being the locally focused papers which Southam wanted them to be. And in unfavorably comparing the *Herald* to the *Journal*, *The Star* was oblivious of the fact that O'Callaghan, the former *Journal* publisher, had been the one who hired Stephen Hume.[3]

— II —

Following April's frenetic activity, the Edmonton Jewish Federation leaders looked to May 9 as the day on which they would be able to air their grievances directly to Peter Lougheed. But there was little respite during those next two-and-a-half weeks. The planning continued apace.

At various meetings, ways of dealing with Keegstra, the ATA and hate literature were discussed. The possibility of attempting to have Keegstra prosecuted for promoting hate was deemed not viable. Programs to sensitize young people in Eckville, and to distribute material on Jews there, were suggested. Katz and Boroditsky met with the Alberta Human Rights Commission.[4]

The final preparations for the meeting with Premier Lougheed were made on Friday, May 6. Joe Shoctor was selected to be the spokesman of the delegation. The other members were to be Katz, Boroditsky, Howard Starkman, Aaron Shtabsky, Myer Horowitz, Mel Hurtig, Peter Owen and Norman Witten, all of Edmonton. From Calgary, the representatives were to be Gert Cohos, the Jewish Council president, Norman Green and Harry Cohen.[5]

When Herb Katz joined the other Alberta Jewish leaders prior to the Lougheed meeting, icy stares met him from one corner of the room.[6] The stares were from people who had seen that morning's *Edmonton Journal*, with Katz's "demand" that the Premier act. What Katz had done was exactly what the rest of the Edmonton group had decided should be avoided. Boxing Lougheed into a corner would only make him more difficult to deal with, they believed.

If there was coolness from one direction, Katz felt daggers from the other. That was because the Calgary delegates had not wanted to come up to Edmonton for the meeting from the start. Gert Cohos was pleased that Stiles had been censured: it made people realize that what he had said was "unacceptable and unaccepted." Eviction from the Conservative caucus, however, was not on her agenda. Nor did it seem to be on the mind of Henry Cohen or Norman Green. Apparently, they feared the possibility that such an action might make Stiles into a martyr.

The delegates had gotten together to formulate a common position prior to the meeting. All shared the general perception that Lougheed was not sensitive to the feelings of ethnic or minority groups, but they were unable to agree on what their goals should be. Predictably, the delegation divided itself along geographic lines. The time for the meeting with Lougheed approached, and no policy had been established.

The eleven men and one woman walked the few blocks to Government House and up the stairs. The media was waiting. The delegation stood around for awhile until they were ushered into a conference room, and sat down at a large boardroom table. After a few moments, Lougheed's assistant entered, followed by the Premier himself. "Good afternoon, ladies and gentlemen," he said. "I have to tell you that I have one hour to give to you." Walking around the room, and noticing the familiar faces, he shook everyone's hand. He appeared cold and businesslike. This is, apparently, his normal demeanor for business matters when he is relating to more than one person. The Jewish delegates were apprehensive.

"We are greatly disturbed; we are greatly concerned," Starkman said in a prepared opening statement. "The rising tone of racism, and in particular anti-Semitism, which has manifested itself recently in this province has affected and alarmed us most profoundly." He then introduced Joe Shoctor, who sat across the table from Lougheed. Shoctor tried to impress on Lougheed how uneasy the Jews of Alberta felt as a result of the Keegstra and Stiles affairs. He spoke to the issues of school board accountability and curriculum material, following which comments were heard from those around the table.

Lougheed tried to reassure the group that Keegstra and Stiles were not representative Albertans. He recalled his own efforts on behalf of minority groups, including the Individual Rights Protection Act. He noted that Dave King, the Minister of Education, would be looking into making changes in the school system.

Concerning Stephen Stiles, he had done what he felt he should have done. What he had done was very important; it had been accomplished very quickly and it was to the point. He was, he told the delegation, not prepared to do anything else.

Joe Shoctor was not impressed. In an emotional and dramatic way, he reminded the Premier that they had known each other a long time. He had even helped the young gridiron athlete to get his first job, with the Edmonton Eskimos football team. That long relationship entitled him to speak frankly, Shoctor continued. Severe action had to be taken against Stiles; he had to be booted out of the Tory caucus. Lougheed shot back that Stiles had been given an opportunity to retract his statement and he had done so. But Shoctor, on the verge of a roaring argument, persisted in countering Lougheed's view. Raising his steely blue eyes, the Premier ended the conversation. "I will do no more," he said.

Myer Horowitz, the President of the University of Alberta, was disturbed as well. He heard Lougheed emphasizing the need for changes to the school system—a totally miguided plan of attack, in Horowitz's view. He heatedly told him that he didn't think he was making much sense. Finally, Lougheed was asked if he intended making a statement on these matters. He replied that he would do so when he chose to do so. And with that, he got up and walked out of the room.

Lougheed revealed nothing to the waiting reporters. "I didn't make any commitment," he told them. "I'll be discussing the representation with my caucus and cabinet colleagues."

The Jewish leaders sought to look on the bright side. "We are hopeful the Premier will make a very positive and demonstrable statement condemning the racist-like comments that are spreading through the province," Starkman said. These two different perceptions of the outcome of the meeting were presented in the press. The *Edmonton Journal* headlined its story: "Lougheed backs off from Jewish pressure for public statement." The *Calgary Herald* reported that "Jewish leaders say Lougheed to battle racism."[7]

— III —

Following the meeting, the immediate concern of the Edmonton delegation was what to say that evening. In response to the pressure which Starkman sensed was building up on the Federation leadership to make the strongest possible stand, he had scheduled an emergency community rally. Boroditsky, who felt that "our process as a Jewish community" had been satisfied by "going to the top and speaking to the premier," was concerned about the possibility of hot tempers resulting in an unruly meeting. Nonetheless, there was agreement in Edmonton that the Federation had to communicate with its constituents, and be accountable to them.

The gym at the Edmonton Jewish Community Centre was too small that evening to accommodate all of those who wanted to attend the rally. Boroditsky estimated the audience at more than 700, but the police figure was 1,000 people—which would have represented about twenty-five percent of the total Jewish population of Edmonton.

In a lengthy and detailed report, Katz recounted the activities of the Community Relations Council which he headed. All references to his own efforts were put in the plural form. Shoctor, speaking extemporaneously, described what the delegation had achieved from the Lougheed meeting.

Nearly two dozen questions were then taken from the floor. Murray Jampolsky, the ATA's assistant executive secretary, expressed resentment over Katz's comments about the organization, but several others attacked the conduct of the ATA. There were calls for various steps to be taken against Stiles, including a letter writing campaign to have him ousted from the Tory caucus. One person suggested that a peaceful demonstration be held at the Legislature during rush-hour. Alan Shefman, the Director of the League for Human Rights of B'nai B'rith (in Toronto) praised the Edmonton community leadership, and offered to make available resource material from the organization.

The media had not been told of the meeting, and perhaps the only non-Jew present at the rally was Michael Power, a senior vice-president of the insurance brokers Reed Stenhouse, and a former president of the Edmonton East Liberal Association. He said that he wanted everyone to know that there are others like him who wanted to help. He remembered pre-war Alberta which, he said, had been a "neo-Nazi place." Pledging to organize other non-Jews to exert pressure on the government to take action against Stiles, he announced that he intended to "ask a question" at the Premier's Dinner in two days.[8]

Power didn't need to do any organizing. The Keegstra and Stiles affairs had "galvanized the anger of so many people in the province," Katz correctly noted. In a spontaneous outpouring of feeling during the next few days Albertans, as well as some people outside of the province, made it clear that the time had come for action, even in Government House.

When Lougheed told a press conference on May 10—the day after the meeting with the Jewish delegation and the Jewish community rally—that the Stiles matter was over, Herb Katz disagreed. It was will "a raging issue" for Jews, he told the *Edmonton Journal*. The next day, a *Journal* editorial was headed "Speak up Peter."

When one part of society is under attack, we look to our leaders to inject some sanity. It is time for Premier Lougheed to condemn the anti-Semitic wave rippling through the province. . . . It is hard to understand why the premier continues to dilly-dally on the matter. . . . This isn't an oil policy or business diversification project we are talking about. When something as powerful and abhorrent as anti-Semitism is involved, surely a political leader can shed his caution. Lougheed should speak out—now.

Similar sentiments were voiced in an editorial on the other side of the country. "Mr. Lougheed blows it," the *Montreal Gazette* declared.

It's a rare politician who, when offered a painless opportunity to condemn a pernicious evil—to declare himself on the side of right, to stand as a symbol of what is best in his society—turns the opportunity down. Premier Peter Lougheed of Alberta is a member of that strange fraternity.

Mr. Lougheed was approached the other day by a delegation of Jewish community leaders seeking "a statement condemning the racist-like comments" that have surfaced in Alberta recently.

But all he could bring himself to do was temporize. "I didn't make any commitment," he said. "I'll be discussing the representation with my caucus and colleagues." It is a sad commentary on Mr. Lougheed's qualities of leadership that an abhorrence of racism, far from a reflexive action, should be a matter for committee palavering.

Let there be no mistake: Racism is out in the open in Alberta. . . . By ducking the issue, Mr. Lougheed abets twisted views like these. He should be ashamed of himself.

Michael Power kept his promise on May 11, at the $250-a-plate Tory fundraising dinner attended by as many as 850 people. In anticipation of a tense event, security guards kept the media away from the ballroom at the Edmonton Inn.

Questions followed the meal, and Power asked the Premier if he was going to make a statement about the Keegstra affair. "I will," he replied. Power was cheered and applauded as he spoke, and people stopped to shake his hand as he left. He told waiting reporters that "As long as there is venom spewing forth from worms like Keegstra and Company we're going to have to fight them."[9]

As Lougheed prepared to act, others condemned bigotry and racism. In Eckville, the Chamber of Commerce was calling on Keegstra to resign as mayor. In Montreal, Keegstra and Stiles were the subjects of discussion at the plenary assembly of the Canadian Jewish Congress.

On May 11, the Alberta government received a joint telex from Simon Wiesenthal, the famed Nazi hunter from Vienna, and Rabbi Marvin Hier, Dean of the Simon Wiesenthal Center in Los Angeles. They were critical of the support shown for Keegstra by members of the Social Credit Party of Canada, and of Stephen Stiles. The two called on Lougheed to launch an intensive education program on the Holocaust, and to "speak out publicly and unequivocably to all the citizens of Alberta and Canada about this ugly matter.[10]

Attention was fixed on Lougheed on May 12, when he rose in the Legislature to speak. The two Edmonton morning papers had already announced that he was to make a public statement on racism, and the Legislature was packed. He said that he was "deeply disturbed" when he heard of the Eckville teacher's case, and had personally looked into the matter. Hardly looking up from his prepared speech, he referred to Keegstra's views as "bigotry," "anti-Semitic" and "unequivocally racial, religiously prejudiced, historically inaccurate and distorted." Citing statistics from the Alberta Human Rights Commission which indicated a reduction in complaints received by them during the past year, Lougheed asserted that there had been no "resurgence of bigotry and prejudice" in the province.

Nonetheless, he recognized the responsibility of legislators and government officials in this matter, and announced three actions to prevent a recurrence of the Keegstra affair. The Human Rights Commission was to conduct the public education campaign to combat racism which it had first proposed after the May 4 meeting with the Jewish Federation of Edmonton. Dave King, the Minister of Education, was to review the school curriculum (to "better foster greater tolerance and respect for minority groups and individuals in our society") and assess the classroom monitoring procedures (to insure an immediate reponse to bigotry in the classroom). In concluding, Lougheed asked Albertans "to renew their commitment to tolerance and respect for the dignity, ideas and beliefs of others."

Though few questioned the sincerity of Lougheed's speech, there were few who were satisfied with it either. It was long overdue; it dealt with Keegstra but not with Stiles; and it lacked any passion or emotion. "Where was the ringing denunciation?" wondered the *Edmonton Journal* in an editorial headed "Peter speaks out but not too loudly." George Oake, writing in the same issue of the newspaper, mocked the Premier's entire approach to anti-Semitism. "Holocaust survivors are not going to start dancing the Horah on the basis of the premier's assertion that the Human Rights Branch complaints about racism have dropped," Oake wrote, adding that

> It is perhaps indicative of this government that it would measure the number of insults to human dignity over the length of a fiscal year. . . . The premier was undoubtedly sincere in his remarks. It was just that they read like they were prepared by a committee of drones in the Department of Economic Development.

From Montreal, Jim Fleming, the Federal Minister of State for Multiculturalism, called Lougheed's words "much too slow and feeble." Irwin Cotler, President of the Canadian Jewish Congress, was disturbed at the delay. "These things must be immediately rebutted with all the moral and political resources available," he said. [11]

— IV —

If there was one issue which seemed to have escaped much attention it was the issue of the non-Jewish response to Keegstra and Stiles. By the end of April, with the notable exception of the Presbyterian Church in Canada, only individuals had joined the media and the Jews in their battle against bigotry. What seemed particularly surprising—in light of the diligent outreach efforts of the Edmonton Jewish community—was that there had been so little demonstrated ethnic or religious support for the Jews in that city.

There were formidable obstacles hindering action on the part of ethnic and religious groups. If Christians wanted to speak in unison, for example, who would represent them? The Canadian Council of Christians and Jews had for years done little in Alberta other than hold fundraising dinners. And when its director, Victor Goldbloom, attempted to become involved, Harry Cohen in Calgary told him to tread carefully, and Joe Shoctor in Edmonton told him to forge ahead. So he did nothing other than write Lougheed a letter. No functioning central independent organization existed for Alberta's ethnic groups. [12]

There were other problems as well. Like the Jews, the different Christian faiths in Alberta were disunited; in some cases, one did not recognize or speak to another. Christians organized in a centralized, hierarchical manner had representatives who could speak on behalf of their followers. Those organized congregationally naturally found such an effort more difficult, although this did not prevent some Calgary evangelicals from coming forward individually to protest Keegstra's actions.

The media played a subtle role in keeping Christians in Alberta relatively silent. By focusing on the Holocaust denial aspects of Keegstra's teachings (especially after Stiles' statements), it may have misled many Christians into thinking that this was more a matter for comment by historians than theologians. Never during the height of the controversy, in 1983, nor after that, did the media deal with the acknowledged Christian roots of Keegstra's thought. It is probably too much to expect that it could have done so. Yet if it had, Christians might have been more attuned to the moral outrage of the Jewish community.

Ethnic groups in Alberta had their own, more immediate, concerns. They also lacked the confidence to draw attention to themselves in this relatively homogeneous province. And they did not relate to anti-Semitism. As far as is known, the ethnic press did not comment on, or cover, the Keegstra affair at this point.[13]

When one writer investigated the Christian response to these instances of anti-Semitism in the province, she did not find much activity. "So, once again, it has fallen to the Jewish community to come to its own defense," Nancy Millar wrote in the *Calgary Herald*. "And that's the most disappointing rub of all, as far as Jews are concerned." She was not the only non-Jew to point this out. In stronger terms, J. Leslie Beel, in an impassioned essay entitled "J'Accuse," wrote: "I accuse: the non-Jews of Alberta of culpable indifference, of historical know-nothingness, of consent by silence, for having learned nothing, for having remembered nothing."

A few church leaders in Calgary did not believe the criticism was valid. "I'm sick and tired of reacting to things like this," said the Most Rev. Paul O'Byrne, Bishop of the Calgary Roman Catholic diocese. He felt that the news media had excessively emphasized the Keegstra affair. In Edmonton, Roman Catholic Archbishop Joseph MacNeil agreed. Though he stood by the Church's official abhorrence of bigotry, he told the *Western Catholic Reporter* that the controversy surrounding Keegstra and Stiles "has been drummed up by the press. I don't want to make a big thing about this." The Rev. George LeDrew, chairman of Calgary's United Church presbytery, claimed that "It would be an over-reaction for every presbytery and all Christian churches to denounce Keegstra."[14]

Calgary members of the League for Human Rights of B'nai B'rith Canada, a national organization founded in 1966 to deal with anti-Semitism and racism in Canada, were angered and upset by this perceived silence. One of them—Carl Bond—believed it was time church leaders spoke out. With the support of other people in the League, Bond decided to attempt to get a public statement from Calgary Christians.

He began making phone calls on May 2. Not knowing whom to contact, he flipped through the Yellow Pages and called everyone who seemed important. Over lunch, he and another League member discussed a public statement on anti-Semitism with the Very Rev. John Blyth, administrator for the Anglican Diocese of Calgary; the Rev. John Bastigal, of the Council of Social Affairs of the Catholic diocese; Pastor R. Wayne Lewry, the vice-president of the Evangelical Ministerial Association; and Blaine Hudson, the regional representative of the Lutheran Church. Other leaders Bond met personally.

After one such meeting, a Christian leader left with tears in his eyes, upset that he had to be approached by (and did not first approach) the Jewish community, and that thousands of his congregants had not sought out Jews to see how Christians could be helpful. When Bishop O'Byrne told Bond that he was not interested in participating in a public statement, Bond contacted a leading Roman Catholic in Ontario, who intervened. The Rev. John Bastigal later represented the Calgary diocese.

Eight Christian and three Jewish leaders participated in a joint press conference on May 12, at the International Hotel in downtown Calgary. In their statement denouncing "all forms of hatred, bigotry, and racism," anti-Semitism was termed "inherently an attack against Christianity." Calling the Holocaust "an evil so profound that it borders on the imcomprehensible, and thus must never be forgotten or in any manner trivialized," the statement urged all "believers in the Lord" to "renounce hatred and mistrust and treat one another with mutual respect and love."

In June, a survey of eleven non-mainline churches in Edmonton revealed that all of the representatives opposed anti-Semitism, accepted the reality of the Holocaust and did not believe that God had abandoned the Jews. They were also convinced that churches must speak out on anti-Semitism.[15]

The League for Human Rights' success in organizing what was probably the first Christian-Jewish press conference in Alberta brought them into contact with a forceful local activist, Jack Downey. A Calgary entrepreneur, Downey had decided to launch a "conspiracy of one" against Jim Keegstra. In the first of many independent actions stressing the importance of multicultural awareness, Downey announced that public contributions would be accepted for "Project Windmill." The purpose of the project was to send two Eckville students to Europe to visit concentration camps. Then—in response to Keegstra's claim that he was willing to have his ideas disproven in a debating forum—Downey publicly challenged the Eckville teacher to a debate. Keegstra, however, refused.

The Calgary Chapter of the League for Human Rights continued its action, in spite of opposition from leaders of the Calgary Jewish Community Council. In the May 27 issue of *The Jewish Star*, it called for renewed efforts to have Stiles expelled from the Conservative caucus.[16]

— V —

During the month of May, there was turmoil throughout the province. Albertans just couldn't stop thinking about the public teacher and the Tory politician.

In Eckville, where it had all begun, an initial effort was made to bring some historical sense to the town. On May 3, the National Film Board Holocaust documentary "Memorandum" was shown to grade seven to twelve students in the high school gym. The film's non-Jewish director and writer, Donald Brittain, was present as 250 students viewed scenes of concentration camp cruelty. After the film he was prepared to answer questions. But no one had any to ask. Blair Andrew (whose mother Margaret had been one of the most persistent critics of Keegstra) said afterwards that perhaps eighty percent of his fellow grade eleven students denied that the Holocaust occurred and believed in a Jewish world-conspiracy. Students interviewed after the film showing by Robert Lee of the *Red Deer Advocate* indicated that the film had not changed their lack of belief in the Holocaust. Keegstra was later quoted as saying that the "NFB film was a documentation of hate. I would challenge is authenticity."[17]

Efforts on behalf of the students continued. On May 17, Dr. Lew Hamburger, director of the Edmonton Jewish Community Centre; Dr. Bill Meloff, director of Camp B'nai Brith; and Hillel Boroditsky met with Marg Andrew; Ed Olsen, principal of Eckville High; and others to plan a social interaction program at Camp B'nai B'rith in Pine Lake. About fifty students and parents had a day of "fun and fellowship" at the camp on Sunday, July 10.[18]

Also in May, six grade twelve Eckville students flew to Vancouver at the invitation of the local B'nai B'rith lodge to attend the annual Holocaust symposium. About one thousand British Columbia students participated in the two-day event, held at the University of British Columbia. Later in the year, two Jewish Holocaust survivors from Montreal and one from Vancouver spoke to seventy Eckville high school students. Several students were reportedly moved to tears after watching the documentary film "Genocide."[19]

Eckvillians were becoming touchy about the national attention they were receiving. "Eckville, as a community, is taking such a beating across Canada that it's now [urgent] that the problems being created by the mayor be finished off," and *Eckville Examiner* editorial stated. "The sooner . . . responsible groups and organizations speak out the better it will be for the community."

The advice seems to have been taken to heart. At its May 16 meeting, two councillors unsuccessfully attempted to get Keegstra to resign as mayor, claiming that his anti-Jewish views had colored his judgment. One of them, George Schmidt, then announced that he would attempt to have the Alberta minister for municipal affairs investigate Keegstra's conduct as mayor. The Eckville branch of the Royal Canadian Legion condemned Keegstra (though it did not seek his resignation at the time). Len Schultz, the head of the town's Chamber of Commerce, said the Chamber was concerned about the negative publicity which Eckville had received.

These efforts did not accomplish much. It still seemed to more than one observer that some townspeople held attitudes that were "as repugnant as Keegstra's anti-Semitism." On May 16, the attempt to oust Keegstra as mayor failed by a four to two vote in council. Yet the anger in the town against Keegstra continued, and so did the publicity. There were twenty members of the media roaming the streets of Eckville on May 16. "Red Deer's going to get pretty well known since it's so close to Eckville," one man quipped.[20]

Later that month, an effort was made to measure local attitudes towards Keegstra. Kevin McEntee (the Lacombe County School Board trustee who had been involved in Keegstra's firing), Dr. Alexander Dougall, a local physician and about ten others circulated two petitions. Residents were asked to sign either of them—one calling for Keegstra to resign as mayor, and the other for him to remain.

Judging from the results of the Eckville mayoral elections in October, the petitions of the "Concerned Citizens Group" turned out to reflect the attitude of the townspeople to their mayor. In all, 369 residents were canvassed, representing about ninety-seven percent of the electorate. Of those who signed the petitions eighty percent wanted Keegstra to resign as mayor, and twenty percent did not. Of those who did not want him to resign, thirty-seven percent listed their occupation as "Retired."

The petitions were presented to the Town Council meeting on June 6. Keegstra, however, spurned the effort. "I don't think these petitions were legitimate," he told Robert Lee of the *Red Deer Advocate*. When Lee asked him if he thought "they were part of a worldwide Jewish conspiracy to enslave the world," Keegstra replied that he was unable to comment, because he had not examined them. Dougall had not expected more. He said that the purpose of the exercise had been "to show people in other towns in Canada we do not support his views."[21]

May was a month of turmoil, but also—at last—of action. More people in more places began to publicly reject the views of Keegstra and Stiles. Condemnations of racism, bigotry or anti-Semitism, and affirmations of the reality of the Holocaust were heard from an increasing number of public officials. At the end of May, Jim Fleming, the Federal Minister of Multiculturalism, announced a government proposal to establish a parliamentary committee to investigate racial intolerance.[22]

Also at this time, articles on Keegstra appeared in *The New York Times, International Herald Tribune* (published in Paris), and in *Ma'ariv,* an Israeli daily newspaper.[23]

The reactions were not always spontaneous. Most people had to be roused from lethargy, convinced to take action and persuaded to overcome self-interest. The movement to action involved a process, which culminated in an understanding that what had happened was a violation of what is (or should be) normative in society. Only when that occurred did a response become possible. Only then could one say that society had handed down its judgment of Jim Keegstra.

10

The Trial

DURING THE SIX MONTHS following Premier Lougheed's statement on Keegstra, the Alberta government remained undecided on what to do with the man himself. It is true that the Alberta Premier had announced programs aimed at preventing others from imitating Keegstra's teachings. Yet he had made no move to deal with the teacher.

Even in April, before Lougheed spoke out, the Alberta Attorney General, Neil Crawford, had considered laying charges against Keegstra for violating the hate promotion section of the Criminal Code of Canada. According to law, only an Attorney General can take such an action. Crawford was not, however, keen about the possibility, and at the time did not believe that there was enough evidence to prosecute the Eckville teacher. He indicated that a hate trial might "attract other irrationals," and that the effort would be negated if the accused were acquitted. "Not everything that expresses an opinion on race, color or religion is hate literature," he told a reporter. "There's not a lot of control on this literature right now and I'm not sure there should be, even if you and I disagree with what is said."

At the same time, but entirely independent of Crawford's efforts, a group of lawyers brought together by the

Jewish Federation of Edmonton was also considering the matter. This Ad Hoc Legal Committee concluded that any attempt to have Crawford lay charges would be costly and time-consuming, might become a civil liberties issue and was not likely to gain the Attorney General's approval. In this way, the Committee's view coincided with, though it did not follow, a recommendation made by Ben Kayfetz, of the Canadian Jewish Congress in Toronto. In a phone call to Hillel Boroditsky, he suggested that the Federation write to Crawford to encourage him to prosecute Keegstra under section 281. The purpose of such a letter, Kayfetz said, would be to elicit a refusal to utilize that Criminal Code section from yet another Attorney General. This could then be used by the Congress in its continuing efforts to get the law changed. The letter was never sent.

Crawford completed his study of the transcript of the Board of Reference hearing in May, but was still not certain about laying charges. At the end of July, he ordered the RCMP to gather evidence on exactly what Keegstra had done. On September 16, after interviewing Keegstra, hundreds of Eckvillians and others, the RCMP submitted a report to Crawford. Then there was silence until January 11, 1984, when Keegstra was charged with promoting hate under section 281 of the Criminal Code.[1]

Why had Crawford been so hesitant to lay charges, and what in the end moved him to change his mind? The basis of his reluctance seems clear. The section of the Criminal Code of Canada under which Keegstra could be charged was perceived by law authorities and scholars as an inoperative law. According to Section 281.2, subsection 2, "Every one who, by communicating statements, other than in private conversation, wilfully promotes hatred against any identifiable group" is guilty of an offence. But what is a "private conversation" and how does one establish will-fulness? According to the B'nai B'rith League for Human Rights, the word "wilfully" alone had apparently caused Crown Attorneys to shy away from using the law, "because of difficulties in establishing what was in the accused's mind."

And there were other problems with this section of the Criminal Code, in that it allowed four defences (besides those normally available).

> No person shall be convicted of an offence under subsection (2)
> (a) if he establishes that the statements communicated were true;
> (b) if, in good faith, he expressed or attempted to establish by argument an opinion upon a religious subject;
> (c) if the statements were relevant to any subject of public interest, the discussion of which was for the public benefit, and if on reasonable grounds he believed them to be true; or
> (d) if, in good faith, he intended to point out, for the purpose of removal, matters producing or tending to produce feelings of hatred towards an identifiable group in Canada.

In a study of hate propaganda laws undertaken at that time for the Attorney General of Ontario, Patrick Lawlor, Q.C, found particular difficulties with the "sincere fanatic" defence of section C, and the "good faith" one in section D. "Keegstra on the Holocaust is probably in good faith," Lawlor wrote in March 1984. These clauses, he added, "are clearly difficult, if not impossible, to enforce."[2] Indeed, at that time there had been no successful prosecution under this section since it became law in 1970.

Crawford's thinking was undoubtedly also influenced by several non-legal considerations. The Alberta conservative, for example, were probably hesitant to pursue a criminal prosecution for philosophical reasons. They believed in a cautious, disciplined government guided by *laissez-faire* attitudes. In the course of studying a problem, contemplating an action and following the public mood, an issue might resolve itself.

But Crawford also weighed other factors which encouraged him to prosecute. The Keegstra affair seemed to let loose a flood of hate. In May 1983, Ku Klux Klan posters surfaced in Edmonton, and hate literature was sent to two Manitoba universities. In June more hate literature appeared in Edmonton and in Olds, Alberta. In July, an 83-year-old Keegstra supporter, Louise Huseby, handed out the current issue of Ron Gostick's *On Target* in the street in Eckville. The issue was devoted to presenting the "facts" about the conspiracy behind "The 'Keegstra Affair'." Huseby also mailed it and Pastor Sheldon Emry's anti-Jewish *America's Promise Broadcaster* to local residents. In Saskatchewan, the Human Rights Commission began looking for the distributor of that same issue of *On Target*. In nearby Idaho, the annual Aryan World congress, a convention of racist rhetoric, anti-Semitism, weapons training and gun-swapping, convened in July. The Christian Defence League, an Alberta-based organization founded to give financial and legal support to Keegstra, was established in September. In October Keegstra attended a Calgary meeting of the right-wing Canadian League of Rights.[3]

Was Alberta reverting to where it had been in the 1930s, when anti-Semites openly preached their doctrines in churches and the government tolerated and helped finance the distribution of anti-Semitic propaganda? It was not, of course, but Crawford may well have felt that dramatic and strong action was necessary to combat the negative image Alberta had developed inside and outside Canada as a result of Jim Keegstra and the government's slow response. Perhaps he felt it was necessary to placate the Jewish community. Or perhaps he concluded that—win or lose—the Attorney General could only look good for having tried to enforce the law.

In the end, it was the evidence itself, unearthed by the RCMP in their investigation, that decided him. Crawford was shocked and outraged by what Keegstra had been teaching; it was far worse than he had ever suspected. Not to take action would surely raise questions about the moral character of the Lougheed government.

So in late December 1983 or early January 1984, Crawford walked into the Premier's office in Edmonton with a stack of material from the RCMP investigation. He told Lougheed that he wanted to lay charges. Lougheed pondered the matter for a few moments. Then he gave Crawford permission to go ahead.

— I —

Even before the Attorney General decided how he was going to deal with Jim Keegstra, the Alberta government was implementing the programs which Lougheed had announced in May. The cost of two of them approached one million dollars.[4]

When Jewish leaders met with Dave King, the Minister of Education, on May 30, they found him relaxed and well prepared. Among other things, they had considered proposing that an anti-racism program be adopted in the schools. Instead, King ended up telling the meeting of specific items on his agenda. He talked about the review of the curriculum. He told them there were going to be changes to the procedure whereby complaints can be initiated against teachers, since he believed that it had taken too long for Keegstra to be fired from his job. In all, the group was "exceptionally pleased," as Herb Katz said, with what they had heard. The purpose of the meeting had been to emphasize to government politicians the importance of the topic to Alberta Jews, and they felt this had been achieved.[5]

A month later, on June 27, King announced the establishment of a special committee to combat racism in the province's classrooms. Headed by Calgary lawyer and former Conservative MLA Ron Ghitter, the twelve-member "Minister's Consultative Committee on Tolerance and Understanding" was to travel the province seeking citizens' advice on how to promote ideas in Alberta schools which would help to develop a harmonious society. At the same time, Alberta Education (the regional office of the Ministry of Education) was to review procedures for decertifying teachers; to establish a policy for regular monitoring and supervision of teachers; to assess current teacher training programs in Alberta universities; and to review curricula from the perspective of promoting the teaching of tolerant ideas in the classroom.[6]

The Ghitter Committee, as it came to be known, crisscrossed Alberta for five months to hear 375 formal presentations. It issued four "discussion papers" and two reports, which ended up having very little to do with the Keegstra affair.

What caught the attention of the Committee was the state of private (particularly religious) and Native school education in Alberta. Ghitter found nothing ironic in the thought that the intolerance which his Committee discovered in private schools had been revealed as the result of Keegstra's teachings in the public system. Although in its early months it awakened lively interest in "tolerance and understanding," the Ghitter Committee was hardly noticed by the time its final report was released in February 1985.[7]

The second government program begun in response to the Keegstra affair was a newspaper, radio and television advertising campaign to combat racism in the province. Conducted by the Alberta Human Rights Commission, the program got off to a shaky start when news about it was leaked to the press almost three weeks before the official announcement on October 4, 1983. In television and radio spots, and in prominent newspaper advertisements, the message that "Alberta is for all of us" was proclaimed during a three-month period. The multi-media effort—which contained no reference to Keegstra—won awards for the Hayhurst advertising agency, which co-ordinated the campaign. According to a Commission survey, the campaign also proved successful in making people think about discrimination.

Despite this, it was criticized as government interference by some, and as not hard-hitting enough by others. *The Jewish Star,* which referred to the program as "tokenism," maintained that "the government could have saved taxpayers the $500,000 which is going to be spent on this program, had it chosen to act on its beliefs, rather than to advertise them." A related effort by the Commission to get

Alberta newspapers to print a series of ethno-cultural profiles at their own expense was never carried out. The province's two major dailies refused to participate in the government plan.[8]

— II —

On that Monday morning, June 4, 1984, as Jim Keegstra walked up the stairs of the Provincial Courthouse in Red Deer with his lawyer Doug Christie and a retinue of followers sporting "Freedom of Speech" buttons, he had already suffered several setbacks. As the preliminary hearing into criminal charges against him was about to get underway, Keegstra was no longer the mayor of Eckville. He was no longer a member of the Alberta Teachers' Association. And he was no longer a certified teacher in the province of Alberta.

First, he had been defeated in the Eckville mayoral contest on October 17, by a 278 to 123 margin. Then on February 16, a three-man Teaching Profession Appeal Board upheld the Alberta Teachers' Association decision to terminate Keegstra's ATA membership, and to recommend the suspension of his license. Finally, on April 11, Dave King revoked his teaching license, making it impossible for him to teach in an accredited school in Alberta.[9]

Related events, however, kept Keegstra in the news and, unintentionally or otherwise, fueled support for his ideas. Following in the footsteps of Stephen Stiles, Calgary MLA Bowdan "Bud" Zip became the second Alberta Conservative to question the Holocaust. "I think maybe some of the figures [relating to the number of Jews murdered by the Nazis] were overstated," he told an *Edmonton Sun* reporter on February 22. That same day, he wrote Herb Katz that his views had been "distorted," and he publicly apologized for his remarks (apparently at Lougheed's insistence).[10]

In April, the League for Human Rights of B'nai B'rith Canada persuaded Canada Post to ban the importation of a notable, though obscure, pseudo-scholarly work on the

Holocaust entitled *The Hoax of the Twentieth Century,* by Arthur R. Butz. Curiously enough, it was not until Keegstra's preliminary hearing that the ban attained public notice. The book, by a professor of electrical engineering and computer sciences at Northwestern University near Chicago, attained further notoriety when it was subsequently seized by the RCMP from the University of Calgary Library.

Direct support for Keegstra came from the Christian Defence League, which had been working to provide financing for Keegstra's impending court battle. On September 10, 1983, at a meeting of the group in the town of Bentley, near Eckville, the treasurer Jim Green "stressed [the] need to support Keegstra—now with money and any other means." Soon Keegstra himself, who was originally planning to handle his own case because "most lawyers, as well as politicians, are completely terrorized by the Zionist Jewish A.D.L.," was seeking prayers and financial assistance. In February Green was offering founding memberships in the Christian Defence League at a hundred dollars, while a twenty-dollar donation would put one on the mailing list. "Please pray for Jim, he really needs our help," Green wrote to one person. "If it were not for his strong belief and blessed assurance he would not be able to carry on the good fight." A postcript stated: "We are Israel."[11]

The purpose of the preliminary hearing in Red Deer was to determine if there was sufficient evidence to proceed with the charge against Keegstra. It was expected to last four days. But like the trial a year later, the hearing lasted twice as long as expected.

Indeed, the 1984 judicial proceeding turned out to be a rehearsal for the 1985 courtroom case in several ways. In both instances, Doug Christie—the 37-year-old Victoria lawyer, "anti-Eastern Canadian" and self-styled defender of free speech—served as Keegstra's attorney. Bruce Fraser and Larry Phillippe were the Crown Prosecutors. Christie's tedious cross-examination of student witnesses consistently focused on the accuracy of their classroom notes. He tried to show that Keegstra had not spoken against all Jews (an identifiable group), but only the supposed conspirators among them. He maintained that the Crown had failed to demonstrate that Keegstra's anti-Jewish teachings had succeeded in promoting hate. On several occasions there were sharp exchanges between Christie and Fraser, and even in the preliminary hearing the judge warned Keegstra's lawyer to stop interrupting the witness and to avoid theatrics.

Such conduct apparently impressed one spectator, who first saw Christie in action in Red Deer, and later hired him for his trial in Toronto. That spectator was Ernst Zundel, the Canadian Publisher and author of Holocaust denial literature.

The Crown utilized some of the same tactics in both court cases. Fraser and Phillippe based their case on the notebooks, essays and exams of Keegstra's students (reading from some sixty items), and on their courtroom testimony. The less convincing, less confident student witnesses—who often turned out to be clearly sympathetic to their former teacher—were called first, and used to establish the precise nature of what had been taught. Most of the Crown's witnesses in the preliminary hearing returned for the trial.

Christie found some of his own evidence so impressive (such as the 1920 article by Winston Churchill on "Zionism versus Bolshevism" from the *Illustrated Sunday Herald*, in which Churchill wrote about a Jewish world-conspiracy) that he entered it again a year later. He also twice read long passages from the Talmud, which he claimed supported his client.

Reporters from across Canada came to the preliminary hearing in Red Deer in full force, at least for the first few days. At the outset, half of the sixty seats in the courtroom were taken by them. But soon their attendance fell off, and Keegstra supporters frequently outnumbered media representatives. There was a lot of sensational news to report, and Christie wanted it all covered. He had refused to request a ban on publicity (as Fraser had desired), maintaining that the media had presented a great deal of anti-Keegstra material, and he wished his client's point of view to receive public attention.[12]

As in the Board of Reference hearing in March 1983, the nature of Keegstra's classroom conduct was spelled out in the preliminary hearing by his former students on the witness stand. By the third day of testimony, spectators could grasp the conspiratorial world-view. Reading from various classroom materials, students noted that Keegstra had taught them that the Jews had provoked the French and Russian Revolutions, the American Civil War, both World Wars and the 1930s Depression. He maintained that Henry Kissinger was a KGB agent, Nelson Rockefeller was a born-Jew who became a Baptist and the United States Federal Reserve was controlled by Jewish conspirators. Keegstra also taught that, hundreds of years ago, a Jewish-controlled group held a "Feast of Reason" during which young girls were killed and their blood poured over the bodies of prostitutes.

Trudi Roth testified that Keegstra got a "certain look" in his eyes when he began to talk about the ongoing Jewish world-conspiracy. Richard Denis reported that he received a sixty-five percent mark for an essay in which he wrote, "We must get rid of every Jew in existence so we can live in peace and freedom." Dana Kreil was given a seventy-five percent grade on her essay praising Hitler and warning against Jewish "satanic hate."

Some former students still admired their teacher, and had adopted his views. For example Danny Desrosiers told Fraser that Keegstra "showed us pictures of the gas ovens [in Nazis death camps]. They weren't very big. The Jewish people must have been very short." He added that the international finance conspirators were not all Jewish, though "most took the Jewish religion. You knew [Keegstra] isn't talking about Sam Jew who owns a bakery."

On the other hand, seventeen-year-old Blair Andrew, whose mother Marg had been instrumental in having Keegstra fired, spoke of a man who called rich Jews "money thugs" and other Jews "gutter rats." One's marks depended on whether or not one expressed belief in the Jewish conspiracy, he said, and all the students knew that. "As far as I can determine, [Keegstra] hated the whole race," he added. Sherron Wolney, a class valedictorian at Eckville High, said that "Mr. Keegstra's lectures, I gathered, were 'Love your neighbor as yourself' as long as they . . . weren't Roman Catholic or Negroes."

Christie was grueling in his detailed cross-examination of the nine students who appeared at the preliminary. One of them broke down in tears on the stand. In the hot, stuffy courtroom some spectators murmured "that's right" at certain of the students' negative statements about Jews, and Judge Crowe had to warn them twice against snickering and laughing.

One of the few moments of humor during all of Keegstra's trials came when a student, under cross-examination by Christie, indicated that Judaism was related to Communism, socialism, fascism and to the "WCC." Christie, a co-founder of the Western Canada Concept Party—a separatist movement—was joined in laughter by courtroom spectators when he said, "I submit [Keegstra] was talking about the World Council of Churches."

Fraser and Phillippe had told reporters that they had thirty witnesses to call, and that the preliminary could last three weeks. But during lunch on June 15, the ninth day of testimony, Fraser decided the Crown had made its point. Judge Crowe agreed. "There is, in my mind, no doubt that these statements, or some of them . . . are capable of promoting hatred of the Jewish people." Keegstra was committed to trial.

— III —

Fraser and Christie lost no time in readying themselves for the trial. While both were busy preparing to argue Christie's claim that the charge against Keegstra was unconstitutional under the new Charter of Rights and Freedoms, Fraser was also busy learning about Judaism. Actually, he had been at work on the case since charges were first laid in January 1984. He was in contact with the B'nai B'rith League for Human Rights and the Canadian Jewish Congress, and he consulted with historians, Talmudic scholars and other experts. One of these was Rabbi W. Gunther Plaut of Toronto. Fraser told Plaut that Christie was expected to cite modern-day anti-Talmudic works as evidence supporting Keegstra's teachings. Plaut replied that he did not approve of allowing the trial to degenerate into a medieval disputation. In such an event, the Talmud, Judaism and the Holocaust would be on trial, rather than Keegstra, and that had to be avoided.[13]

There would be no trial of Jim Keegstra at all, however, if Section 281 of the Criminal Code was in violation of the Charter of Rights (which was to become effective on April 7, 1985). This issue was raised by Christie and dealt with before Court of Queen's Bench Justice Frank H. Quigley, in Red Deer, on October 10 and 11, 1984.

To assist him in the defense case, Christie invited the Calgary-area lawyer Duncan McKillop to participate in presenting the legal arguments. McKillop was quick to quash potential rumors that his involvement with Keegstra indicated that he supported his views. But in February 1985, McKillop (who was the Chairman of the Canadian Bar Association's southern Alberta constitutional law subsection and the President of the Alberta Chamber of Commerce) became embroiled in a public controversy when he told a reporter that "I have doubts about the numbers in the Holocaust and who they were—but not to the point of believing it never happened."[14]

To McKillop and Christie, the hate propaganda section of the Criminal Code represented an unreasonable limitation on freedom of expression, as guaranteed under the Charter of Rights. They were not the only ones who felt that the anti-hate legislation was unconstitutional. The Canadian Civil Liberties Association agreed. Although they did not publicize their view, in June 1984 they made an unsuccessful attempt to convince the Canadian Jewish Congress to join them in having this constitutional matter referred to a special hearing of the Supreme Court of Canada. Such a hearing required Cabinet assent, and there had been fewer than ten such "references" to the country's highest court during the past quarter-century. Had the

Supreme Court ruled on the matter, and in agreement with the Civil Liberties Association position, the Keegstra trial would not have taken place.

In countering the position of McKillop and Christie, Fraser responded that the charge against Keegstra dealt with the promotion of hatred, not its expression. "I'm not saying [Keegstra] said: 'I hate Jews,'" Fraser explained. In addition, free speech is not an absolute right, asserted the Crown Prosecutor (who had been assisted in preparing his arguments by R. F. Taylor, a constitutional expert from the Alberta Attorney General's office).

On November 5, in a fifty-one-page statement which took eighty minutes to read, Quigley ruled in agreement with the Crown's argument: "It is my opinion that section 281.2(2) cannot rationally be considered to be an infringement which limits 'freedom of expression,' but on the contrary it is a safeguard which promotes it." Therefore the hate propaganda section was constitutional.[15]

— IV —

When Jim Keegstra's third trial in three years began in Red Deer on April 9, 1985, many expected that it would be the most spectacular one of all, maybe even the trial of the century.[16]

But Canadians were getting used to such trials. In early 1985 Ernst Zundel, a Toronto graphic artist, had been tried and convicted for violating Section 177 of the Criminal Code of Canada:

> Everyone who wilfully publishes a state-ment, tale, or news that he knows is false and that causes or is likely to cause injury or mischief to a public interest is guilty of an indictable offence . . .

The German-born Zundel had become Canada's most infamous publisher of anti-Jewish hate material, and one of the world's most active distributors of anti-Semitica. Zundel's material, printed in Canada by Samizdat Publishers, was regularly distributed in Canada, the United States and Germany. By the early 1980s he concentrated on pro-Nazi and Holocaust denial literature, prompting the laying of a charge against him under Section 177 by Mrs. Sabina Citron of Toronto, a Holocaust survivor.

Zundel's trial was dramatic. For weeks Canadian newspaper headlines reflected the bizarre goings on in the packed Toronto courtroom. The prosecution produced a string of Holocaust survivors and historical experts whose testimony was challenged by Zundel's lawyer, Doug Christie. Christie tried to cast doubt on the truth of the Holocaust by asking survivors such questions as, "What color were the walls of the Auschwitz-Birkenau gas chambers?" He then produced a string of defence witnesses—all Holocaust deniers.

When Zundel took the stand in his own defence it soon emerged that he was a confirmed Nazi. Under cross-examination he was shown to be a cynical and calculating defender of his hero, Adolf Hitler. Zundel would do almost anything to advance Hitler's political views. It took the jury less than a day of deliberation to convict him.

In Toronto, Christie had failed to win his case. Yet his abrasive cross-examination technique—a sort of verbal scorched-earth policy—plus his confrontations with the judge and the extensive media attention all seemed to herald an extraordinarily sensational trial in Red Deer. So much pressure was expected on the 110 available courtroom seats that reporters were required to register in advance, and were strictly limited in numbers. It was necessary to pass through a metal detector watched by two RCMP officers and a bailiff in order to enter room 201 in the Red Deer Court House.

The trial, the first in Alberta to test this section of the Criminal Code, and one of the longest in the province's history, never became the anticipated "event." The testimony of the students was repetitious and often boring, and Christie's cross-examination was plodding and tedious. Keegstra spent much of his time on the witness stand reading from literature that set out the conspiracy theory. There were few fireworks.

After a few weeks, the reporter for the Toronto *Globe & Mail* left Red Deer to take another assignment. The Keegstra trial, which began on the front pages of many newspapers, was soon pushed back into other sections. On most days the courtroom was less than half full.

Crown Prosecutor Bruce Fraser's approach to the case was built on the evidence of the student notebooks, essays, exams and courtroom testimony (as it had been in the preliminary hearing). He was determined to leave no doubt about what had gone on in Keegstra's classrooms. Day-in and day-out, Fraser examined a parade of former students, twenty-three in all, who referred to notebooks and essays. It was a repeat of previous testimonies.

Christie was calm and deliberate in cross-examination. He was tenacious, he was methodical and he was sometimes sarcastic. But like John MacKenzie, the presiding Justice, he was courteous, even deferential. Some expected that Keegstra, when put on the stand in his own defence, would prove—as had happened with Zundel—to be his own worst enemy. Nothing he said, however, seemed to have any catastrophic effect. He appeared totally unaffected by the ordeal. Tall, well-proportioned, with broad shoulders and grayish hair, Keegstra would move easily about among his supporters during the daily recesses, often smiling as he chatted with them or with his family. He was neatly dressed, affecting western-style belts. One could imagine how he would appear as an authority figure to high school students.

Christie seemed uncertain about his own approach, or perhaps he was being pragmatic. At first, he questioned the accuracy of the student notes. Later, however, he seemed to accept that they were a faithful record of what had occurred, and turned his attention to an attempt to demonstrate that Keegstra had formed his views about the Jews in "good faith" and on "reasonable grounds." Christie entered 140 books, pamphlets and documents as evidence in an attempt to make this point. (In the Zundel trial, 200 exhibits were introduced.)

Christie relied on two defences—"good faith" and "reasonable grounds"—under Section 281.2 during the twenty-six days that Keegstra was on the stand. Standing in the dock, Keegstra would, on some days, lecture to the ten-man, two-woman jury about his beliefs, answering far more than he was asked. Occasionally he was rebuked by MacKenzie for this.

Trying to anticipate every move Christie might make, Fraser and Phillippe worked fifteen to eighteen hours a day during the trial. When it seemed necessary, as a result of Keegstra's testimony, for Fraser and Phillippe to familiarize themselves with the Talmud, Fraser got in touch with Rabbi Peter Hayman of Calgary. Hayman, the spiritual leader of a local synagogue, was a Ph.D. candidate in Talmudics at Yeshiva University in New York. During eight sessions lasting as long as three hours each, Fraser and Hayman studied the Talmud together, focusing on the texts cited in diatribes such Pranaitis's *The Talmud Unmasked* and Dilling's *The Jewish Religion*. They also spent several other sessions discussing Jewish attitudes to Christianity, the "chosen people" concept and related subjects.

In the end, Fraser decided not to call Hayman as a witness. His purpose in Red Deer was not to dispute the Talmud; it was to get a conviction. The trial was dragging on for too long. Besides, Keegstra had already discredited his own assertions about the Jews when he tried to label almost everyone he disagreed with, from Alberta Premier Peter Lougheed to External Affairs Minister Joe Clark, as Communists and dupes of the Jewish conspiracy.

In a decision reminiscent of the preliminary hearing, Fraser abruptly ended his cross-examination of Keegstra on July 9. Christie's final argument was delivered in fifteen hours over three days. Fraser was content with a three-hour summation. The judge took about the same length of time to deliver his charge to the jury.

On July 20, on the seventieth day of the proceedings, and after deliberating for thirty hours over a four-day period, the jury unanimously found Keegstra guilty of wilfully promoting hatred against the Jews. He was fined $5,000 for this criminal offense.

— V —

What was accomplished by trying Jim Keegstra? In spite of its great length, the trial revealed little that was new. Keegstra had, after all, always been quite forthcoming in describing his views and his teachings. His statements were part of the record from the beginning, and could be found in newspaper reports and in the transcript of the Board of Reference hearing.

Notwithstanding the conviction, which—if upheld under appeal—will be a precedent-setting verdict, it is difficult to discern any direct benefit from the trial to the "identifiable group" which had been the object of Keegstra's hate promotion—the Jews. The weeks of testimony of Keegstra and his former students contained numerous half-truths, distortions and lies about Jews, Judaism, a Jewish world-conspiracy and the Talmud. None of them was ever rebutted in the courtroom.

But here, too, there was nothing new. Both the Talmud and the myth of the Jewish world-conspiracy had been on trial before. One hundred years before Keegstra was found guilty in Red Deer, August Rohling—a canon and professor of Catholic Theology in Prague—was challenged for having published *Der Talmudjude (The Talmud Jew)*, an anti-Semitic polemic against the Talmud. The 1885 judgment obtained against Rohling stated in part that "not a single text exists in the whole of the Talmud in which Christians or pagans or idolators are given the name of an animal." Nonetheless, Rohling continued to publish anti-Semitic tracts, and *Der Talmudjude* remained in print into the 1930s. (J.B. Pranaitis utilized Rohling's writings in *The Talmud Unmasked*.)

The Protocols of the Elders of Zion, the 1890s work which purports to reveal plans of a Jewish world-conspiracy, was put on trial fifty years ago in Berne, Switzerland.

Following proceedings which spanned nearly two years, the judge ruled that the book was a "trashy forgery." His concluding words seem remarkably timely even today. "I hope," he wrote,

> that there will come a time when nobody will any longer understand how in the year 1935 almost a dozen fully sane and reasonable men could for fourteen days torment their brains before a court at Berne over the authenticity of these so-called 'protocols,' these *Protocols* that, despite all the harm they have caused and may yet cause, are nothing but ridiculous nonsense.

Of course the Berne trial, which attracted worldwide press coverage, did little to put an end to this myth. Jim Keegstra showed that it still flourishes.[17] Moreover his trial neither dispelled nor countered myths about the Jewish people or promoted understanding about them. This was not the mandate of the Crown Prosecutors. Their job was to gain a conviction, and in that they were successful.

Can the judicial system be used effectively to deal with hate mongering? Recent American experience suggests that it can be. In 1979 the Los Angeles-based Institute for Historical Review offered a $50,000 reward to anyone who could prove that a single Jew had been gassed to death during the Holocaust. When the Institute refused to pay Mel Mermelstein, a Holocaust survivor who responded to the offer, Mermelstein launched a seventeen-million-dollar libel suit against the Institute. In 1981, for the first time in American history, a California court ruled the "Jews were gassed to death at Auschwitz concentration camp in Poland during the summer of 1944." In July 1985, two weeks prior to the court date, an out-of-court settlement was reached. The terms were tangible and far-reaching: the Institute was required to pay Mermelstein $90,000, agreed to apologize in writing to him and other Auschwitz survivors for maintaining that the Holocaust was a myth and was required to publicly declare that "the fact that Jews were gassed at Auschwitz is indisputable."[18]

However, the lasting significance of the Keegstra affair does not lie in his trial. Society itself, and not the court of law, remains the most effective place to counteract hatred. Bigotry will not be eliminated by the Criminal Code of Canada. In the end, what was important about the Keegstra affair was that there were those in the community who recognized the danger which Keegstra posed to Canadian society and were determined to do something about it. Outraged parents, a handful of school officials, the Jewish community and a sensitive media were willing to wage a public battle against the danger. That is what counted.

Afterword

FOR NEARLY THREE YEARS, Jim Keegstra has been in the forefront of public attention. He is not likely to be quickly forgotten by friend or foe, for many have been affected by his "lessons in hate."

From the weeks of court testimony by Keegstra's Eckville students, it is apparent that a number of them were either confused by their teacher's instruction, or have incorporated it into their thinking about the world. They may indeed become the bearers for the future of the medieval myths about a Jewish world-conspiracy.

Beginning in 1984, a number of initiatives were undertaken to prevent a recurrence of the Keegstra situation in the classroom. In March, the Alberta Teachers' Association amended its Code of Ethics to require teachers to teach "in a manner that respects the dignity and rights of all persons without prejudice as to race, religious beliefs, color, sex, physical characteristics, age, ancestry or place of origin." Several weeks later, Alberta Education issued a discussion paper. It proposed new requirements for those wishing to qualify as certified teachers, regular evaluations of those who wished to remain as certified teachers and ongoing assessments of the teacher education programs at Alberta universities. In early 1985, after four failed attempts in five years to get the ATA to agree to a new teaching profession act, Minister of Education Dave King finally established a Council on Alberta Teacher Standards. The ATA claimed it was underrepresented on the Council and open war erupted between it and King. A compromise was finally reached in June 1985. The first priority of the new Council was to devise guidelines for classroom inspection of teacher competence.

King has clearly used the Eckville High School precedent as a means of achieving previously contemplated changes in the Alberta education system. "I do not consider 'the Keegstra affair' to have been an 'important historical event,'" King wrote to the authors of this book before the establishment of the new Council. "It is significant not in itself, but rather for the window of opportunity it opened, which lent focus and power to a number of initiatives that had commenced in the years 1979-1982."[1]

Before the Keegstra trial ended, the Jews of Alberta started to work in concert for the first time, and to consult with each other. Prodded by Milton Harris, President of the Canadian Jewish Congress, the two communities established an Alberta Region of the Canadian Jewish Congress in July 1984. A year later, representatives of the two communities joined together to prepare a response to the Keegstra trial verdict.

Whatever progress was made in increasing the interaction and understanding between Alberta's Christians and Jews was due principally to the determination of Fritz Voll, who was appointed the regional director of the Canadian Council of Christians and Jews in the fall of 1983. In July 1985, following the Keegstra trial, a press conference called by the Angelican Bishop of Calgary and attended by some Christian leaders condemned anti-Semitism as anti-Christian. Notably absent was any Roman Catholic representation, although Calgary Catholic Bishop Paul O'Byrne later held a separate press conference. Although Christian and Jewish relations are now light years away from where they were five decades ago, they are still far from where they should be.

In at least one instance, the torrential media coverage of the Keegstra affair had an effect on distributors of hate literature in Canada. Wally Klinck—the Sherwood Park, Alberta, owner of C.H. Douglas Social Credit Supplies—voluntarily ceased selling Holocaust denial literature in April 1983. But Ron Gostick's Canadian League of Rights in Flesherton, Ontario (with a warehouse run by Eric Boswell in Brooks, Alberta, and another in Vancouver) continued doing business.[2]

In recognition of its coverage, the *Edmonton Journal* was given a B'nai B'rith Media Human Rights Award in 1983. The Jewish Federation of Edmonton received a special citation for its "outstanding community relations programme in confronting blatant anti-Semitism in the classroom" from the Council of Jewish Federations, in New York, in 1984. In October 1983 the Federation lodged a formal complaint against the *Journal* before the Alberta Press Council for publishing an "offensive and odious" cartoon comparing Israeli Defense Minister Ariel Sharon to Klaus Barbie, the Nazi "Butcher of Lyon." The Council agreed with the Federation that care should be taken not to "trivialize the Holocaust," and that the cartoon should not have been printed.[3]

What has become of those who fought the battle of Eckville?

In Edmonton, Herb Katz was unanimously commended by the Jewish Federation Board for his efforts as head of the JCRC. He continued his participation in the Federation until the spring of 1985, when he ceased all involvement in its work. Hillel Boroditsky, the Federations director, became the Executive Director of the United Way of Edmonton. Howard Starkman completed his two-year term as the Federation's first president. In Calgary, Harry Shatz retired as the Executive Director of the Calgary Jewish Community Council after twenty-three years. Gert Cohos finished her term as the Council president, and was followed by Bruce Libin, a lawyer, who set the Council in a new direction with an historic emphasis on outreach work for the Community Relations Committee.

Keith Harrison, Executive Assistant of the ATA, was promoted to Co-ordinator of Member Services for the organization. Arthur Cowley was succeeded by a new president of the ATA. Frank Flanagan, the former Superintendent of the County of Lacombe School Board, is now with the Alberta Department of Education. Sandra Weidner, the chairman of Lacombe School Board, was appointed to serve for two years on the Council on Alberta Teaching Standards.

In Eckville, Susan Maddox and Margaret Andrew, the parents who were instrumental in having Keegstra fired from his teaching position, declined to be nominated for the 1983 *Edmonton Journal* "Citizen of the Year" award by the Jewish Federation. However, they were recognized by the Canadian Jewish Congress in 1984 with citations of merit "for dedication and advancing the cause of human rights for all Canadians."

Ross Henderson of the *Eckville Examiner* joined the *Red Deer Advocate* as a staff reporter and covered part of the Keegstra trial. Robert Lee of the *Advocate*, who is now Ottawa bureau chief for the Edmonton and Calgary *Sun* newspapers, wrote an important article on "Keegstra's Children" for *Saturday Night* magazine. Ben Kayfetz of the Canadian Jewish Congress retired after thirty-seven years with the organization. Ron Ghitter, the head of the Committee on Tolerance and Understanding, ran for leadership of the Alberta Conservative Party after the retirement of Peter Lougheed in 1985. Ghitter, a Jew, ran headlong into anti-Semitism in trying to win delegates in parts of rural Alberta.

Doug Christie, who represented both Keegstra and Ernst Zundel in their hate promotion trials, wrote a private letter to raise money for the Keegstra defence fund. This letter found its way into circulation in July 1985. One excerpt read: "Every day [during the Red Deer Trial] a representative of the Canadian Jewish Congress sits in court and walks in and out of the prosecutor's office at the breaks, as well as advises the media, showing us who is the real power in the land."[4]

Although Keegstra paid the $5,000 fine, Christie has appealed the conviction on thirty-two grounds. The Alberta

Court of Appeal, which will rule on the matter and on the Crown's appeal of the "manifestly inadequate" sentence, could set aside the verdict or order another trial. In the meantime, Jim Keegstra works as an auto mechanic. Even without his provincial teaching certificate, he could still return to the classroom in one of Alberta's two dozen "category four" private schools, which are not required to hire certified teachers.[5]

Jim Keegstra taught his lessons in hatred for at least a decade before he was dismissed. He got away with it primarily because of complacency, misguided loyalty and the failure of colleagues and school officials to understand the depths of his fanaticism. He was eventually brought to account not because the system finally began to function, but because a handful of parents—ordinary, decent people—did not want their children to learn his lessons in hate. And he was brought to account because there *were* people in the school system in Lacombe County who would not tolerate his gross misuse of the classroom. The drama was played out in Eckville, Alberta, but it could have happened anywhere—wherever loose teacher training standards, haphazard teacher evaluation and weak supervision of teachers provide the opportunity.

The myth of the Jewish conspiracy has been a part of modern folklore for hundreds of years. The anti-Semitism that spawned it has been part of western civilization for much longer. The guilty verdict in the Keegstra trial will change nothing. Keegstra still believes as he did. His supporters, in Canada and around the world, still believe in their myths and continue to purvey their medieval Jew-hate. This irrationality will not be stamped out any more than physical disease can be completely conquered. But that doesn't mean we are powerless to deal with the problem. The career of Jim Keegstra revealed the weaknesses of a democratic society, but the ending of that career revealed its strengths. For the sake of its children, society must be vigilant.

Appendix

Document 1: R. K. David to James Keegstra, December 18, 1981

Dear Mr. Keegstra:

Further to our conversation of today's date in the presence of Mr. Ed Olsen, I wish to state my impressions of our meeting and confirm the position I have taken with regard to the way in which you have been presenting information in your Social Studies 30 program.

Parents in Eckville have complained that you are presenting prejudiced and biased views of history and that these biased views are particularly directed against Jews. In their complaints, parents have stated that you are presenting theories of history and your biased point of view as if they were facts. A review of your personnel file indicated that these concerns and similar complaints date as far back as November 1978, when a number of letters were received by the Superintendent and these complaints were discussed at length by you and Mr. Frank Flanagan.

My discussion with you this morning leads me to believe that you do have a highly biased and prejudiced view of history which is not held by most reputable historians or by curriculum developers in the Province of Alberta. My perusal of student notebooks, interviews with students in your Social Studies 30 class and an examination of a term paper written by one of your students leads me to believe that you are teaching these biased and prejudiced views as if they were confirmed by historical fact and not merely as your own particular point of view.

All of the students I interviewed confirmed that you teach an "International Jewish Conspiracy" interpretation of history as if it were fact. Furthermore, the students interviewed say they believe your teaching to be true. None of the students confirmed these beliefs by independent study and research, although they did say you mentioned literature was available if they wanted to read it.

I believe you are teaching your particular views and biases in a vigorous, forceful and persuasive way so that students are convinced that what you are saying is the truth, although they have not confirmed these views by any independent study.

Your teaching of history and the biased views you are presenting, also the extent to which you are emphasizing these biased views as indicated by my review of this concern, is simply not acceptable. It is my impression that students are being subtly indoctrinated into your point of view. This approach to teaching Social Studies 30 is not in keeping with the constraints of the curriculum or the expectations of the Board of Education and the community of Eckville, and must cease.

I am not giving you this directive to muzzle your academic freedom or to limit your intellectual integrity, but simply to insist that all sides of a historical question must be presented in as unbiased a way as possible, so that students can judge contradictory points for themselves. Furthermore, the "Jewish Conspiracy" must not be taught as if it were fact instead of just another view of history.

If there are any further complaints with regard to this matter, and if it is confirmed that these complaints are justified, I will expect you to appear before the Board of Education to express your point of view and teaching procedures. Furthermore, I will recommend at that time that serious disciplinary action be considered by the Board to prevent further exposure of our students to a very slanted and one-sided view of history.

I wish to confirm that this matter will be brought to the attention of the Board of Education and that my directives in this letter can be considered a lawful order of the Board in accordance with clause 79(1)(a) of the School Act. If you have any reactions or responses to this letter, I would appreciate them in writing.

Yours truly,

R. K. David
Superintendent of Schools

Document 2: R. K. David to James Keegstra January 19, 1982

Dear Mr. Keegstra,

The Board of Education will be considering the possible termination of your contract of employment as a teacher with the County of Lacombe at its meeting on February 9th, 1982. The reasons for this consideration are as follows:

> 1) Your failure to comply with the Alberta Social Studies Curriculum.
> 2) Your teaching of discriminatory theories as fact.
> 3) Your failure to modify sufficiently your teaching content and/or approach to reflect the desires of the Board of Education, its officers and the local community.

If you wish an opportunity to be heard by the Board of Education before a decision is made, you are invited to attend the meeting at 1:00 p.m. on February 9th in the Board of Education Chambers at the County Office. You may be represented by legal council, the A.T.A. or other as you so wish.

Please advise me before February 1st in writing if you will be attending the meeting.

Yours truly,

R. K. David
Superintendent of Schools

Document 3: R. K. David to James Keegstra March 9, 1982

Dear Mr. Keegstra,

I wish to inform you of the decision made by the Board of Education as a result of the hearing held on February 9, 1982.

At the hearing, you reviewed the historical background for your beliefs and presented to the Board of Education this background and beliefs as historical fact. Thus, you verified my impression as stated in the third paragraph of my letter to you dated December 18. You further confirmed that what you are teaching is not according to commonly accepted historical interpretation of historical fact. Furthermore, you confirmed at the hearing that the substance of my views and conclusions with regard to your teaching methods, style and content, are accurate. In particular, you confirmed that you teach an international Jewish conspiracy interpretation of history as if it were fact. During your presentation to the Board of Education, you outlined this theory at length and explained to the Board how you go about teaching it.

The issue under review at the hearing was not your competence as a teacher or your ability to teach the subject matter. Nor was the issue the esteem or regard that is held for you by your colleagues in Eckville or by the Town Council of Eckville, but simply, the content, approach and emphasis placed in your Social Studies program on questionable and controversial theories of history.

The Board of Education has resolved not to terminate your contract of employment at this time. However, the Board of Education wants you to clearly understand that your teaching practices, as reviewed with the Board at our February 9th meeting and referred to in my letter of December 18th, are not acceptable and are not to continue in the future. Specifically, the Board of Education directs:

1. That in your teaching of Social Studies, you comply with the "Alberta Social Studies Curriculum" guide with particular reference to the following clauses:

• 'Development of understanding of distinctive human values" . . . "The Alberta Social Studies Curriculum accepts that values derive from all aspects of culture, and that schooling must demonstrate sensitivity to the values of community, parents and social institutions while assisting students to deal in positive ways with the value conflicts that exist in the 'real world'" . . . (Page 4)

• "Development of competencies in processes of value analysis, decision-making and moral reasoning"

. . . "If people are to acquire the qualities of intellectual independence and moral maturity that characterize effective citizenship, they must be provided opportunities to analyze values critically, choose carefully from alternatives and reflect on the implications of their choices beyond the personal and the immediate." . . .

. . . . "Students are assisted in developing these skills by being provided the following types of experiences:

• Value analysis, including consideration of the value priorities of self and others; reflections upon value conflicts, competing courses of action and alternative consequences of actions; distinguishing between factual and value claims; and identifying logical inconsistencies." . . . (Page 5)

• "Development of positive attitudes towards self, others and the environment"

. . . "Learning in a free and open inquiry atmosphere. The following provide the framework for specific attitudinal objectives that are prescribed for curriculum topics:

• An attitude of commitment toward intellectual processes of inquiry. Such an attitude includes demonstration of skepticism, objectivity, tolerance for ambiguity, open-mindedness, tentativeness of interpretations and respect for evidence." . . . (Page 5)

2. You must not teach discriminatory theories as if they were fact. This is particularly applicable to the Jewish conspiracy theory of history. Commonly held interpretations of history must be presented to your class as the major emphasis of the course. If controversial theories or not commonly accepted theories are presented by you, they must not be presented as fact. No one theory must be emphasized or highlighted and students must be given the opportunity to judge for themselves the merits of these theories. [This too, is in keeping with the intent of the Social Studies Curriculum Guide as stated on Page 6, . . . "The process of developing, testing and substantiating (or falsifying) generalizations is amongst the most important qualities of true inquiry." . . .]

The purpose of these directives is to clarify for you the expectations and intent of the Board of Education so that you fully understand what is required of you, if you wish to continue teaching in the County of Lacombe. If you do not comply with the directives in this letter, the Board will again consider the possible termination of your contract of employment.

The Board of Education requires your written assurances that you will follow the directives in this letter at all times in the future.

Yours truly,

R. K. David
Superintendent of Schools

Document 4: James Keegstra to R. K. David, March 18, 1982

Dear Mr. David,

Re: Your letter of March 9, 1982

The quote from the Alberta Social Studies Curriculum Guide confirms that I have been and am teaching in accordance to this guide. I can assure you and the Board of Education that I will not disappoint your expectations and will continue to teach in accordance to the Alberta Social Studies guide.

I count it a privilege to be able to teach the students of Eckville in accordance to the Christian ethics, values and principles as required by the Alberta Department of Education. I will present to them all the facts at my disposal so that they will be able to discriminate carefully between alternatives and thus become solid thinking citizens producing a stable, peaceful society.

May the God of Wisdom guide you.

Yours sincerely,

Jim Keegstra

Document 5: R. K. David to James Keegstra, April 7, 1982

Dear Mr. Keegstra,

Your letter of March 18th was presented to the Board of Education at their regular meeting on April 6th.

The wording of your letter is not entirely satisfactory to the Board. I refer specifically to the first paragraph of your letter in which you suggest that you have been and are teaching in accordance with the quotations from the curriculum guide that were in my letter of March 9th. It is the position of the Board of Education that you were not teaching in accordance with this guide and it is their directive that you must change so that your teaching does conform to the intent of the curriculum.

I wish to inform you that if there are any further complaints with regard to this matter, they will be investigated further.

Yours truly,

R. K. David
Superintendent of Schools

Document 6: Susan Maddox to R. K. David, October 11, 1982

Dear Mr. David,

Pursuant to our telephone conversation of October 7, I am writing a formal complaint against Mr. J. Keegstra, teacher at Eckville Jr.–Sr. High School, specifically with reference to his teaching of Science and Social Studies 9. My son, Paul Maddox, is a student in these classes and it is his reports, both verbal and written, which form the basis of my complaints which I will outline for you.

During the initial days of the current school year, Mr. Keegstra spent most of the time in Science class presenting Creation and Evolution. This is in what I understand to be a physical science class. Apparently Creation was given a short hearing and Evolution a long one with the theme being strongly pro-Creation and very anti-Evolution with the message coming across loud and clear that anyone who believes in Evolution is a Communist. Firstly, I feel nothing contradictory in believing in both Creation/Evolution; secondly, I see nothing in believing in the adaptation of species to their environment as either heresy or Communism; thirdly, these two subjects are out of context in a physical science course. According to my son, Mr. Keegstra has been teaching subject matter with frequent outbursts of political and religious fervor including a lengthy dissertation against the metric system—"a communist conspiracy," he states.

Social Studies is a continual presentation of bigotry and prejudice. Attached to this letter you will find a photocopy of Paul's notebook including dictated and blackboard notes from the beginning of term up to and including October 8. The numbers in red at the top of each page are mine, and following each point of complaint I will place in brackets the number of the page on which you will find the reference.

In the process of studying English history from circa 1500–1700 the students have been told that Oliver Cromwell was a "good man because he was a staunch protestant" but they have not been told that Cromwell, indeed a dictator, slaughtered and maimed thousands of Irish, Scots and English, in the name of God. I do not appreciate my son being convinced to admire a historical figure of that character. I find it interesting that all comments on the Puritans are positive and those on the monarchy and Roman Catholics are very negative. There is no inclusion of beneficial reforms contributed by parliament during the reign of the monarchs. The notes are all slanted in the point of view of the Puritans as if they were the focal point of history and all events revolved around them. (5, 6, 7, 8, 9)

He has also been taught that the origins of slavery are founded in the establishment of the Bank of England and that all bankers are crooks because they create credit for interest which is usury which in turn is immoral. Therefore, he says, people who invest money for interest are thieves. (10 & bottom 13) Mr. Keegstra is misusing the word "usury" because it is defined in the Concise Oxford Dictionary as meaning "the practice of lending money at exorbitant interest especially at higher interest than is allowed by law." It is my understanding that our chartered banks operate well within the law. This teacher has also told the students that all judges are corrupt and judges are lawyers who couldn't make the grade as lawyers (verbal report).

Another objectionable feature of Mr. Keegstra's teach-ings are the repeated derogatory remarks against Jews. He first mentions them as backers of the Society of Masons which he says became the conspiracy overthrowing Richard Cromwell in 1660. (8) He then teaches that the Jews returned in 1664 as if the event was of major historical im-portance immediately preceding calamitous events caused by the wrath of God as vengeance for ill treatment of the Puritans. (9) The climax of all this anti-Semitism is a fanatical tirade found on pages 13–15 of the notes. I will not paraphrase this lengthy annotation but instead implore you to read this yourself. I ask, why is valuable class time being wasted on an insignificant individual, Adam Weishaupt, whose background is very obscure?

I would like to conclude this letter by summarizing my objections. By reading Paul's notes I have deduced that Mr. Keegstra has presented the historical facts that support his slanted views and has failed to present many facts of history. What he has omitted are not only interesting but also essential to our understanding of Britain, her parliamentary system on which our own is based and on the impact of British history on the shaping of the modern world. This is further emphasized by Paul telling me that their course began with A.D. 1500 because that is when Reformed (Puritan) belief began. Therefore he has performed errors of omission as well as commision. I fear my son will not have adequate Social Studies background for post-secon-dary courses.

We have always taught our children to accept people regardless of race, color or creed and to judge each on his individual merits. Therefore I find Mr. Keegstra's racial and religious bigotry and prejudice intolerable.

His radical opposition to judges, lawyers and banks, et cetera is an undermining of the institutions we value as contributing to an orderly society.

Of all the notes on this course I feel that 90 percent is indoctrination and 10 percent facts. As our children are being sent to school for education, not indoctrination, I appeal to you to dismiss Mr. Keegstra from teaching classes in which our children will be enrolled.

Thanking you for your consideration, I am
Yours respectfully,

Susan Maddox

Document 7: R. K. David to James Keegstra, October 21, 1982

Dear Mr. Keegstra,

The Board of Education will be considering the possible termination of your contract of employment as a teacher with the County of Lacombe at its meeting on November 22, 1982. The reasons for this consideration are as follows:

> 1) Your failure to comply with Alberta Education's prescribed curriculum and, in particular, the social studies curriculum.
> 2) Your failure to modify sufficiently your teaching content and/or approach to reflect the desires of members of the local community and the Board of Education, as communicated to you by the Superintendent of Schools.
> 3) Your refusal to comply with the directives of the Board of Education as found in my letter of March 9, 1982.

If you wish an opportunity to be heard by the Board of Education before a decision is made, you are invited to attend the meeting at 1:00 p.m. on November 22nd in the Board of Education Chambers at the County Office. You may be represented by legal council, the ATA or other as you so wish. If you wish to bring persons in addition to council to make representations on your behalf, feel free to do so.

Please advise me before November 15th in writing if you will be attending the meeting.

Yours truly,

R. K. David
Superintendent of Schools

Document 8: R. K. David to James Keegstra, December 7, 1982

Dear Mr. Keegstra,

This will confirm your attendance at the Board meeting of December 7, 1982 together with your representative, Dr. A. K. Harrison of the Alberta Teachers' Association. After having heard the representations of those persons who appeared before the Board and after considering same, the Board, by motion, resolved that your contract of employment with the County of Lacombe No. 14 Board of Education be terminated in accordance with the provisions of the School Act, 1980.

Accordingly, I have been directed to advise you that your contract of employment with the County of Lacombe No. 14 Board of Education is terminated effective thirty (30) days from the date of receipt by you of this notice of termination. Further, the reasons upon which the County of Lacombe No. 14 Board of Education based its decision to terminate your contract of employment are as follows:

1) Your failure to comply with Alberta Education's prescribed curriculum and, in particular, the social studies curriculum.

2) Your failure to modify sufficiently your teaching content and/or approach to reflect the desires of members of the local community and the Board of Education, as communicated to you by the Superintendent of Schools.

3) Your refusal to comply with the directives of the Board of Education as found in my letter of March 9, 1982.

Further, this will advise that in accordance with the provisions of the School Act, 1980, you are hereby suspended forthwith from your duties as a teacher until the effective date of this notice of termination.

As you are aware, the provisions of the School Act, 1980, provide that you may, within fourteen (14) days of receipt of this notice of termination, appeal the decision to terminate your contract of employment to the Minister of Education. The relevant provisions of the School Act, 1980 (Section 95 to 99 inclusive) are included for your reference.

Yours truly,

R. K. David
Superintendent of Schools

Document 9: Alberta Teachers' Association, April 20, 1983

News Release: ATA Comments on Keegstra Case

President Arthur Cowley of The Alberta Teachers' Association today issued the following statement with respect to the Keegstra case.

Last December, the County of Lacombe Board of Education terminated James Keegstra's employment as a teacher in Eckville. The board alleged Keegstra had not adhered to the prescribed curriculum and had introduced objectionable material.

Under the laws of Alberta, a teacher whose employment is terminated in this manner has the right to appeal to a Board of Reference. Currently, a Board of Reference is a one-person board, drawn from a panel of judges. For the last forty years, The Alberta Teachers' Association has provided legal assistance to teachers in Board of Reference cases. This ensures that all teachers have access to the due process of law.

When such a case arises the Association does not hold a hearing of its own; in fact, it is not legally entitled to do so. The Association's legal services are withheld only when the teacher's conduct has previously been the subject of an

Association investigation that has proven grounds for non-support. In short, the teacher has a right to the "day in court" and the Association has an obligation to ensure that legal services are available so that the teacher's right is not abridged by lack of adequate defence.

In the case of Keegstra, all of this proceeded as it should. The Board of Reference has upheld the termination and the Association is satisfied that due process has been observed.

This does not mean that the Association condones or would defend the teaching content which, as alleged, Mr. Keegstra taught. In fact, the Association has taken a public stand against both racism and stereotyping, and advocates the teaching of mutual respect among groups. To this end, the Association has prepared material to assist teachers in eliminating or countering such aspects in text and resource materials and eliminating them from formal and informal class discussion.

The Association has not been granted the legal authority to judge teacher competence. It does, however, have the authority to judge ethical behavior of its members. This process begins when a complaint is registered in proper form with the Association's executive secretary. Any teacher may request an investigation and any person may lay a charge. Investigation by an Association representative follows and if sufficient grounds are revealed a hearing by the Association's Discipline Committee is held. If this quasi-judicial procedure results in a verdict of guilty, a penalty is imposed. Penalties range from a reprimand to expulsion from ATA membership and/or cancellation of the teacher's certificate by the Minister of Education. An appeal from such decisions may be made to the Teaching Profession Appeal Board. Once the discipline process has been properly initiated, the Association is unable to engage in public discussion of the case.

The Association is not permitted authority in teacher certification, teacher competence and professional practice. Government has persistently refused to accept the Association's offer to assume full responsibility in these matters.

Document 10: Herb Katz to Arthur Cowley, April 26, 1983

Dear Sir:

Thank you for meeting me and Mr. H. Boroditsky, Executive Director of the Edmonton Jewish Federation, at your office on April 22, 1983. Further to our discussion and following upon your suggestion, allow me to summarize our views and formally put forward some matters for the consideration of your Provincial Executive Council.

The Edmonton Jewish Federation and its Community Relations Council are deeply concerned about a number of recent events which have occurred in Alberta. We refer to the discovery of an Eckville Junior-Senior High School Social Studies teacher, Mr. James Keegstra, having taught a hateful and distorted view of history over a number of years; to the realization, during the course of Mr. Keegstra's Review Appeal Board hearing, that his efforts were supported by a well entrenched network engaged in the distribution of literature, the purpose of which is to incite hatred against the Jewish people, and; the statements of a government side member of the legislative assembly of this province, calling into public question the historical veracity of the Holocaust in such a manner as to impugn the character of the Jewish people.

It is our view that these events, although separate, are cut from the same cloth: we see them as echoing an earlier day in the history of Alberta, when unfounded social and political theories of a racist nature were openly expounded and supported by government and other responsible institutions of our society. We do not believe that the maintenance of a sane and a tolerant society must fall only on the shoulders of the victims of derision or upon an outraged news media. Based upon the overwhelming expression of support which the Edmonton Jewish Federation has received from both Jewish and non-Jewish citizens of Alberta and from all parts of Alberta, we conclude that a large number of Albertans are deeply concerned about maintaining and even enhancing the delicate fabric of tolerance without which few would care to visualize existence.

We believe that among the institutions of Alberta society, its education establishment, and foremost in it, the Alberta Teachers Association has not only a responsibility but also an outstanding opportunity and a great ability to lead Alberta in publicly addressing these recent and distressing manifestations of intolerance and by its actions and its example, in correcting them.

The Jewish Federation of Edmonton proposes to the Provincial Council of the Alberta Teachers' Association that the ATA Council address itself to the specifics of ways in which and programmes through which the ATA might actively support the spread of racial and religious tolerance in Alberta. These might include the preparation and conducting of in-service teacher programmes on the Holocaust and Judaism as well as racism in general or, work in conjunction with the curriculum development department on Holocaust and Jewish religious material for our students."

We are aware of the ATA's insistence on "due process." We respect this concept. We hasten to point out however that "due process" is a concept in law and does not necessarily find succor in the idea of justice. Where the concept of "due process" meets with justice is in our view in the idea of "the spirit of the law." In this regard, we believe that the active involvement in combatting anti-Semitism through programmes, would lend publicly to the ATA a sense of following "the spirit of the law" which has hitherto been absent, in spite of what we know is your revulsion at the teachings of Mr. Keegstra.

On this issue we should also like to express our concern about the public statements of Mr. Keith Harrison in his capacity as an officer of the ATA. These statements left the clear public impression that Mr. Harrison and the ATA had little if any difficulty supporting Mr. Keegstra's activities in the classroom. It is our impression that these statements are not only disturbing in themselves but also do not fairly represent the position of the ATA. We would like to know if upon deliberation, you support Mr. Harrison's remarks and if not, what action or statement you might envision making to correct it.

Thanking you for your attention in this matter and looking forward to your reply, we remain,

Yours truly
Jewish Community Relations Council

Herb Katz
Chairman

Document 11: A Sample Student Essay, 1981

Judaism and Its Role in Society from 1776-1918*

Judaism is a religious cult that claims to trace its origin to Abraham. But most Jews in the world today are strictly Jews by religion. This mixture makes the Jews very dangerous. The Jew today follows the writings of the Talmud. The Talmud is a set of ancient rules set down by many of the scribes and pharisees from before Christ's era. This Talmud teaches the Jews to hate Christians. They call Christians Goyim (dog) and say that the Christians are cursed. But Christ said that the Jew was a curse and would be a curse to all nations they were allowed into.

The Jews believe that by the year 2000 they will control the world. They are going to do this through welfare states and bloody revolutions. They want to set up their "New World Order" with the Headquarters in Israel. Israel must be the head because this is the only way they can fool the Christians into believing that they are the chosen race.

The Jews are the controlling heads behind all communist and socialist governments in the world today. They either have direct involvement in the policy making or they support the government with money. They are planning to get all governments grouped together into one world

---

*Jim Keegstra gave this essay, by one of his students, to R. K. David when they met on December 18, 1981. In the following transcription, the errors appearing in the text have been retained.

dictatorship. They are doing this today through groups like the United Nations, NATO, and the WARSAW pact. These groups are so large that they are easily infiltrated and controlled by the Jews.

The first large Jewish controlled organization was the Weishouption "Illuminate". It was formed on May 1st 1776. It was a direct plan for the destruction of Christianity and the setting up of a one world government. His plan contained five specific points:

1. Destroy All Monarchies and Legitimate Government
• Monarchies cannot be infiltrated and poisoned by Jews.
• A Legitimate Government cannot be tricked into doing revolutionary things.
• This would also keep the people confused.

2. Destroy All Religions, Especially Christianity
• Religion makes people moral, so they can therefore tell right from wrong.
• Christian people do not worship false Gods and natural goods, therfore, they will not worship the Jews.

3. Abolish Marriage and Have Children Raised by the State
• Marriage makes men and women responsible.
• State raised children will be taught that the state is supreme.

4. Abolish Private Property (land) and All Inheritances
• Private Property gives man a little piece of power. This power keeps them free.
• An inheritance makes a child receive some of the things his father worked for. This creates respect between son and father.

5. Abolish All Loyalty and Allegiances to God, King, and Country
   • Everything will have to be in writing because a man's word will mean nothing.
   • People will no longer fight for freedom because their country will mean nothing to them.

The Illuminate used the five pointed Red Star as a symbol. Wieshoupt used deception to gain followers in his group. Weishoupt found that the clergy and the intellectuals were the easiest to dupe. He had more trouble convincing the middle class business men and farmers. These men were levelheaded and could see through the lies of the illuminate. Weishoupt did find that when telling a lie don't tell a small lie, it will be picked up, tell a whopper. The people will think it so outrageous that they will think it will never become possible.

The first revolution to start the takeover of the world to One World Government by the Jews was the French Revolution. The Jews were the organizers of warehousing. They would store and distribute the food in France. In the spring of 1789 they held back the food and created a period of extreme starvation in France. This, however, did not readily break the loyalty of the French people toward their King. Finally the Jews sent in small groups of anarchists and rebelists to incite some riots. This worked well and in July of 1789 the French Revolution began. The German Jews Weishaupt and Clootz were the organizers of the revolution. They had many lackies like Robespiere to carry out the Reign of Terror which lasted from August 1789 until July 1793.

The first people killed during the Reign of Terror were the small business men and farmers. They would butcher the farmer, kill all the working animals and burn the crops. This created more problems in France. Food was really scarce and trust was non-existant. The French people started to become immoral and steal from one another. Lords and police officials were taken completely by surprise when the barbarionism hit Paris. The Jewish anarchists would lead the people in attacking and killing the Lords. The anarchists set up the Guillotine and would kill anyone who disagreed with them. Things in France were in total chaos.

Near the end of the "Reign of Terror", Napoleon came onto the scene. Napoleon was a very good orator and socialist. He would tell the people in very enthusiastic speeches about how they were going to destroy the autocratic monarchy for the people. Then when Napoleon finally took over he set up a dictatorship of his own. Napoleon started many of the steps toward a New World Order. He put into effect his new International Metric System of Weights and Measures. Napoleon also started a French National Bank in 1802. This bank was completely controlled and organized by the German Jew company under Loaw Rothschild. Napoleon brought France much debt when he borrowed from these banks for his wars. Napoleon also codified the law and called it the "French Civil Code". This code was based on many of the laws in the Jewish Talmud. Napoleon was finally wiped out in 1815 at the Battle of Nations at Liepzig.

The next fight for the advancement of Judaism was the American Civil War in 1860-1864. It started over who was going to control trade and commerce in the United States. The South was already under the control of the Jews. Meanwhile the North still had full control of its money. The anarchists and rebelists in the United States at the time had to get the people incited to fight. They brought up two strong arguments to get the peoples' emotion going. The first one was that the slaves would have to be freed. The second argument was over having a strong central government or having a confederacy of many small governments.

When the war had started, Lincoln needed money to manufacture guns, ammunition, and pay soldiers. He went to the Bank for the money and the Jews were going to charge him 10-15˙ on the money he borrowed. He decided that this was not right and the government would make its own money. He came up with the Union Greenback. This war created great debt in the South but did not financially bother the North. The Jews had supplies brought from France to the South but they did not arrive quick enough or in enough number to help. Lincoln won the war and took over the South.

Lincoln observed the destruction that had happened in the South during the war. He decided to rebuild the south using the government's money, the same way he had during the war. The Jews did not like this because it would create no debt. In 1865 the Jews hired an actor named John Wilkes Booth to assasinate Lincoln. When Lincoln was dead the Jews wanted to destroy the South. They had roving bands of thugs move into the South and they destroyed many of the great plantations, bridges, railroads, and towns. The people were put into great debt paying war reparations. The Jews still did not have control of the treasury however.

Germany was another country that was put through the treachery of the Jews. In 1860 William I of Germany became King. He was a power hungry King and started to raise a large army. The larger his army became, the more disobedient he became toward parliament. In 1863 William appointed a German Prime Minister. This man was a German named Auto Von Bismarck, a great believer in Realpolitik. Realpolitik is the belief that the end justifies the means. He used this way of doing things many times. Bismarck had an alter-ego, this man was the Jew, Lasalle. Lasalle controlled Bismarck's every move. Before making any decision Bismarck would consult with Lasalle. Bismarck was a very devout anti-christian. He wanted to destroy all christianity and unionize all the German states. This was a start of Planned Wars.

When Bismarck went into a war he wanted the other country to start it. The first war was against Denmark. In 1864, through the use of shrewd diplomacy, Bismarck got Denmark to start the war. He then moved his army in and promptly crushed Denmark. Bismarck picked up the areas of Schlezwig-Holstein. He then went to work on Austria. He used the same methods with Austria. Austria attacked Germany in 1865 but Bismarck's army quickly moved over the Austrians and picked up some parts of Austria that were "mostly German".

There was one more country that Bismarck wanted to get some land from. This country was France, and Bismarck wanted the rich, industrial area of Alsace-Larraine. William of Germany sent a letter to the King of France protesting what was going on in France at this time. The King of France replied saying that France would like to solve this problem without having to fight. Bismarck intercepted this letter before it was delivered to King William. He wanted to find out what this was about. After he read it he had it delivered to the king. William then replied very nicely to France but Bismarck also intercepted this letter and changed it to sound very abusive. Napoleon therefore declared war on Germany and the France-Prussian war of 1868 was on. Bismarck moved his great German War Machine into France and in the Palace of Mirrors in Versaille the New German Empire was formed. After this Bismarck demanded very cruel reparations from the French. He took Alsace-Larraine but could not get any of the French farmland because the French farmers were too land oriented and would not give it up. By hard work and dedication the French farmers and small businessmen paid off the debt to Germany in a mere three years.

Bismarck formed the triple Alliance with Italy and Austria-Hungary in 1882. He also brought socialism into Germany with the excuse that he must "fight fire with fire". In 1888 William I died. He was succeeded by William II. Bismarck and William II did not get along too well. William finally got rid of Bismarck and took over on his own. After a while William II got used to listening to his German Jewish advisors. They kept telling William that the Germans were the chosen people and the superior race. They told him to build up the War Machine to take over and unite all the Germans. William started to do so. This building of German's power was one of the main causes of World War I.

One of the places that the Jews had a stronghold in the 18th century was in Russia. Catherine the Great started to let Intellectuals into Russia who promoted anarchy, rebelism and chaos in Russia. They found their least success in the Klazzar Jews. These people were very rebelous and easy to incite into riots. Catherine thought of herself as an intellectual and started the destruction of the Monarchy and the Roots of the New World Order. Catherine did, however, lighten the clamps of the Feudal System and started to give the serfs much more freedom.

Alexander I took over after Catherine and continued the freeing of the Serfs. He ran into complete opposition from the nobels. The nobels started to back the Jewish Intellectuals. This started the split between the Russian Czars and their Worlds. When the French attacked Russia in the Neopoleonic Wars the Jews tried to break down Russia but the serfs were too loyal to the King. Russia beat back the French with the help of the worst winter on record.

In 1825 Constantine refused the throne, therefore Czar Nicholas I took over. The Jewish intellectuals started the story that Constantine was going to give a constitution and Nicholas I had siezed cover from Constantine because of this. The story was false but the Jews were able to incite a small revolution. After this was put down, Nicholas started to travel in England and Holland. There he saw much progress and freedom. Nicholas came home and started many good reforms. The Jewish mob did not want this. They knew that if the people were going to revolt they would have to have something to revolt about. The Jews therefore prevented these reforms by way of assassinations. One of Nicholas' men would get a reform all ready to go through and then he would be assassinated. In one year alone, the Bolshevek Jews assassinated about 625 of Nicholas best men. Nicholas finally got fed up and became "Reactionary". He formed a Secret Police to shut down all secret societies. He formed some of the first concentration camps for political prisoners. He got rid of many Russian Jews. Nicholas was severely smeared by the western press. Nicholas was one of the first people to be called Antisemetic. At this time Jewish sympathizers put out a book that told of autocratics of Christians against Jews.

In 1851 Engles and Marx got the Crimenn War started between Russia and Britain. They did so by using discrete control of the news media. The news that went around in Russia was that the Jews were chasing out the Moslems in Palestine. Russia became prepared to go straighten the Jews out. Then the British media was told the story that Russia was heading for Palestine to take it over. Palestine was still a British Colony at this time so Britain would not let them enter. This was the time of the "Charge of the Light Brigade" and Florence Nightengale. The war lasted until 1856 and thousands of men were killed. Before the war was over Nicholas I died and Alexander II took over in 1855. Alexander II started many of Nicholas' reforms going after he finished the war.

Alexander was a great believer that Russia could be as free as England and Holland were. He freed the serfs, sold them land, gave them interest free loans, built good schools and industries, and set up local municipal governments. Alexander also wanted to get Russia moving. He built many new roads, bridges, and the world's longest railroad. Alexander also beautified Russia by building many large Russian Orthodox Churches and the Kremlin. Everything was going fine but the evil groups were starting to grow in Russia. Alexander had let the secret polices grip on the Revolutionary Jews slip and now they were starting to assassinate more of Alexander's government officials. Alexander was determined to set up a constitutional monarchy in 1881 but on the day he was going to unveil it, on his way back from a friend's funeral, he was attacked. A group led by a gal named Sofi bombed the Czar's carriage when he was reviewing his guard. The Czar was not injured but many of his soldiers were. Instead of staying in his carriage, he went to aid his men. The attackers threw another bomb and this time killed the Czar.

Alexander III took the throne in 1881. When his father's murderers were caught he had them tried and hung for murder and treason. The western press smeared Alexander for this. Alexander really clamped down on the Jews and drove many of them from Russia. In 1886 Herzl

officially formed Political Zionism which pushed the Jew
being the chosen race and their right to Palestine. This was
later the base of the Bolshevik party.

Alexander III died in 1894 and Nicholas II came to the
throne. Nicholas had a goal, to bring Russia into the 20th
century. To do this he had to relax the hold on the evil
groups. He went by the same plan that Alexander II had.
Russia advanced so far by 1910 that they did not even feel
the depression of 1910-11 in Russia.

In 1903 twenty three of the leading Jews in the world
met in London. They were talking about forming the
Bolshevik party. They all agreed that Russia had to be
brought to her knees. They were going to do this through:
   1. Needless Wars
   2. Riots, strikes, and sabotage
   3. Revolution
   4. Control of Credit and Trade
The first war they started was the Russian-Japanese
war. It was a naval battle between the quick agile ships of
the Japanese and the slow tubs of the Russians. The
Japanese won easily and destroyed the entire Russian Navy.
They also staged a revolution in 1905 but it was put down.
They then started revolutions in the Bulcan countries from
1905-1913. Finally they saw a way to finish Russia in 1914.
They would involve Russia in a world war.

Bosnia was under the control of Austria. Serbia said
that Bosnia should be independent and if anyone should
control Bosnia it should be Serbia. Russia put its support
behind Serbia while Germany put its support behind
Austria. This created a very heated situation. To set the
whole thing rolling all the Jews had to do was send in a
Bolshevik Jew to assassinate Prince Ferdinand of Austria
while he was in Bosnia. Austria heard the assassin was a
Bosnian-Serb and sent an ultimatum to Serbia telling them
to do certain things. When Serbia undertook to meet all
except two, on which requested arbitration, Austria treated
her reply as a refusal and declared war on July 28th, 1914.
Germany declared war on Russia on August 1 in support of
Austria. France declared war on August 3 against Germany.

Germany was now in a tight spot, they were heading into a war on two fronts. They decided that they could beat France fairly quick so they went into France first. Germany however, made a mistake and went through Belgium on their way to France. All of a sudden a secret pact between England and Belgium shows up and Britian joins the war against Germany. Germany is now fighting three of Europe's greatest powers.

With the help of England and the rest of the Commonwealth countries, the Germans could not take France as fast as they had wanted to. However, because of Jewish Bolshevik work in Russia the Russian army was not as strong as it should have been. The Russian supplies would be misshipped, usually to Germany. The Russians had to fight without food and ammunition against Germans with new machine guns. The Bolsheviks also sabotaged factories, railways, and destroyed food supplies in Russia. Early in 1917 the Czar went to the front lines to see what was going on. When he got there he saw the shape his army was in and started to ask questions. The bolsheviks told the Czar that the only way that they would allow supplies through was if the Czar would resign. He did so on March 15, 1917, and the Duma set up a provisional government under Prince George Lvor. Lvor wanted to have the men retreat, rest, and regroup, but the others in the provisional government would not let the army do this. Lvor resigned and Kerenski took over. He called back all the Bolshevik Jews that were exiled in other countries. This is when Lenin and Trotskey came on the scene. Lenin came from Germany in a sealed boxcar with $5 million in gold. Trotskey came from New York by boat. They took over the Bolshevik party and on November 7, 1917, took over Russia.

The Bolshevik Jews and the German Jews signed a peace treaty which took Russia out of the War. Before the war the United States under Woody Wilson had passed the Federal Reserve Act. The Jews now had to move the control of the money from London to New York. They also wanted to secure themselves a homeland. They found that

Germany was very unsympathetic to the Jew but England, on the other hand, would fall for their story. So Rothschild and Weismann took a trip to England. They told Prime Minister Belfort that if England wanted any help from the United States they would have to agree to certain things. These things made up the Belfort Declaration:

1. Palestine would be given to the Jews.
2. Center of Finance would be moved from London to New York.
3. All Scripture would be removed from Parliament and schools.

Belfort agreed. The United States came into the war in the summer of 1917. On November 2, 1917, Belfort delivered his report to Parliament. Now the Jews decided to turn the tide on Germany. Things deteriorated quickly for Germany in the war. The Czar of Germany wanted to sue for peace as early as July, 1918, but peace did not come until October, 1918. Finally on November 11, 1918, the Armistice was signed. The Jews wrote up the treaty of Versaille which was the main document of the Peace Agreement.

As you can see the Jews are truly a formidable sect. They work through deception and false tales to achieve their ends. They are very powerful and must be put in their place.

Notes

List of Abbreviations

AR	*Alberta Report* (Edmonton)
CH	*Calgary Herald*
CJC	Canadian Jewish Congress (Toronto)
CJN	*Canadian Jewish News* (Toronto edition)
CJS	Calgary edition, *The Jewish Star*
CP	Canadian Press news service
CS	*Calgary Sun*
EE	*Eckville Examiner*
EJ	*Edmonton Journal*
EJS	Edmonton edition, *The Jewish Star*
ES	Edmonton Sun
GM	*Globe & Mail*, national edition
JFE	Jewish Federation of Edmonton files
JWB	*Jewish Western Bulletin*, Vancouver
LG	*Lacombe Globe*
RDA	*Red Deer Advocate*
RKD	Robert K. David file, Lacombe
VS	*Vancouver Sun*

All dates are given in the form of month, day, and year ("12/10/82" stands for December 10, 1982).

Preface

1 Lueger's statement, and the reference to the Jew as "an evil principle," are from George L. Mosse, *Toward the Final Solution: A History of European Racism* (Madison, Wisconsin: University of Wisconsin Press, 1985), pp. 113, 142

Chapter 1: The World of Jim Keegstra

1 Unofficial transcript, CBC's *The Journal,* May 2, 1983
2 *Homesteads and Happiness* (Eckville Historical Society, 1979), pp. 13-20; "Alberta Locations: Town of Eckville" (Government of Alberta Publications, June 1984)
3 Statistics Canada, 1981 Census Returns
4 CS 05/22/83
5 CH 10/29/83
6 Howard Palmer, *Land of the Second Chance* (Lethbridge, Alberta: Lethbridge Herald, 1972), pp. 14-25
7 R. M. Lee, "Keegstra's Children," *Saturday Night,* May 1985
8 C. B. MacPherson, *Democracy in Alberta* (Toronto: University of Toronto Press, 1953), pp. 93-141
9 Myrna Kostash, "Eckville, Alta. The Agony of a Small Town," *Chatelaine,* Feb. 1984

10 CH 06/03/83
11 Ibid
12 RDA 04/06/83
13 Ibid, 04/02/83
14 Justinus Bonaventura Pranaitis, *The Talmud Unmasked: The Secret Rabbinical Teachings Concerning Christians* (Reedy, West Virginia: Liberty Bell Publications, n.d.)
15 *Extremism on the Right: A Handbook* (New York: Anti-Defamation League of B'nai B'rith, 1983), pp. 69-70
16 Ibid, pp. 61-4
17 E. Dilling, *The Jewish Religion: Its Influence Today* (Torrance, California: Noontide Press, 4th ed., revised, 1983)
18 Mosse, *Toward the Final Solution*, pp. 138-40, Cohn, *Warrant for Genocide*, pp. 55-6, and especially Joel E. Rembaum, "Medieval Christianity Confronts Talmudic Judaism," *Judaism* (New York), vol. 34 (Summer 1985), pp. 373-384
19 RDA 04/06/85; AR 05/30/83; CH 06/03/83; EE 12/14/82; on premillennialism, see Ernest R. Sandeen, *The Roots of Fundamentalism: British and American Millennarianism, 1800-1930* (Chicago: University of Chicago Press, 1970), pp. 12-13, 20-2, 164, and RDA 04/02/83
20 CS 05/08/83
21 RDA 08/22/84
22 RDA 04/06/85
23 EE 10/83

8 ES 05/19/83
9 AR 05/30/83
10 CH 06/03/83; 08/26/84
11 Lee, "Keegstra's Children," as cited
12 RDA 08/22/84
13 C. H. Douglas, *The Big Idea* (Liverpool, England: K.R.P. Publications, Ltd., n.d.)
14 H. Palmer, *Patterns of Prejudice* (Toronto: McClelland & Stewart, 1982), pp. 154-8
15 Alberta Social Credit Board, Annual Report, p. 32
16 John J. Barr, *The Dynasty* (Toronto: McClelland & Stewart, 1974), pp. 127-30
17 H. Palmer, "The Keegstra Affair in Historical Perspective," *Humanities Association of Canada, Newsletter*, Spring 1984
18 B'nai B'rith League for Human Rights, "Ron Gostick, Social Credit Movement and Canadian Intelligence Service"
19 Ibid. Gostick's own version of the history of the Canadian League of Rights can be found in the *Canadian Intelligence Service*, vol. 31, no. 9 (Sept. 1981)
20 *Enterprise*, no. 17 (March 1983)
21 Mark Silverberg, "Memorandum: The Canadian League of Rights" (CJC, Vancouver)
22 CH 06/03/83
23 EJ 04/17/83
24 *Canadian Intelligence Service*, vol. 33, no. 7 (July 1983)

Chapter 2: The Roots of Anti-Semitism

1 See the two brilliant works by Norman Cohn, *Warrant for Genocide* (London: Eyre & Spottiswoode, 1967), pp. 21ff, and *The Pursuit of the Millennium* (New York: Harper & Row, 2nd ed., 1961), chapter 1
2 Cohn, *Warrant for Genocide*
3 Ibid
4 Ibid
5 CBC's *The Journal*, May 2, 1983
6 CH 04/16/83
7 EE 12/14/82, p. 1 and 01/25/83, p. 1

Chapter 3: Keegstra and the Classroom

1 Keegstra's views on this can be found in the notebooks of his students; testimony at the Red Deer trial, May 29, 1985; Board of Reference Hearing, vol. 1, pp. 89, 136; and CH 06/05/85
2 EJ 03/07/83
3 *Responding to Change: A Handbook for Teachers of Secondary Social Studies* (Edmonton, 1975), p. 5
4 *1981 Alberta Social Studies Curriculum*

5 Board of Reference hearing, vol. 1, pp. 113-7
6 Ibid, vol. 2, p. 161
7 EE 04/05/83
8 Board of Reference hearing, vol. 2, pp. 166-7, 162-3, 174-5
9 CH 06/06/85; Board of Reference hearing, vol. 2, pp. 152-3
10 CH 05/25/83
11 AR 05/02/83
12 Board of Reference hearing, vol. 1, pp. 119-22, 127-30, 134, 148-9
13 George Johnson, *Architects of Fear* (Los Angeles: Jeremy P. Tarcher, Inc., 1983), esp. pp. 12-13, 15, 24-5
14 Board of Reference hearing, vol. 2, pp. 89-90; CH 05/30/85
15 Board of Reference hearing, vol. 2, p. 63
16 CH 06/01/85
17 Board of Reference hearing, vol. 2, pp. 113-5
18 See Keegstra's testimony at the Board of Reference hearing (vol. 2), and CH 06/05/85, 06/08/85
19 CH 05/29/85
20 AR 06/25/84; CH 06/12/84; CH 06/06/84
21 "Judaism and its Role in Society from 1776-1918" (RKD)
22 ES 06/07/84
23 CH 06/09/84

Chapter 4: The Alberta School System

1 Board of Reference hearing, vol. 2, pp. 177-9
2 Ibid, vol. 1, p. 228
3 CH 05/25/85
4 RDA 05/24/85
5 CH 05/25/85
6 CBC, *The Journal*, May 2, 1983
7 Interview with A. Carritt, 03/03/85
8 AR 05/02/83
9 CH 05/24/85
10 RDA 05/24/85
11 Ibid
12 EE 12/21/82
13 Interview with Marg Andrew, 01/27/85
14 AR 05/02/83

15 Interview with Gerald Wilson, Director of the Calgary Regional Office, Alberta Department of Education, 04/04/85
16 Interview with Bob David, 02/11/85
17 *ATA Manual*, p. 150
18 RDA (clipping from M. Andrew)
19 AR 05/14/84
20 Board of Reference hearing, vol. 1, p. 244
21 AR 07/11/83
22 Interview with Gerald Wilson, as cited
23 A. K. Harrison, "Procedures and Reasons for Termination of Teacher Contracts in Canada," pp. 47ff
24 CH 11/19/83

Chapter 5: Dismissal

1 Interview with Bob David, 02/11/85
2 Ibid; Board of Reference hearing, vol. 1, pp. 5-7
3 Interview with Bob David, 02/11/85; Board of Reference hearing, vol. 1, pp. 7-20
4 R. K. David to J. Keegstra, 11/18/81 (RKD)
5 Interview with Bob David, 02/11/85
6 Interviews with Bob David, 02/11/85, and Sandra Weidner, 04/11/85; Board of Reference hearing, vol. 1, pp. 21-2
7 R. K. David to J. Keegstra, 01/14/82 (RKD)
8 J. Keegstra to R. K. David, 01/25/82 (RKD)
9 Interview with A. K. Harrison, 03/27/85
10 Ibid
11 Interview with Bob David, 02/11/85
12 R. K. David to J. Keegstra, 03/09/82 (RKD)
13 J. Keegstra to R. K. David, 03/18/82 (RKD)
14 R. K. David to J. Keegstra, 04/07/82 (RKD)
15 Interview with M. Andrew, 01/27/85; Board of Reference hearing, vol. 1, pp. 223-5

16 Petition (undated; M. Andrew collection)

17 Teacher Visitation Report, 05/17/82 (RKD)

18 M. Andrew to D. King, 06/11/82 (M. Andrew collection)

19 M. Derieu to M. Andrew, 06/18/82 (M. Andrew collection)

20 D. King to M. Andrew, 10/12/82 (RKD)

21 S. Maddox to R. K. David, 10/11/82 (RKD)

22 Ibid supra, 10/19/82 (RKD)

23 R. K. David of F. Crowther, 10/21/82 (RKD)

24 R. K. David to J. Keegstra, 10/21/82 (RKD)

25 Teacher Visitation Report, 10/28/82 (RKD)

26 Interview with A. K. Harrison, 03/27/85

27 A. K. Harrison to R. K. David, 11/12/82 (RKD)

28 F. Crowther to R. K. David, 12/03/82 (RKD)

29 Board of Reference hearing, vol. 1, pp. 276-283

30 RDA 04/16/83

31 CH 12/08/82

32 Ernest Hodgson, "The Keegstra Mess: An Administrative Report Card," *Canadian School Executive*, March 1984, pp. 15-17

Chapter 6: The ATA's Dilemma

1 EJ 04/17/83

2 Interview with A. K. Harrison, as cited

3 Board of Reference, vol. 2, p. 301

4 "Reasons for Decision of the Board of Reference," 04/14/83

5 RDA 04/15/83

6 Alberta Teachers' Association, News Release, 04/20/84

7 Interview with A. K. Harrison, as cited

8 Ibid

9 EJ 04/24/83

10 Unofficial transcript, CBC, *The Journal*, 05/02/83

11 CH 05/17/83

12 EJ 04/26/83

13 Alberta Hansard, 04/18/83

14 EJ 04/19/83

15 RDA 10/12/83; EJ 11/16/83

16 CH 10/12/83

17 EJ 02/03/84

Chapter 7: Early Warnings, Cautious Responses

1 Interview with Ross Henderson, 02/07/85; telephone interview with George Lee, 08/14/85

2 Telephone interview with Bob Warwick, 07/01/85

3 B. Warwick, CH 12/08/82, B12, and also Jim Isbister, RDA, 12/08/82. p. 1; R. Henderson, EE, 12/14/82, p. 1; G. Lee, LG, 12/15/82, p. 1; EJ 12/09/82 and GM 12/10/82 carried CP reports

4 The information about the Lacombe informant is based on interviews with that person, the School Board member and with Harry Shatz (01/30/85)

5 Interviews with F. Schwartz (04/08/85), G. Cohos (01/22/85), H. Shatz (01/30/85)

6 "Canadian Jewish Congress" (pamphlet, no author, n.d. [but 1981]), p. 5; see editorials in CJS: "How to Win the West," 01/23/81, p. 4 and "The Cotler Era," 05/27/83, p. 4; Harvey Rich, "The Calgary Jewish Community" (undated draft copy, subsequently published by the Center for Jewish Community Studies, Temple University, Philadelphia, 1974), p. 5

7 The undated memo is in JFE. The first published reports announcing the Board of Reference Hearing in Edmonton were in EE (01/25/83, p. 1) and RDA (01/27/83, p. 2B)

8 B. Kayfetz to H. Boroditsky, 01/18/83; Kayfetz to H. Shatz, same date (both in JFE); interview with Fay Schwartz, 04/08/85. In March, 1982, a suggestion was made from Edmonton to form an Alberta Jewish Council, but it was not until July

1984 that an Alberta Region of the CJC was inaugurated (EJS, 03/82, p. 1; CJS 08/17/84, p. 1).

9 Telephone interview with H. Katz, 04/20/83; telephone conversation with H. Boroditsky, 04/19/85; see CJS 02/25/83, p. 1

10 This section is based on Max Rubin, "Alberta's Jews: The Long Journey" (MS, 1981); H. Rich (as cited above, fn. 8); Harold M. Waller, "Power in the Jewish Community," in *The Canadian Jewish Mosaic*, ed. by M. Weinfeld, W. Shaffir and I. Cotler (Rexdale, Ont.: John Wiley & Sons, 1981), 151-60; "The Jewish Community of Edmonton 'Welcomes' You to Our City" (Edmonton: Jewish Community Council, typescript, [1980]); and on personal knowledge

11 EJS 12/80, p. 1; telephone interview with M. Silverberg, 02/01/85

12 "Pretty disappointed," RDA 05/05/83, p. A2; AR 03/14/83, p. 35; "lunatic fringe," EJ 05/09/83; "it's going to cost them," EJ 05/05/83; Wally Klinck, ES 04/24/83

13 Interview with H. Katz, 12/23/84

14 EJS, 05/82, p. 1; Minutes of the Meeting of the JCRC, 10/14/82; H. Katz, ES 10/10/82, p. 10; EJS 11/82, p. 1; the Edmonton rallies took place on June 10 and August 23 (EJS, 07/82, p. 1 and 09/82, p. 1); interview with H. Katz by Michael Solman, JWB 05/26/83, p. 3

15 Interview with H. Boroditsky, 12/24/84, H. Katz, 04/20/83, 12/23/84. The significance of *None is Too Many* was not lost on others: see EJ 04/30/83; editorial, *Western Catholic Reporter* (Edmonton), 05/02/83, *Alberta Sonshine News* (Edmonton), 06/83, p. 4

Chapter 8: The Stiles Affair

1 Interviews with H. Katz, 04/20/83, 12/23/84

2 Interviews with H. Starkman, 03/11/85, B. Warwick, 07/01/85 and Kevin Peterson, 05/22/85; *Jewish Standard* (Toronto), 04/15/83, p. 4

3 EJ. p. 1, CH, p. A17 (both 04/12/83); RDA, p. 1, EJ, p. A15, ES, p. 11, (all 04/13/83); EJ, CH (both 04/14/83); RDA 04/15/83, p. B2; interviews with H. Katz (as cited); on Lastman, see also CJN (11/10/83, p. 35); RKD to M. Lastman (04/20/83; RKD file); Thorsell: EJ 04/14/83 (and another defence of Lastman, EJ 04/24/83); B. Kayfetz to H. Katz, 04/14/83 (JFE); Confidential Minutes of JCRC, Ontario Region Meeting, 05/04/83, p. 1; "never intended to visit": EJ 04/18/83

4 King: ES 04/19/83, p. 11, EJ 04/20/83, p. B2; Hoeksma: RDA 04/15/83, p. B2; AHRC: EJ, RDA 04/18/83; EE 04/19/83, p. 1; Hattersley: RDA, CH 04/20/83; EE 04/26/83, and see EJ 04/18

5 Transcript of taped interview with Stiles, EJ 04/21/83, p. A10

6 EJ, CH, RDA (all 04/20/83); EJ 04/21/83, pp. A1, 14; Crawford: CH 04/20/83, p. 2, EJ (same date), B1; CH 04/21/83, p. A3 (and EJ, RDA, same date); ES 04/22/83

7 Diamond: RDA 04/21/83; Katz: telephone interview, 04/20/83 (and see ES 04/21/83, p. 3)

8 Interview with H. Katz, 12/23/84; EJ 04/21/83, p. B1

9 EJ 04/21/83; CH 04/21/83, p. A3 and 04/22/83, p. 2

10 *Alberta Hansard*, 04/21/83, pp. 1-3

11 RDA, p. 1; CH, p. 1; George Oake in EJ (all 04/22/83)

12 D. Braid, EJ 04/21/83; for similar views, see Stephen Hume, EJ 04/23/83, p. A6; editorial, ES 04/22/83, p. 10; Geoff White, CH 04/22/83, p. A8; William Gold, CH 04/25/83, p. A8

13 Confidential interview with D. Wertheimer; telephone interview with H. Boroditsky, 04/21/83; Jack Tutty (AHRC Exec. Dir.) to H. Boroditsky, 04/21/83; H. Katz to R. Vivone (Exec. Assist. to Dave King), 04/21/83 (reply, April 26; all letters in JFE)

14 Howard Palmer, "Social Credit and

Anti-Semitism," CJS 04/29/83, p. 5;
interviews with H. Starkman,
03/11/85, H. Katz, 12/23/84, M.
Horowitz, 03/11/85; rough notes by
H. Boroditsky on the April 22 meeting are in JFE

15 Interview with S. Hume, 01/28/85;
the quote is from EJ 04/23/83, p. A6;
for other editorials, see 04/16/83 and
05/07/83; background features: EJ
04/30/83, p. B3; 05/05/83, p. B8; for
commendatory letters, see EJ
05/07/83, 05/12/83; unpublished correspondence, Dr. J. M. Kirman to R.
T. Baker (Pulitzer Prize Administrator), 05/10/83. Hume was ineligible for the award, which is given
only for material published in the
United States (R. C. Christopher to
J. M. Kirman, 05/18/83)

16 CS 05/08/83, p. 12; ES 05/08/83;
Lethbridge Herald 06/07/83, p. A7;
CH 05/07/83, p. 1 (letter to the
editor, Ch 05/25/83, p. B8); for protests to CS: CS 05/12/83, p. 10,
05/13/83, p. 11, CJS 05/13/83, pp. 3,
4; and to *Lethbridge Herald*,
06/17/83, p. A6, see the critique by
Eva Brewster, *Raymond Review*
(Raymond, Alberta), 06/22/83, p. 9,
and correspondence between Hy
Calman and B. Kayfetz, June 29,
July 4, 12 (JFE). For criticisms of the
media's treatment of racism, see Julian Sher, *White Hoods: Canada's Ku
Klux Klan* (Vancouver: New Star
Books, 1983)

17 Keegstra's "theories": McFadyen, EJ
04/19/83; see also Marlene Antonio,
CS · 05/13/83, p. 11 ("historical
theories"), and EE 04/19/83, p. 1
("Jewish conspiracy theory"); excerpts from Norman Cohn's brilliant
book, *Warrant for Genocide*, were
printed in EJS, 04/84, pp. 7-8, CJS
04/13/84, pp. 8-9, and see two columns in CJS 05/27/83, p. 4, 06/10/84,
p. 4; Stiles: EJ 05/05/83, p. B6

18 CBC: Braid in EJ 05/05/83, GM
05/04/83; Smith: CJN 05/12/83; Congress: "Confidential Minutes of the
Meeting of the JCRC, Ontario Region," 05/04/83, p. 2

Chapter 9: A Month of Turmoil

1 Interview with H. Katz, 12/23/84;
the phrase "shaken by passion" was
used by Lionel Fine to describe the
attitude of Jews of Alberta (EJ
05/11/83, p. B5)

2 Interview with K. Peterson,
05/22/85; *Canadian Newspapers:
The Inside Story*, ed. by Walter
Stewart (Edmonton: Hurtig, 1980),
pp. 163, 169

3 Interviews with K. Peterson and S.
Hume, 01/28/85; letter of J. P. O'Callaghan in CJS, 05/13/83, p. 5, personal knowledge

4 Agenda of the "Community Relations Council—Ad Hoc Outreach
Committee," and a list of those who
were called to attend the meeting,
are in JFE; RDA 04/29/83; AHRC:
interview with H. Katz, 12/23/84;
"Statement by Marlene Antonio,"
05/04/83 (JFE); CH, EJ, ES, GM (all
05/05/83)

5 Rough notes by H. Boroditsky,
05/06/83; for names of those in the
Jewish delegation, see CJS 05/13/83,
p. 2

6 The following description of the Jewish delegation's meeting with
Lougheed is based on interviews
with six of the twelve Jewish participants. Lougheed, and some Jewish
delegates, refused to be interviewed

7 Lougheed, Starkman: EJ, CH, RDA
05/10/83

8 Interviews with H. Starkman,
03/11/85, H. Boroditsky, 12/24/84,
H. Katz, 12/23/84; mass rally: the
only media coverage appeared in
EJS, 05/18, p. 1, CJS, 05/13/83, p. 1,
and see the rough notes of the rally
by H. Boroditsky (JFE); "Report to
the Edmonton Jewish Community
on actions undertaken by the Community Relations Council with regard to the Keegstra-Stiles Affair and
recent manifestations of anti-
Semitism in Alberta," by Herb Katz
(typescript, 05/09/83)

9 Katz: EJS 05/83, p. 2; editorials: EJ
05/11/83, *Montreal Gazette* 05/12/83;
Tory dinner: EJ 05/12/83 gives 700
present, ES 05/12/83, p. 14, 850
people

10 Condemnations of Keegstra, bigotry,
and racism were made by the follow-
- ing types of groups: churches: CJS
05/13/83, p. 3; university: W. H.
Worth to Dave King, 05/13/83; public school: CH 05/11/83, and the
advertisement, 05/19/83; Ernest
Manning: EJ 05/12/83, CJS 05/13/83;
ACFA: News Release, 05/12/83, and
Le Franco, Edmonton, 05/18/83, p.
1; AUPE: News Release, 05/12/83;
Edmonton Mayor Cec Purves: EJ
05/13/83, p. B2, ES 05/15/83; Eckville: EJ, CH, RDA 05/12/83; Congress: *Montreal Gazette*, 05/13/83;
Wiesenthal: EJ, CH, RDA 05/12/83;
RDA 05/13/83, p. 1; 15 Social Credit
members had opposed the attempt
to have Keegstra ousted from the
party (RDA, CH, EJ 05/03-05/83),
and Hattersley, their head, attempted to oust Erhart and Green
from the party (ES, CS, CH,
05/04/83; CS 05/08/83; AR 05/16/83).
AR 05/16/83. Those two said they
also denied the reality of the
Holocaust (EJ 05/03/83)

11 Legislature was packed: GM
05/13/83; the text of Lougheed's
statement was reprinted in EJ
05/13/83, EE 05/17/83, and CJN
06/02/83; remarks overdue: RDA,
CH, Ron Collister in EJ (all
05/13/83); comment on Stiles
needed: EJ 05/13/83, quoting Ray
Martin (NDP leader), H. Starkman,
H. Katz; editorial in CJS 05/13/83,
EJS 05/83; lacking emotion: EJ
05/14/83, and see Peter Gorrie in ES
05/15/83; Fleming: *Montreal Gazette*, CH, EJ, RDA (all 05/14/83);
Cotler: EJ, RDA 05/14/83. The sole
known positive editorial was in *Toronto Sunday Star,* 05/15/83

12 Goldbloom: CJS 06/01/84, p. 2;
RDA, EJ, CH 05/04/83; Keegstra:
CH 05/12/83, p. A2

13 In July 1984, a request was made to
nine ethnic newspapers published in
Alberta to provide us with clippings
relating to the Keegstra affair. No
replies were received. Letters were
sent to: The *Canadian Chinese
Times, La Opinion,* (Spanish), *Le
Franco-Albertain, Moshi-Moshi*
(Japanese). *Nyugati Magyarsa* (Hun-
garian), *Philippine Bayanihan,
Prairie Link* (Southeast Asian), *Scan-
dinavian Centre News, Ukrainian
News. The Western Catholic Reporter,* in Edmonton, sent two
clippings

14 Millar: CH 04/03/83, p. G10; Bell:
CJS 05/13/83, p. 4; criticism rejected: Ch, EJ 05/06/83, RDA
05/07/83, *Western Catholic Reporter,*
05/16/83

15 Interview with C. Bond, 06/23/85;
CJS 05/13/83, p. 3; Christian-Jewish
statement: "A Public Rebuke of
Ethnic and Religious Hatred in Alberta"; CH, CS, RDA, CJS (all
05/13/83); survey: *Alberta Sonshine
News* (Edmonton), 06/83, p. 5; personal knowledge

16 Downey: "Project Windmill": CH
05/13/83, CH 05/16/83, RDA
05/19/83; debate: EJ 05/17/83, CH
05/18/83, EE 05/24/83, RDA
06/01/83; Downey meeting: EE
08/09/83, CH 09/22/83, personal
knowledge; League: interviews with
C. Bond, 06/23/85; G. Cohos,
01/22/85; A. Narvey, 05/21/85; F.
Schwartz, 04/08/85; H. Shatz,
01/30/85; personal knowledge

17 RDA, EJ, CH 05/04/83; Keegstra:
CH 05/12/83, p. A2

18 E. Olsen to R. K. David, 05/24/83
(RKD); EJ 05/18/83, RDA 0/20/83;
E. Olsen, etal., to Eckville Parents,
06/24/83 (M. Andrew collection)

19 RDA, EJ 05/27/83; JWB 06/02/83,
06/16/83, VS 06/11/83; H. Leon to
M. Elterman n.d., and reply, also
n.d. (CJC-Vancouver); "Genocide,"
shown Sept. 19: CJN 08/11/83,
09/15/83, 09/29/83; EJ, RDA
09/14/83 and RDA 09/20/83; CH
09/20/83; CS 09/21/83; EE 09/27/83;

Jewish Post (Winnipeg), 09/29/83; *B'nai B'rith Messenger* (Los Angeles), 09/30/83

20 Editorial: EE 05/17/83, p. 4; Schmidt: EE 05/17/83, p. 1; observer: Olive Elliott, EJ 05/14/83, editorial in ES 05/18/83, *Montreal Gazette*, 05/14/83; "close to Eckville": RDA 05/17/83, p. 1B

21 McEntee: ES 05/05/83; petition: EE, RDA, CH (all 06/07/83); "Concerned Citizens Group" petition, and submission to Town Council (A. Carritt collection)

22 Condemnations were made by Peter Elzinga: CJS 05/13/83, p. 2; BC Teachers' Federation: News Release, 05/13/83 (JFE); Western Canada Concept Party: RDA 05/16/83, p. 1B; E. Neilsen: EJ 05/17/83; BC Socreds: *Vancouver Province*, 05/16/83, JWB 05/20/83; ATA: CH 05/17/83; Dave King: EJ 05/18/83; Alberta MPs: CH, RDA 05/20/83, EJS 06/83; Presbyterians: RDA 05/21/83; United Church: News Release, 05/24/83 (JFE); Ottawa: CH 06/03/83; Alberta Ku Klux Klan: ES 05/20/83, p. 18; Fleming: EJ 05/27/83

23 *The New York Times*, 05/26/83; *International Herald Tribune*, 05/27/83 (see EE 07/12/83), *Ma'ariv* 05/27/83 (see EJ 06/08/83)

Chapter 10: The Trial

1 Crawford: ES 04/24/83, p. 26, and 04/21/83, p. 3; transcript review: CH 05/27/83; RCMP: EE 08/02/83, RDA 08/03/83, EJ 08/04/83, CJN 08/11/83, Ross Henderson to H. Katz, 08/10/83 (Katz collection); report submitted: CJN 09/01/83, p. 29; "Summary of the Recommendations of the JCRC Ad Hoc Legal Committee" (JFE); interview with S. Chumir, 04/83; RDA 04/18/83 and 04/27/83, p. B1, EE 04/19/83, ES 04/24/83; rough notes, undated, of a telephone conversation between B. Kayfetz and H. Boroditsky (JFE; and see the letter of Kayfetz to Boroditsky, 07/13/83)

2 *Martin's Criminal Code, 1979*, pp. 262-3; Patrick D. Lawlor, *Group Defamation: Submissions to the Attorney General of Ontario* (n.p., March 1984), pp. 34-6

3 Crawford interview: EJS 09/83, CJS 09/07/83; KKK: EJ 05/18/83; Manitoba: *Winnipeg Sun*, GM 06/01/83, *Jewish Post* 06/02/83; Edmonton: ES 06/05/83, p. S7; Olds: EJ, RDA, CH 06/15-17/83; VS 06/16/83; Huseby: EE 08/09/83, p. 1, enclosure to A. Carritt, M. Andrew to S. Chumir, 07/23/83; Saskatchewan: CH 08/05/83, EE 08/09/83, RDA 08/27/83, CJN 09/15/83; Aryans: EJ 07/08/83; CDL: RDA 09/16/83; CLR: CH 10/30/83, p. B2; for articles at this time on hate literature, see *Winnipeg Free Press*, 06/06/83, p. 1; ES 06/05/83, p. S7; CH 07/18/83, EJ 08/10/83, and the 3-part series by K. Warden, CH 07/18/83

4 $400,000 was spent on the Ghitter Commission (CH 02/08/85, p. A3) and $540,000 on the Alberta Human Rights Commission media campaign (CH 02/03/84, p. B7)

5 Interviews with H. Katz, 12/23/84, H. Boroditsky 12/24/84, M. Horowitz, 03/11/85, J. Kirman 04/30/85; EJ 05/05/83, EJ, RDA 05/31/83, CJN 05/19/83, p. 10

6 EJ, CH 06/27/83; ES, RDA 06/28/83; EJ 06/30/83; CH 07/20/83; AR 07/11/83

7 "Nothing ironic": AR 03/12/84, p. 27

8 News leak: EJ 09/16/83, 09/19/83; *Alberta Communications Network*, 06/06/84; "too soft": *Collage* magazine (Calgary), 03/84, pp. 2, 4; editorial, CJS 11/04/83, p. 4

9 ATA: CH, EJ 02/03/84; CH, CS, EJ, ES 02/17/84, N. I. Bass (Qualifications Secretary, ATA) to J. Keegstra, 05/11/84 (RKD); King: CH 04/12/84, p. A9, CS 04/13/84, p. 3, CJN 04/19/84, p. 7

10 ES 02/22/84; Zip to Herb Katz, 02/22/84 (H. Katz collection); CJS 03/16/84, p. 4; Butz: RDA 06/09/84,

Le Journal De Montreal, 06/10/84,
CJS 09/21/84, pp. 1, 4

11 CDL Minutes of Meeting, 09/10/83;
Jim Green to "Dear Christians,"
n.d.; J. Keegstra to "Dear Friend &
Supporter," 11/27/83; J. Green to
[name withheld], 02/09/84

12 On Christie, see RDA 06/04/84;
Monday Magazine (BC), 02/24/84;
CH 05/01/85; Claude Adams,
"Through the Fingers," *Canadian
Lawyer,* April 1985, pp. 17-19

13 On Plaut, see Confidential Minutes
of the Meeting of the Joint Community Relations Committee (Ontario),
06/27/84, p. 4

14 CP file copy, 09/26/84; CJS 02/15/85,
p. 1

15 CCLA: Confidential Minutes of the
Meeting of the JCRC (Ontario Re-
gion), 06/27/84, pp. 4-6; CH, CS,
GM, RDA, 10/11/84; CH, CS, EJ,
ES 10/12/84; RDA 11/05/84; CH, EJ,
ES, GM, RDA 11/06/84

16 Unless otherwise noted, the description of the trial and the proceedings
is based on personal knowledge

17 Rohling: Mosse, *Toward the Final
Solution,* as cited, pp. 138-41, *Encyclopedia Judaica,* XIV, 224; Berne:
Cohn, *Warrant for Genocide,* as
cited, chapter 10

18 *The New York Times,* 07/26/85, p. 9,
Baltimore Jewish Times, 08/02/85

Afterword

1 ATA Code: CH 03/26/84, p. B1, ATA
News Release, 03/29/84; Alberta
Education News Release no. 14,
05/07/84; Teaching Council: CH
06/19/85 and 06/22/85; King wrote:
letter to D. Wertheimer, 02/22/85

2 EJ 04/23/83, p. A8; ES 04/24/83.
Klinck and Boswell estimated that
they were selling about $1,000 worth
of books a year, with sales increasing
during the past two to three years

3 Federation: EJS 02/84, p. 3; *Edmonton Journal:* EJS 12/83, p. 3; Press
Council: EJS 10/83, 11/83, 12/83
(p. 4)

4 CH 07/21/85, p. B6, EJ (same date),
p. A2; RDA 07/11/85, p. 1B

5 Katz: Minutes of the Jewish Federation of Edmonton Board, 05/16/83,
p. 4; Maddox and Andrew: Minutes
of the JFE Board Meeting, 12/06/83,
p. 6, EJS 02/84, p. 2, Keegstra: CH
07/23/85, p. A3, EJ 07/31/85, CH
08/20/85, p. A7, RDA 08/15/85, p.
1B

Index

ABOUT THE AUTHORS

DAVID BERCUSON is a writer and historian who teaches at the University of Calgary. His most recent book is *The Secret Army*.

DOUGLAS WERTHEIMER is the editor and publisher of *The Jewish Star*, a bi-weekly newspaper published in Calgary and Edmonton. Both authors live in Calgary and closely followed the Keegstra case from beginning to end.

**For the millions who can't read
Give the gift of literacy**

More than four million adult Canadians can't read well enough to fill out a job application or understand the directions on a medicine bottle. You can help. Give money, volunteer with a literacy group, write to your MP, and read to your children.

For more information, contact:

Canadian Give the Gift of Literacy Foundation

34 Ross St., Suite 200,
Toronto, Ont. M5T 1Z9
(416) 595-9967

The Canadian Give the Gift of Literacy Campaign is a project of the book and periodical industry of Canada, in partnership with Telephone Pioneers of America, Region 1-Canada.

SEAL BOOKS

Offers you a list of outstanding fiction, non-fiction and classics of Canadian literature in paperback by Canadian authors, available at all good bookstores throughout Canada.

THE BACK DOCTOR	Hamilton Hall
THE IVORY SWING	Janette Turner Hospital
NEVER CRY WOLF	Farley Mowat
THE KITE	W.O. Mitchell
BIRD IN THE HOUSE	Margaret Laurence
ANNE OF GREEN GABLES	Lucy Maud Montgomery
BEST CANADIAN SHORT STORIES	John Stevens, Ed.
LADY ORACLE	Margaret Atwood
AN INNOCENT MILLIONAIRE	Stephen Vizinczey
BORDERLINE	Janette Turner Hospital
AND NO BIRDS SANG	Farley Mowat
THE DANCE OF SHIVA	William Deverell
STONE ANGEL	Margaret Laurence
STRAIGHT FROM THE HEART	Jean Chretien
BLUEBEARD'S EGG	Margaret Atwood
JOSHUA THEN AND NOW	Mordecai Richler
MY DISCOVERY OF AMERICA	Farley Mowat
A CERTAIN MR. TAKAHASHI	Ann Ireland
THE CANADIAN ESTABLISHMENT	Peter C. Newman
A JEST OF GOD	Margaret Laurence
HOW I SPENT MY SUMMER HOLIDAYS	W.O. Mitchell
ANNE OF WINDY POPLARS	Lucy Maud Montgomery
SEA OF SLAUGHTER	Farley Mowat
THE HANDMAID'S TALE	Margaret Atwood
THE CANADIANS (seven volumes)	Robert E. Wall
JACOB TWO TWO MEETS THE HOODED FANG	Mordecai Richler
HEART OF A STRANGER	Margaret Laurence
THE DOG WHO WOULDN'T BE	Farley Mowat
WHO HAS SEEN THE WIND	W.O. Mitchell
THE ACQUISITORS	Peter C. Newman
LIFE BEFORE MAN	Margaret Atwood

The Mark of Canadian Bestsellers